HEGEL'S THEORY OF THE MODERN STATE

Cambridge Studies in the History and Theory of Politics

HEGEL'S THEORY OF THE MODERN STATE

SHLOMO AVINERI

The Hebrew University, Jerusalem

CAMBRIDGE UNIVERSITY PRESS

CAMBRIDGE

LONDON   NEW YORK   NEW ROCHELLE

MELBOURNE   SYDNEY

Published by the Press Syndicate of the University of Cambridge
The Pitt Building, Trumpington Street, Cambridge CB2 1RP
32 East 57th Street, New York, NY 10022, USA
296 Beaconsfield Parade, Middle Park, Melbourne 3206, Australia

Library of Congress catalogue card number: 70–186254

ISBN 0 521 08513 6 hard covers
ISBN 0 521 09832 7 paperback

First published 1972
First paperback edition 1974
Reprinted 1974 1976 1979 1980

First printed in Great Britain by
Western Printing Services Ltd, Bristol
Reprinted in Great Britain by
Redwood Burn Limited, Trowbridge & Esher

CONTENTS

... so philosophy too is its own time apprehended in thoughts.

Hegel, Preface to
Philosophy of Right

PREFACE

Ever since Hegel's death in 1831, his political philosophy has continuously remained the focus of an agitated and heated discussion. The emergence of a 'Young' Hegelian school alongside the orthodox 'Old' Hegelian tradition pointed to some of the astounding ambiguities and potentialities inherent in the Hegelian system, as did the controversy between Karl Rosenkranz and Rudolf Haym about the political implications of Hegel's philosophy. Since then, almost every shade of political philosophy had protagonists claiming to state its case in what they considered to be a legitimate interpretation or derivative of Hegelianism. Socialists like Moses Hess, Karl Marx and Ferdinand Lassalle related their philosophies to Hegel in one way or another, just as did liberals like T. H. Green, Bernard Bosanquet and Benedetto Croce, and fascists like Giovanni Gentile; though interestingly enough, one would be hard-pressed to recall a comparatively prominent conservative thinker who could be termed a Hegelian. During World War II one British commentator credited Hegel with maintaining that 'might indicates right',[1] whereas more recently others would tend to follow Pelczynski's contention that Hegel's conception of the state postulated 'an ethical community'.[2]

Surely such a dichotomic view calls for some clarification. It is the aim of this study to attempt to reconstruct the development of Hegel's political philosophy as seen through his various writings over the whole period of his activity. Because it was the *Philosophy of Right* that had such an impact on subsequent students of Hegel, so much of the traditional discussion of his social and political philosophy tended to focus on this work to the exclusion of many of

[1] E. F. Carritt, 'Hegel and Prussianism' (*Philosophy*, April 1940), reprinted in W. Kaufmann (ed.), *Hegel's Political Philosophy* (New York, 1970), p. 43.

[2] Z. A. Pelczynski, *Hegel's Political Philosophy: Problems and Perspectives* (Cambridge, 1971), pp. 1–29. These two collections of essays, edited by Kaufmann and Pelczynski respectively, show how lively is the contemporary interest in the problem.

Preface

his other writings; and though it is without doubt his most systematic work on political philosophy, many of its themes cannot be fully understood unless related to some of his other works. Moreover, when Hegel's early writings on religion, society and politics were published for the first time by Nohl in 1907 under the title *Hegels theologische Jugendschriften*, this did little outside of Germany to change the traditional interpretations of Hegel which had by then already hardened into rival orthodoxies.

Other posthumously published works by Hegel had a similar fate. Hegel's critique of social and political conditions in Germany around 1800 was published by Mollat in 1893, at the height of German nationalism, and the political context of its publication, symbolized by the title *The Constitution of Germany* given it by the editor, further complicated any attempt to relate Hegel's arguments in the essay to his general philosophical position. The publication in the early 1930s by Hoffmeister of two sets of early lectures by Hegel known as the *Jenaer Realphilosophie* hardly evoked any adequate response: the destruction of intellectual life in Germany by the Nazis made the *Realphilosophie* as forgotten for almost two decades as Marx's *Economic-Philosophical Manuscripts*, which were rescued from obscurity and oblivion at about the same time. Nor was there much sympathy in the West for a German philosopher who certainly did not fit neatly into the categories of individualist liberalism: and Marcuse's *Reason and Revolution* has been for three decades almost the only extensive study in English that attempted to incorporate the *Realphilosophie* into its interpretation of Hegel's philosophy.

I have tried to draw on all of Hegel's writings on social and political problems so as to present as comprehensive a picture as possible of the variety and richness of his concerns: I have thus relied on published theoretical writings, lecture notes, political essays, excerpts from his reading as well as on Hegel's private correspondence. Consequently the study will try to cover a much wider scope than the traditional discussion of the state proper, grounded as such a discussion is in just one section of the *Philosophy of Right*. I shall try to approach Hegel's theory of the state in the context in which it appears in Hegel's system, where it is related not only to his general philosophical concerns but also to the other spheres of social and economic life. It is in this sense that Hegel's theory of the state is also a theory of social relations in a much wider sense. As Pelczynski has recently shown, Hegel's usage of the concept 'state' differs so much from its customary connotation as to be responsible for many of the misunderstandings surrounding Hegel's political philosophy.

It is also for this reason that I do not follow the tradition of many of Hegel's translators and commentators of capitalizing the term 'state'. Once one writes 'State' rather than 'state', Leviathan and Behemoth are already casting their enormous and oppressive shadows. Of course Hegel capitalizes *Staat*: but then all nouns are capitalized in German, as in Shakespearean English, and if one likes to follow this custom for some reason or other and capitalize the State, one ought to do the same with Right, the Individual, Freedom, Family, Civil Society, as well as with all Animals, Vegetables and Minerals. Unless one decides to adopt such a system in its entirety, a selective capitalization of the State is as arbitrary and intellectually scandalous as any other willful misrepresentation.

Any writer trying to deal with only one aspect of Hegel's philosophy – and this volume very clearly tries to limit itself to just one such aspect – has to be aware that in a very basic way his study is in danger of not being able to overcome either of the following pitfalls. If he tries to trace in depth the connection between Hegel's political thought and his general philosophical system, he may find himself immersed in an explication of the systematic edifice of Hegel's philosophy without ever reaching his political theory. Alternatively, he may try to condense the general system into a tight and concise introductory chapter which will stand very little chance of doing justice to it while at the same time being almost certainly so dense as to be more obscure than illuminating; the writer may thus raise more problems in his introductory section than he will later be able to answer adequately in the detailed discussion of Hegel's political philosophy proper.

It would be foolish on my part to assume that my own approach to the problem succeeded in overcoming these difficulties. All I can say is to try and state what I set out to do – namely, to identify as much as possible the *problems* of political and social theory that Hegel addressed himself to and attempt to render them in a context that is both autonomous as well as related to the general systematic issues of Hegel's philosophy. By drawing on all possible sources of Hegel's writings, I also intended to bring out the interplay between Hegel's reactions to the upheavals of his own time and his general philosophical concerns.

My main contention is that Hegel emerges from such a confrontation as a philosopher acutely conscious of the achievements and the limitations of the modern age. Since medieval times, traditional political philosophy has not recognized the dimension of historical change as fundamental to a discussion of the normative order. Hegel, on the other hand, tried to answer the problem of historicity which confronted Rousseau, for example, with his most agonizing problem. But while Rousseau was never able to bridge the gap between history and the Good Life – a dichotomy epitomized in what appears as the irreconcilable tension between the Second Discourse and *Émile* – Hegel attempted to relate political philosophy to history and make his understanding of history into a vantage point from which problems of political philosophy could be viewed. Some of the problems bequeathed to Hegel by the Kantian heritage could also be thus approached, and, armed with Montesquieu and Herder, Hegel set out to answer the problems left open by Rousseau. It is in this sense that Hegel can be seen as the first major political philosopher of modern society: the break in historical continuity ushered in by the historical developments leading to the French Revolution made the traditional paradigms of classical political philosophy totally unresponsive to the new needs. Thus while political philosophy before Hegel was preoccupied with legitimacy, Hegel introduced the dimension of change and historicity which has since become central to modern political thought.

This is exemplified most vividly in the treatment of historical figures. To classical political thought before Hegel, it is the founders of polities and states that count: the semi-legendary legislators, the institutionalizers and legitimizers. It is the names of Moses, Lycurgus, Solon, Cyrus and Romulus that one finds in the writings of political thinkers from Machiavelli to Rousseau. To Hegel, the only historical figures significant enough to be incorporated into his system are those who had been central to the processes of world historical change: Alexander, Julius Caesar, Napoleon – and on another level, Socrates and Luther.

It is for this reason that for Hegel all discussion of political issues is immediately a discussion of history: not because of the quest for origins, for a secularized version of the legitimacy implied in the Book of Genesis, but because history, as change, is the key for meaning, and this meaning, as actualized in the world, is the hieroglyph of reason to be deciphered by the philosopher.

If, then, Hegel's political philosophy is modern in this sense, its shortcomings are as much a reflection of this age as are its achieve-

Preface

ments: no philosopher has been as much aware as Hegel was that while the task of philosophy is 'to apprehend what is', every individual, and this includes the philosopher, 'is the child of his time'. Ultimately, political philosophy, as philosophy in general, is an eternal pilgrimage.

Since there is yet no full critical edition of Hegel's works, I had to follow various editions with respect to Hegel's different works. Whenever an English translation exists, I have quoted from it; otherwise I have rendered my own translation. In each case, the edition I followed is pointed out in the footnotes. It is to be hoped that the thorough work now done at the Hegel archives at Bochum under the excellent supervision of Professor Otto Pöggeler will come up with a definitive edition of Hegel's *Werke* before too long.

I would like to thank the American Philosophical Society and the Eliezer Kaplan School of Economics and Social Sciences at the Hebrew University of Jerusalem for research and travel grants that enabled me to pursue and complete this study.

For stimulation and challenge I am indebted to a devoted group of graduate students and teaching assistants at the Hebrew University who sometimes gave me a very hard time in my Hegel seminars. Colloquially referred to as 'the young Hegelians', they include Yosef Avner, Raphaëla Edelman, Edna Marbeh-Fast, Rivka Ginton, Shmuel Harlap, Leah Lieberman, Uri Maimon, Shulamit Nebenzahl and Maly Shafrir. As the talmudic saying goes, one learns most from one's students. I also owe a special debt to my friend and colleague Brian Knei-Paz for his invaluable editorial help.

I finished the manuscript while spending a year as a Fellow at the Center for the Humanities at Wesleyan University. It gives me great pleasure to acknowledge my gratitude to the Center, and especially to its director, Professor Victor Gourevitch, for the friendliness and warmth with which I felt myself surrounded while at Wesleyan.

I have discussed many of the ideas which appear in the book with numerous colleagues both in Israel and abroad: I would like to thank them all, knowing that if it would not have been for them, this book would have been even more inadequate than it is now.

4 April 1972   S.A.

Chapter One

BEGINNINGS

Valedictory addresses are rarely original, and if one tries to find in them the mature man hiding inside the adolescent student, one is apt to be disappointed. Yet in reflecting the conventional wisdom of an age as viewed through the somewhat idealistic prism of youth, they give an indication of the intellectual climate nurtured by a culture.

Hegel's valedictory address on graduating in 1788, at the age of eighteen, from the Stuttgart Gymnasium, is no exception. The subject is slightly outlandish and somewhat stilted: a comparison between the Germans and the Turks. As one may expect, the theme is edifying: the barbarity of the Turks should not be ascribed to any lack of talent in that martial nation; rather it should be recognized as a consequence of the fact that the Turkish state neglected the education of its subjects: 'So great is the influence education thus has on the whole welfare of a state!'[1] Education, *Bildung*, is hailed as the foundation of the body politic: manners, arts, sciences constitute the elements of society, and it is the prime duty of the state to further education and learning.

All the basic beliefs of the German Enlightenment are clearly visible in this speech: like many other of Hegel's expressed views at that period, they attest to the humanistic background of his education prior to his entering the Tübingen Stift, where he studied for five years (1788–93). As Rosenkranz, Hegel's first biographer, has put it, Hegel's education combined the principles of the *Aufklärung* with the study of classical antiquity;[2] similarly, Hoffmeister shows that not only Kant and Fichte constituted the educational background of Hegel, but the whole tradition of the Enlightenment.[3]

---

[1] *Dokumente zu Hegels Entwicklung*, ed. J. Hoffmeister (Stuttgart, 1936), p. 52; see also Karl Rosenkranz, *Georg Wilhelm Friedrich Hegels Leben* (Berlin, 1844; new ed., Darmstadt, 1963), pp. 19–21.
[2] *Hegels Leben*, p. 10.   [3] See his introduction to *Documente*, p. viii.

Beginnings

The political aspect of this combination of classicism and humanism comes out very strongly in several of Hegel's juvenalia: one of its features is a very pronounced interest in political matters. At the age of fifteen Hegel writes a short play about the Second Triumvirate, in which Mark Antony, Lepidus and Octavian try to outwit each other in what appears an extremely naïve Machiavellian fashion.[4] The following year Hegel is fascinated by Sophocles' *Antigone*, which he translates into German.[5] His school diary is full of sometimes surprisingly mature speculations about problems of history and cognition. His reading of historical and theoretical works is very intensive during this period, with a heavy accent on such Enlightenment writers as Feder, Sulzer, Garve, Mendelssohn and Nicolai.[6]

In 1787, at the age of seventeen, Hegel drew up a draft of an essay on 'The Religion of the Greeks and the Romans'. As can be expected, it reflects a mature schoolboy's insights into the subject; yet one cannot but record that the subject prefigures some of Hegel's later interests, as does his statement about the historicity of religious phenomena, still couched in Herderian language: 'Only when a nation reaches a certain stage of education (*Bildung*), can men of clear reason appear amongst it, and reach and communicate to others better concepts of divinity.'[7]

This strong attachment to the prevalent notions of the *Zeitgeist*, as well as to the Kantian heritage, expresses itself also in one of his school aphorisms, when he says that 'Enlightenment relates to culture as theory does to praxis, as cognition to ethics (*Sittlichkeit*)'.[8] The education to culture, which appears in his valedictory address, is thus not a mere convenient phrase used by Hegel for the purpose of striking the right note at the moment of a public display of gratitude and platitude. It seems to reflect a deeper involvement, which comes up again a few years later, when he hails Schiller's *Letters on the Aesthetic Education of Man* as a 'masterpiece'.[9]

---

[4] 'Unterredung zwischen Dreien', *Dokumente*, pp. 3–6.

[5] Rosenkranz, *Hegels Leben*, p. 11. *Antigone* always remained central to Hegel's discussion of tragedy and ethical life; cf. *The Phenomenology of Mind*, trans. J. B. Baillie, new ed. (New York, 1967), pp. 484–99. See also Walter Kaufmann, *Hegel* (Garden City, 1965), pp. 142–6.

[6] See *Dokumente*, pp. 54–166.

[7] *Ibid.* p. 46. In the same vein he tries to distinguish between the religion of the 'populace' (*Pöbel*), based on passion and crude representation, and a more 'pure' and rational religion (p. 47).   [8] *Ibid.* p. 141.

[9] Hegel to Schelling, 16 April 1795, in *Briefe von und an Hegel*, ed. J. Hoffmeister (Hamburg, 1952), I, 24.

Beginnings

Yet it is not until Hegel's move to Berne, where he was to spend three years (1793–6) as a private tutor at the household of one of the republic's patrician families, that one finds in him an active interest in political affairs. This interest can be directly traced to the impact of the events of the French Revolution on Hegel, and it was evidently heightened by the tension between these revolutionary events and the oligarchic conditions of Berne.

There is some evidence that even during his relatively secluded period in the Tübingen seminary, Hegel was involved in some student activities mildly connected with revolutionary events in France. Together with his close friend at the seminary, Schelling, Hegel is said to have planted a 'freedom tree';[10] he is also said to have been involved in a political club which came under official investigation. But it is only in Berne that we have any immediate evidence as to his reaction to the revolution in France: when it comes, it combines a social critique of conditions in Berne with a method of philosophical enquiry related to Kant, with whose writings Hegel became acquainted at that time.[11]

A long letter to Schelling attests to his awareness of the changes his surrounding world was undergoing. Hegel starts by describing the immediate political conditions in Berne:

Every ten years, about 90 members of the *conseil souverain* are replaced. All the intrigues in princely courts through cousins and relatives are nothing compared with the combinations that go on here. The father nominates his son or the groom who will bring in the heaviest dowry, and so on. In order to understand an aristocratic constitution, one has to spend such a winter here.[12]

Referring to a philosophical brochure Schelling has sent him, Hegel remarks that he sees it as a continuation of the revolution in the realm of ideas then going on in Germany, adding: 'From the Kantian system and its ultimate consummation I expect a revolution in Germany which will start with principles that are already there and merely require to be worked out and be applied to all hitherto existing knowledge.' He then goes on to relate this philosophical revolution to the changes in the social and political sphere:

10 Cf. report in *Zeitung für die elegante Welt* (1839), nos. 35–7, quoted in Rosenkranz, *Hegels Leben*, p. 29.
11 On the general problem of Hegel's relationship to the French Revolution see the excellent study of Joachim Ritter, *Hegel und die französische Revolution* (Köln/Opladen, 1957).
12 Hegel to Schelling, 16 April 1795 (*Briefe von und an Hegel*, I, 23). This letter is partly quoted, in an English translation, in Kaufmann, *Hegel*, p. 303.

Beginnings

I believe that there is no better sign of the times than the fact that mankind as such is being represented with so much reverence, it is a proof that the halo which has surrounded the heads of the oppressors and gods of the earth has disappeared. The philosophers demonstrate this dignity [of man]; the people will learn to feel it and will not merely demand their rights, which have been trampled in the dust, but will themselves take and appropriate them. Religion and politics have played the same game. The former has taught what despotism wanted to teach: contempt for humanity and its incapacity to reach goodness and achieve something through man's own efforts. With the spreading of ideas about how things should be, there will disappear the indolence of those who always sit tight and take everything as it is. The vitalizing power of ideas — even if they still have some limitation, like those of one's country, its constitution etc. — will raise the spirits.[13]

There hardly could be a more poignant expression of the spirit and program of German idealist philosophy. Philosophy appears here as the great emancipator from the fetters of traditional religion and existing political life. But the accent put by Hegel on the political aspects of this emancipation is much stronger than the one usually to be found in the classical writings of German idealism or, for that matter, in the letters of Hegel's two main correspondents of that period – Schelling and Hölderlin.

Yet there is a further dimension to Hegel's critique of contemporary cultural and political life. The passage from the letter to Schelling just quoted ends with a statement which introduces a completely new note into Hegel's critique. Hegel contrasts with present conditions his vision of man recognizing the power of ideas and being ready to make sacrifices for them, and he then concludes: ·'At present, the spirit of the constitution has allied itself with self-interest (*Eigennutz*), has founded its kingdom on it.'

By itself, this may not appear as more than an isolated remark, couched in what may be seen as merely moralistic language. Yet Hegel's literary activity during his Berne period shows that it was more than that.

During his stay in Berne, Hegel's reading included Montesquieu and Hume, Thucydides and Gibbon, as well as Benjamin Constant.[14] But the deepest influence left on him at this period was Sir James Steuart's *An Inquiry Into the Principles of Political Economy*, which he read in German translation. Such was the impact created

---

[13] *Briefe von und an Hegel*, I, 24. George Lichtheim has pointed out in his *Marxism* (London, 1961), p. 36, the striking resemblance between this letter to Schelling and Marx's earlier writings.

[14] Rosenkranz, *Hegels Leben*, p. 62; Rudolf Haym, *Hegel und seine Zeit* (Berlin, 1857; new ed., Hildesheim, 1962), p. 64.

by the reading of this study, that Hegel wrote a lengthy commentary on Steuart's book, which is now lost, though Rosenkranz still reports to have seen the manuscript in the 1840s. It is from this description of the activity and analysis of the market mechanism by Adam Smith's mentor and contemporary that Hegel derived from that time onwards his awareness of the place of labour, industry and production in human affairs. Alone among the German philosophers of his age, Hegel realized the prime importance of the economic sphere in political, religious and cultural life and tried to unravel the connections between what he would later call 'civil society' and political life.[15] Fichte's *The Closed Commercial State* (1800) conspicuously lacks a comparable grasp of political economy, and thus reads like a latter-day mercantilistic pamphlet, basically out of touch with the realities of modern economic life.

It must have been under the impact of Steuart that Hegel embarked upon a detailed study of the Bernese financial and fiscal system and its social implications. But, like his commentary on Steuart, this study has unfortunately not survived.[16] What has survived is a German translation, prepared by Hegel but published anonymously, of a French tract on social and political conditions in the Pays de Vaud, which had been under the rule of the City of Berne since the sixteenth century. This is a pamphlet by an exiled lawyer from Vaud, Jean-Jacques Cart, originally published in Paris in 1793. In it Cart shows how the Bernese oligarchy used their suzerainty over Vaud to encroach by degrees upon the historical rights of the local population.[17] Hegel prepared a German edition of this pamphlet and published it in 1798 in Frankfurt under the title *Aus den vertraulichen Briefen über das vormalige staatsrechliche Verhältnis des Waadtlandes (Pays de Vaud) zur Stadt Bern.* The German translation includes numerous additions and comments, as well as a preface, by the unnamed translator, and it was only in 1909 that it

---

[15] See Rosenkranz, *Hegels Leben*, p. 86; Ritter, *Hegel und die französische Revolution*, p. 35; Georg Lukács, *Der junge Hegel* (Zürich/Wien, 1948), pp. 228–9. A most fascinating attempt to trace Steuart's terminology in Hegel's later writings has been undertaken by Paul Chamley in his two studies: *Économie politique et philosophie chez Steuart et Hegel* (Paris, 1963), and 'Les origines de la pensée économique de Hegel', *Hegel-Studien*, III (1965), 225–61. Rosenkranz (p. 85) also remarks that at that time Hegel undertook a study of the effect of the English Poor Laws.

[16] Rosenkranz, *Hegels Leben*, p. 61; *Dokumente*, p. 462.

[17] For a fuller résumé of Cart's pamphlet, see Z. A. Pelczynski's introductory essay to Knox's translation of *Hegel's Political Writings* (Oxford, 1964), pp. 9–12.

was discovered and established that the translation and the comments were prepared by Hegel.[18] The preparation of this volume is thus Hegel's first published work.

Though most of Hegel's comments tend only to amplify Cart's argument, there are a number of instances where they represent Hegel's independent judgement. Between the publication of Cart's original pamphlet and the appearance of Hegel's translation, French revolutionary troops liberated Vaud from its dependence on Berne: so the topicality of Cart's booklet was somewhat diminished, though Hegel adds in his preface that there is a general political importance in the study of such conditions as described by Cart.[19]

Most of Hegel's own comments center round the oligarchical, nepotic system of government in Berne itself, and these must reflect his own studies on this subject. He criticizes Berne for not having a written penal code and for its supreme authority exercising both legislative and juridical functions. Though Hegel never followed any strict interpretation of the separation of powers theory, he strongly argues here against 'criminal justice being completely in the hands of the government'.[20] Hegel cites a number of hair-raising cases where evident injustice was done to innocent people because prosecution and adjudication were in the same hands, adding: 'In no country that I know of is there, proportionately to its size, so much hanging, racking, beheading and burning as in the Canton of Berne.'[21]

Moving to another sphere, Hegel attacks a notion which had been used by some of the apologists of Berne, namely that a low level of taxation corresponds to a high degree of political freedom. If this were the criterion, Hegel argues, the English would be the most unfree nation in the world, since 'nowhere does one pay so many taxes' as in England. To Hegel a view that judges the quality of citizenship in terms of financial self-interest represents a basic

---

[18] See Hugo Falkenheim, 'Eine unbekannte politische Druckschrift Hegels', *Preussische Jahrbücher*, cxxxviii (1909), 193–220; see also Jürgen Habermas' *Nachwort* to his edition of Hegel's *Politische Schriften* (Frankfurt, 1966), pp. 344–5.

[19] Hegel always referred back to the City of Berne as an example of corrupt oligarchy. In his marginal notes on Haller's *Restauration der Staatswissenschaften* (1816), Hegel comments: 'Nothing except the views of the Bernese ever enters his consciousness.' See G. W. F. Hegel, *Berliner Schriften*, ed. J. Hoffmeister (Hamburg, 1956), p. 678.

[20] *Dokumente*, pp. 250–3.

[21] *Ibid.*, p. 252.

fallacy; such a view prefers to forgo citizenship for 'a couple of thalers a year'. It is not the quantity of taxation that makes men free citizens, but whether the tax is imposed on them by an external power or whether they tax themselves. Englishmen are free not because they pay low taxes, but because they vote for their own taxation. Hegel then adds:

The duties which the English Parliament imposed on tea imported into America were extremely light; but what caused the American Revolution was the feeling of the Americans that with this totally insignificant sum, which the duties would have cost them, they would have lost their most important right.[22]

Hegel's praise for the English system of taxation through representation is, however, coupled with an oblique criticism of the British system of representation itself. Commenting on Pitt's ability to rule through a parliamentary majority even when this appeared to be contrary to what seemed to be general public opinion, Hegel adds that this became possible because 'the nation can be represented in such an incomplete manner that it may be unable to get its voice heard in parliament'.[23] The reference is cryptic, but its implication about the narrow base of the franchise in Britain at that time is obvious. In view of Hegel's later remarks about British parliamentary representation, this early awareness of the complex link between society and parliament in England is of some significance: it is also rare in a German thinker of that period.

Though it would be impossible to attempt to reconstruct Hegel's political outlook from these fragmentary comments, it is nevertheless possible to come to a number of conclusions. Hegel's general view seems to follow that climate of opinion in Germany which reacted favourably to the principles of the French Revolution, though it did not necessarily subscribe to all its political manifestations. It should be pointed out, however, that there is no reference in Hegel's comments of that period to natural rights. Cart's own pamphlet itself limits its argument to the vindication of the historical rights of the people of Vaud which were taken away from them by the City of Berne; the obvious parallel with the historical claim of the American colonies, mentioned by Hegel himself, is significant. On the other hand, though Hegel accepts the sort of political vision the Revolution stands for, he very sharply criticizes Robespierre. In a letter to Schelling he expresses, in 1794, the same criticism of Jacobin terror which he would reiterate during the Jena period and which foreshadows his description of Jacobinism in

[22] *Ibid.*, p. 149.   [23] *Ibid.*

the *Phenomenology* as 'absolute fear', abstract freedom undeterred by any institutional limit.[24]

Beyond this there appears a specific interest shown by Hegel in the relationship between the economic sphere and political organization. As we shall see in the course of this study, it took Hegel many years to evolve his own theory about this relationship. But even at this early stage it is clear that on this subject he is groping in a direction transcending the facile beliefs of the Enlightenment and the ideas of the French Revolution. Further, in his comments on Cart, Hegel brings out very strongly the economic aspect of the Bernese rule in Vaud: his acquaintance with Steuart's writings must have added a further dimension to the otherwise purely political and legalistic nature of Cart's enquiry.

A similar set of problems is raised in a series of fragments written by Hegel in Frankfurt, where he lived for three years (1797–1800) after leaving Berne. These were published by Hoffmeister as 'Frankfurt Historical Studies', and constitute Hegel's first attempt at a systematic study of history.[25]

Many of the ideas Hegel was to incorporate later into his philosophy of history can be found here, especially those concerning some of the basic characteristics of what he would call 'the Oriental World'. The oriental nations are characterized, according to these fragments, by their complete subordination to external necessity, coupled with a total disregard for immediate reality in their cultural life.[26] Further, oriental society is static, stagnant and unchanging. The subservience to external necessity makes despotism and tyranny into the main ingredients of the oriental political system: 'Lordship and slavery: both conditions are equally justified here, since both are ruled by the same law of force. He is considered a happy man in the Orient who has the courage to subjugate him who is weaker.'[27]

In his discussion in these fragments of Renaissance Italy, Hegel is first seen attempting an adequate definition of the state which would be able to fit into a changing historical context. In central and northern Italy, Hegel argues, the link between the individual and the political entity was incomplete and very loose: 'The history

---

[24] Hegel to Schelling, December 1794 (*Briefe von und an Hegel*, I, 17); *Dokumente*, pp. 359–60.

[25] The extremely complex problem of dating Hegel's early manuscripts has recently received careful attention at the Hegel-Archiv in connection with the preparation of the complete edition of Hegel's works. For a report see Giesela Schüller, 'Zur Chronologie von Hegels Jugendschriften', *Hegel-Studien*, II (1963), 111–59.   [26] *Dokumente*, pp. 257–9.   [27] *Ibid.*, p. 258.

of Italy at that period is not so much the history of a people or a plurality of peoples as a history of a *mass of individuals* . . . Living together in cities was more a cohabitation side by side than a submission under the same laws. The power of the authorities was weak, no idea had yet any power . . . [In the city-states] the exercise of justice was merely the victory of one faction over another.'[28]

Such a system of particularism, lacking a common bond, explains, according to Hegel, the rise to prominence of Roman Law in the Italian universities:

In Italy, legal studies appeared in Bologna earlier than poetry, and the most noble spirits of the people flocked there . . . For only on the judge's dais were they still servants of an idea, servants of law: otherwise they would be only servants of a man.[29]

Yet it is in his description of the modern state that the problems which preoccupied him earlier express themselves most clearly. The modern state, Hegel argues, is characterized by its being an instrument for the protection of property:

In the states of the modern period, all legislation hinges upon security of property; it is to this that most rights of the citizens relate. Few free republics of antiquity have regulated through the constitution strict property rights – the preoccupation of all our authorities, the pride of our states. In the Lacedae-monian constitution, security of property and of industry was a point which did not figure almost at all, which was, one can say, almost completely forgotten. In Athens, it was customary to rob rich citizens of a part of their wealth, though one used an honourable excuse when one set about robbing a person: one saddled him with an office which required enormous expenditure.[30]

The relationship between property and the political order is further amplified in its historical dimension when Hegel mentions that even under the most free of constitutions, the disproportionate wealth of a few citizens would lead to the destruction of liberty. His examples are Periclean Athens, Rome in the period of the Gracchi and the power of the Medicis in Florence.[31] Though we have earlier mentioned Hegel's abhorrence of Jacobin terror, he expresses some understanding for the social motivation and background of the *sansculottes*, saying: 'One does perhaps an injustice to the system of Sansculottism in France when one ascribes to it rapacity alone its attempt to reach a more equal distribution of property.'[32]

The modern state, based on the security of property, is to Hegel

---

[28] *Ibid.*, pp. 269–70 [29] *Ibid.*, p. 269.
[30] *Ibid.*, pp. 268–9. [31] *Ibid.*, p. 269. [32] *Ibid.*

the state of his contemporary world: there does not seem to be much difference in this respect between the *ancien régime* and the revolutionary republic. Hegel says explicitly that the security of property is 'the preoccupation of all our authorities, the pride of our states': such language does not refer to the revolutionary government of France alone, but to all governments and states of his contemporary world. According to Hegel, the ancient world did not pay attention, on the political level, to property; Renaissance Italy disregarded anything beyond the particular power and will of the individual. It is only with the advent of the modern age that a universal system of property became the mainstay of the state and the right to decide upon one's taxation became the cardinal issue of political allegiance and participation. Yet the unequal distribution of property means recourse to political power for the furtherance of economic interests; both Hegel's analysis of conditions in Vaud, as well as his comments on the social movements of antiquity and radical Jacobinism, make it clear how much he was aware of the fact that political power appeared as an instrument of economic self-interest, sanctioned, as he put it in his letter to Schelling, by the 'halo' of political theory and religion.

It is only if one views Hegel's preoccupation in this light that one can grasp the import of some aspects of his studies of the ancient world and early Christianity, undertaken in the Berne and Frankfurt period. Though these studies, which will be discussed in the next chapter, deal with problems of a religious and theological nature, they are oriented towards the *public* realm of religion and culture as well as towards solving the individual believer's quest for personal salvation. In the polis and in the Church, Hegel was looking for a paradigm for a kind of universality which was lacking in the political system of the modern state. Being aware of the achievement of modernity – he quotes Hume as the historian who looked for the integration of the individual in a political universality – Hegel is conscious of its burden as well.

It is with this in mind that one can approach one of the most enigmatic fragments of Hegel's early period, published for the first time by Franz Rosenzweig in 1917 as 'The First Program of a System of German Idealism'.[33] Though the manuscript, dating from 1796, is in Hegel's own hand, there is no doubt today that it is a

[33] 'Das älteste Systemprogramm des deutschen Idealismus', *Sitzungsbericht der Heidelberger Akademie der Wissenschaften*, Phil.-hist. Klasse (1917), 5. Abhandlung.

copy of a common manifesto, not a piece of writing composed by Hegel alone; Schelling's influence, for example, is strongly felt. Yet there is no doubt that it represents a set of ideas which, even if not originating with Hegel, at least received his approval.

This manifesto of the philosophy of subjective freedom culminates in a discussion of the state, and under paragraph 6 the following is stated:

From nature I move to human artefact . . . I shall demonstrate that just as there is no idea of a machine, so there is no idea of the state; for the state is something mechanical. Only that which is an object of freedom may be called an idea. We must therefore transcend the state! (*Wir müssen also über den Staat hinaus!*) For every state is bound to treat men as cogs in a machine. And this is precisely what ought not to be; hence the state must cease to be (*aufhören*).[34]

Beyond that state Hegel sees the 'absolute freedom of all spirits, who carry the intellectual world in them and should not seek God or immortality outside themselves'. To anyone who knows Hegel's later writings this is a most surprising if not startling document; the echoes it evokes of later Marxian thought are too loud to be overlooked or wished away.

But this document can also be very easily misunderstood or misrepresented by attributing its radicalism either to Schelling alone or to a passing early phase of Hegel's intellectual development. A close scrutiny of the document within the context of what we know of Hegel's political thinking in the Berne–Frankfurt period points to a different interpretation: there seems to be a clear link between this fragment and his other writings on political problems of that period. The state that has to be 'transcended' in the *System-programm* is a 'machine' in which individual men are mere 'cogs'. Surely this cannot be the kind of state Hegel would later develop in his political philosophy. The state that has to be 'transcended' and should 'cease to be' is rather the state with which Hegel had dealt in his writings up to 1796: it is the state based on security of property, 'the preoccupation of all our authorities, the pride of our states'; it is the state based on nothing else than self-interest; it is the state as emerging from the theories of natural law. It is the kind of organization which Hegel would later call 'civil society', which he himself characterized as 'the external state, the state based on need, the state as the Understanding envisages it (*Not- und*

[34] *Dokumente*, pp. 219–20.

Verstandesstaat)'.[35] It is this 'state' which has to be transcended, since freedom – which is the subject under discussion in the *Systemprogramm* – cannot be formed in it, and of such a state there can be no 'idea'. Such a state is a 'machine' because, after all, what Hegel would later call 'civil society' is nothing else than the market mechanism. The idea of the state has to be found in something else, representing not an aggregate or a mass but an integrated unity, a universal. And in looking for this idea, Hegel turns his attention to the ancient polis, to the early Church and to the contemporary reality of the Holy Roman Empire of the German Nation – the themes of his early theoretical writings on politics and society.

[35] *Hegel's Philosophy of Right*, trans. T. M. Knox (Oxford, 1942), § 183.

Chapter Two

POSITIVITY AND FREEDOM

While Hegel's early fragments point to his concern and dissatisfaction with the traditional view of the state as a legitimate expression of self-interest, another preoccupation always accompanies his
historical studies and exercises. This is the attempt to confront the
problems raised by institutional religion. Rosenkranz, Hegel's biographer, points out that during his years in Berne, Hegel had
emancipated himself from the orthodox theology which he had been
taught at the Tübingen seminary.[1] Yet this emancipation was not
achieved through an outright repudiation of orthodoxy, nor through
the adoption of a merely anti-religious or anti-clerical attitude.
Hegel was led to confront some traditional theological problems
with contemporary philosophical principles; and just as he moved
away, during 1795–1800, from a Kantian position in philosophy, so
his discourses on problems relating to religious issues came to
reflect subtle changes in emphasis and typology, though the basic
issues discussed remained broadly the same.

The manuscripts dealing with these problems were published
for the first time by Hermann Nohl in 1907 under the title *Hegels
theologische Jugendschriften*, and it is under a similar title that
most, though not all of them, have been published in English.[2]
Nevertheless, despite the fact that most of these fragments deal
with issues related in one way or another to religion, they are not
theological writings in the strict sense of the word. Some of the
fundamental theological problems involved are allowed to remain
more or less open by Hegel when he admits a dichotomy between
reason and revelation – and leaves it at that.[3] The problems which
Hegel does try to confront have far more to do with the historical,
social and even economic aspects of religion, with the relationship

---

[1] Rosenkranz, *Hegels Leben*, p. 45.
[2] G. W. F. Hegel, *Early Theological Writings*, trans. T. M. Knox, introduction
by Richard Kroner (Chicago, 1948).
[3] *Ibid.* p. 292.

between types of societies and types of religious belief, and with the political context of religious institutions. It is as an historian and sociologist of religion, as well as a social critic, that Hegel emerges from these manuscripts. Historical investigations, heavily indebted in their method to Herder, are joined here with a philosophical enquiry speaking the language of Kant. What troubles Hegel are not so much problems of personal belief and individual salvation but issues related to the social dimension of the religious phenomenon.[4] And if contemporary readers justly find a glimpse of Kierkegaard in these early writings, Feuerbachian and even early Marxian themes are no less prevalent.

The main problem which Hegel attempts to come to grips with is that of 'positivity' in religion. By 'positivity' Hegel means a religious system which lays down a set of rules and regulations which the believer has to follow not because each individual act of behaviour represents for him the expression of his own inner conviction and free moral choice, but because it has been so established, set down and 'posited' for him by the institutions of religion. This basically Kantian juxtaposition of 'freedom' versus 'positivity' supplies Hegel with a criterion by which to judge different religious systems.[5] His specific historical problem follows from these criteria and can be conveniently summed up under two headings: firstly, how did it happen that Christianity, which began as an attempt at emancipation from 'positive' Old Testament Judaism, ended up with an ecclesiastical establishment at least as 'positive' as the old Mosaic Hebrew law; and, secondly, how did Christianity succeed in conquering the old pagan world and overcoming the Graeco-Roman religion.

The various manuscripts dealing with these problems, though dating from a number of years, can be roughly arranged in two major sets, the first centering around the manuscript entitled 'The Positivity of the Christian Religion' and the second around 'The Spirit of Christianity and Its Fate'. The first set of manuscripts

---

[4] See Walter Kaufmann, 'Hegel's Early Antitheological Phase', *Philosophical Review* LXIII (1954), 3–18. Lukács, however, goes to the other extreme when he labels any discussion of Hegel's 'theological period' as a 'reactionary legend' (*Der junge Hegel*, pp. 27–45). See Emil L. Fackenheim, *The Religious Dimension in Hegel's Thought* (Bloomington/London, 1967), for a thorough discussion of Hegel's religious thought.

[5] *Early Theological Writings*, p. 98: 'A religion is better or worse according as, with a view to producing this disposition which gives birth to action in correspondence with the civil or moral law, it sets to work through moral motives or through terrorizing the imagination and, consequently, the will.'

dates from the Berne period, while the later one belongs to the Frankfurt years. Though recent research has shown that some of the dating problems are extremely complex,[6] the basic division adopted by Nohl and which was followed in the Knox–Kroner English translation can be maintained. The main dividing line in the manuscripts occurs around 1797 – a date which corresponds to Hegel's move from Berne to Frankfurt – when there appears a clear shift in the argument away from Kantian rationalism to a more speculative mode of reflection.[7] Yet the problem of positivity runs through all these writings and it confronts Hegel with some basic problems of social culture and political allegiance. It is in this context that he develops his views on the socio-political structure of the Greek polis, the Jewish commonwealth and the Christian church. The insights achieved in these discussions were later to become elements in the development of Hegel's theory of the modern state. It is against the background of his preoccupation with classical republican *virtus,* Hebrew law and Christian love that Hegel was able to construct the mode of allegiance which has to supersede the mechanistic, individualistic, modern state, based, as Hegel has already remarked, on the concept of property and its security.

JUDEA, THE 'POLIS' AND 'VOLKSGEIST'

Hegel's investigation of religion in its historical perspective is premised on typical Enlightenment views about religion as deriving from man's rational faculties: 'The highest end of man is morality, and among his dispositions for promoting this end, his disposition for religion is one of the most outstanding.'[8] Following Lessing's *Nathan the Wise,* Hegel is aware that though this disposition for religion is universal, the concrete form in which it appears in the individual consciousness may be different in each particular case. Hegel's distinction here between 'objective' and 'subjective' religion is in line with a parallel distinction by Mendelssohn. Hegel, however, concedes that in order to implant the 'objective' rules of reason

---

[6] See esp. Giesela Schüller's article in *Hegel-Studien,* II, referred to earlier (p. 8).

[7] Knox, prefatory note to *Early Theological Writings,* p. vii, as well as Kroner's introduction, pp. 8–20.

[8] *Hegels theologische Jugendschriften,* ed. H. Nohl (Tübingen, 1907), p. 48. This passage is taken from a manuscript entitled 'Folk-religion and Christianity', not included in the Knox–Kroner English translation. Cf. a similar statement in 'The Positivity of Christian Religion', *Early Theological Writings,* p. 68: 'The aim and essence of all true religion . . . is human morality.'

in the individual consciousness, one has to take into account subjective motivation. Consequently, a rudimentary dialectical relation between the content of religion (rational morality) and its form (imagination) is postulated by Hegel:

> Reason sets up moral, necessary and universally valid laws; Kant calls these 'objective', though not in the sense in which the rules of the understanding are objective. Now the problem is to make these laws subjective, to make them into maxims, to find motives for them; and the attempts to solve this problem are infinitely diverse.[9]

Such a dialectical relationship has obvious historical consequences since it necessarily relates any given religion to the totality of the socio-cultural phenomena of the historical entity under discussion. A shift in the general structure of society and its *mores* would cause a change in the form of religious beliefs, while changes in religion have to be conceived as reflections of changes in the general conditions of the *Zeitgeist*.

Religion thus appears as an aspect of a wider historical totality. Following Herder, Hegel refers to this totality as *Volksgeist*, the sum total of socio-cultural institutions which make up what is then colloquially called 'national character'.[10] Following a tradition which goes back to Bodin and Montesquieu, Hegel maintains that a discussion about religion is necessarily an enquiry into the general historical conditions affecting a particular group. In a paragraph in which he discusses the acceptance of Christianity by the pagan world, Hegel expresses thoughts which must have reflected a parallel phenomenon in the realm of the ideas and social reality connected with the French Revolution:

> Great revolutions which strike the eye at a glance must have been preceded by a still and secret revolution in the spirit of the age (*Zeitgeist*), a revolution not visible to every eye, especially imperceptible to contemporaries, and as hard to discern as to describe in words. It is lack of acquaintance with this spiritual revolution which makes the resulting changes astonishing.[11]

The combination of Herder and Kant appears most strongly in Hegel when he describes folk religion, rooted in popular imagination and consciousness, in terms which attempt to fit Kantian ethics into a Herderian structure:

---

[9] *Ibid.* p. 143.
[10] On the difference between Hegel's usage of the term *Volksgeist* and the way it was used by the Romantics and the Historical School of Jurisprudence, see my 'Hegel and Nationalism', *Review of Politics* xxiv (1961), 474–9, and the literature mentioned there.
[11] 'How Christianity Conquered Paganism', *Early Theological Writings*, p. 152.

Judea, the polis and Volksgeist

We consider it a necessary requirement for a folk religion that it does not force its teaching upon anyone, nor does violence to any human conscience ... [Its precepts] must not contain anything that universal reason does not recognize.[12]

With these intellectual tools Hegel attempts to penetrate the intricate relationship between Christianity and Judaism on the one hand and paganism on the other. Hegel's discussion of the origins of Christianity begins naturally with a description of Jewish religion. Though Hegel's account of Judaism draws very heavily upon prevalent Christian notions about it, Hegel focuses on issues of social practice rather than points of religious belief. Judaism at the time of Jesus is to Hegel a paradigm of a 'positive' religion and Jewish society appears as a totally unfree one; the political subjection of Judea to Rome only exacerbated the basic lack of freedom implicit in Mosaic law:

The Jews were a people who derived their legislation from the supreme wisdom on high and whose spirit was now overwhelmed by a burden of statutory commands which pedantically prescribed a rule for every casual action of daily life and gave the whole people the look of a monastic order. As a result of this system, the holiest of things, namely the service of God and virtue, was ordered and compressed in dead formulas, and nothing save pride in this slavish obedience to laws not laid down by themselves was left to the Jewish spirit, which already was deeply mortified and embittered by the subjection of the state to a foreign power.[13]

Such a system implied a total subsumption of the political sphere under the religious: Judea was a theocracy, in the strict sense of the word.[14] On top of all this, Mosaic law guaranteed the exclusiveness and apartness of the Jews. Hegel's description follows both Herder's views on the Jews, as well as the general view about the Jews held by the Enlightenment, a view which can be seen as a secularized version of the traditional Christian ideas about Judaism.[15]

---

12 Nohl, *Hegels theologische Jugendschriften*, p. 50.
13 'The Positivity of Christian Religion', *Early Theological Writings*, pp. 68–9.
14 *Ibid.* pp. 98–9: 'If an Israelite fulfilled the commands of his God, i.e. if he kept the feasts properly, managed his sacrifices properly, and paid tithes to his God, then he had done everything which he could regard as his duty. These commands, however, which might be moral, as well as religious, were at the same time the law of the land, and laws of that kind can produce no more than legality.'
15 Cf. *Herder on Social and Political Culture*, ed. F. M. Barnard (Cambridge, 1969), p. 231; Arthur Hertzberg, *The French Enlightenment and the Jews* (New York, 1968); Nathan Rotenstreich, *The Recurring Pattern* (London, 1963); Jacob Katz, 'A State Within a State', *Proceedings of the Israel Academy of Sciences and Humanities* (Jerusalem, 1969), IV, no. 3.

Positivity and freedom

This view of Jewish religion as a religion of utter servility appears in an even stronger form in the later essay, 'The Spirit of Christianity and Its Fate'. Here the Jews are shown as utterly incapable of freedom, and their craving after the fleshpots of Egypt serves as a telling example.[16] Abraham, the wanderer, symbolizes the Jews' inability to become attached to any piece of territory; Joseph is seen as having imposed on Egypt the hierarchical system peculiar to Jewish unfreedom and the Sabbath is viewed as a day of rest for slaves – free people do not need it. The cruel fate of the Jews, Hegel concludes, did not arouse pity – only horror, etc., etc.[17]

Though the image of Judaism is less harsh in the earlier manuscripts than in 'The Spirit of Christianity and Its Fate', the general characterization is more or less the same in all of Hegel's writings of that period. The appearance of Jesus as an historical phenomenon is explained by Hegel as a combined reaction against the immanent servitude imposed on the Jews by the Mosaic law and the external, political yoke of Roman imperial rule. Hegel explains the messianic element in Judaism not merely in theological terms but in a socio-historical context, and he is one of the first writers on the subject to give Jewish messianism a highly political explication.

Under Roman rule, the Jews expected 'a Messiah who, girdled with might as Jehovah's plenipotentiary, was to rebuild the Jewish state from its foundations'.[18] Despite his severe criticism of Judaism as a 'positive' religion, Hegel is able to evoke a vivid picture of the tensions in Judaean society under the Romans which helped to nurture the messianic belief:

So long as the Jewish state found spirit and strength enough in itself for the maintenance of its independence, the Jews seldom, or, as many hold, never, had recourse to the expectation of a Messiah. Not until they were subjugated by foreign nations, not until they had a sense of their impotence and weakness, do we find them burrowing in their sacred books for a consolation of that kind. Then when they were offered a Messiah who did not fulfill their expectations, they thought it worth toiling to insure that their state should still remain a state (a nation to which this is a matter of indifference will soon cease to be a nation);

[16] *Early Theological Writings*, p. 190.
[17] *Ibid.* pp. 186, 188, 193, 204–5.
[18] 'The Positivity of the Christian Religion', *Early Theological Writings*, p. 77. Hegel also points out (p. 70) that it was as such a *political* Messiah that Jesus was viewed by his Jewish disciples until the end: 'Even in the last moments of his stay on earth . . . the disciples still displayed in its full strength the Jewish hope that he would restore the Jewish state (Acts 1:6) ["They asked of him, saying, Lord, wilt thou at this time restore again the kingdom to Israel?"].'

they very soon discarded their ineffective messianic hopes and took up arms. After doing everything the most enthusiastic courage could achieve, they endured the most appalling of human calamities and were buried with their polity under the ruins of their city . . . The scattered remnants of the Jews have not abandoned the idea of the Jewish state, but they reverted not to the banners of their own courage but only to the standards of an ineffective messianic hope.[19]

Yet this quite sympathetic presentation of Jewish messianic hope in strongly politicized terms is only brought in by Hegel to accentuate the wholly different character of what he conceived Jesus' intention to have been. Jesus did not want to emancipate the Jewish body politic; he wanted to emancipate the moral element in Judaism from its servitude to 'positive' statutes. Jesus aimed at the precise opposite of what Jewish messianic hopes ultimately became – he wanted to liberate religion from subservience to the political system, since it was this combination in historical Judaism which had turned it into a 'positive' religion.[20] The argument about positivity thus enables Hegel to present a view which manages to combine both the traditional claims of Christianity against Judaism as well as the verdict of the Enlightenment against it. In a second version of the introduction to the manuscript on positivity, Hegel maintains that all religions undergo a period during which what had originally been freely determined appears as 'positive', statutory and legalistic. Jesus is presented as having wished to restore Judaism to its original moral content and the continuity between the message of Jesus and Judaism is strongly stressed.[21] What Jesus wanted to achieve was respect for the moral law through a subject 'in whom the law is itself the legislator, from whose own inner consciousness this law proceeds'.[22] In Hegel's view of Jesus' aim, the Kantian moral imperative was to replace the codification of Sinai.

To this ancient Hebrew servitude to the law Hegel opposes the Hellenic self-determination of the self. While the Jewish commonwealth appears in Hegel as double servitude, the polis, and its religion, appear as the creation of free men.

[19] *Early Theological Writings*, pp. 158–9.
[20] *Ibid.* pp. 98–9; see also Nohl, *Hegels theologische Jugendschriften*, p. 45: 'Nothing is more intolerable than publicly employed guardians of morals.'
[21] *Ibid.* pp. 167–81; cf. p. 75, 'Jesus was a Jew; the principle of his faith and his gospel was not only the revealed will of God as it was transmitted to him by Jewish traditions, but also his own heart's living sense of duty and right.' In 'The Spirit of Christianity and Its Fate', on the other hand, Jesus no longer appears as a possible restorator of original Judaism, but as turning his back totally on the Jewish tradition and introducing the principle of subjectivity which Hegel here characterizes as 'totally foreign' to the Jews (*ibid.* pp. 205, 209).   [22] *Ibid.* p. 144.

Positivity and freedom

Hegel's description of the polis is a panegyric to Hellenism. Paganism, as a religion of beauty, is integral to the spirit of freedom characterized by the polis. The *Volksgeist* wherein 'each nation has an established national trait, its own mode of eating and drinking and its own customs in the rest of its way of living',[23] is the expression of an integral popular culture, where the body politic lives in every individual's consciousness and in the collective imagination:

Every nation has its own imagery, its gods, angels, devils, or saints who live on in the nation's traditions, whose stories and deeds the nurse tells to her charges and so wins them over by impressing their imaginations. In this way these tales are given permanence. In addition to these creatures of the imagination, there also live in the memory of most nations, especially free nations, the ancient heroes of their country's history, i.e. the founders or liberators of their states scarcely less than the men of valour in the days before the nation was united into a state under civil laws. These heroes do not live solely in their nation's imagination; their history, the recollection of their deeds, is linked with public festivals, national games, with many of the state's domestic institutions or foreign affairs, with well-known houses and districts, with public memorials and temples.[24]

Such an integral mode of life, welding together the various aspects of social activity, existed, according to Hegel, only in the classical polis. It was only in this historical context that men lived a truly free life, obeying only their own will:

As free men the Greeks and Romans obeyed laws laid down by themselves, obeyed men whom they had themselves appointed to office, waged wars on which they had themselves decided, gave their property, exhausted their passions, and sacrificed their lives by thousands for an end which was their own. They neither learned nor taught [a moral system] but evinced by their actions the moral maxims which they could call their very own. In public as well as in private and domestic life, every individual was a free man, one who lived by his own laws. The idea of his country or his state was the invisible and higher reality for which he strove, which impelled him to effort ... Only in moments of inactivity or lethargy could he feel the growing strength of a purely self-regarding wish.[25]

Each individual, Hegel adds in a following passage, had 'the picture of the state as a product of his own energies'. The political culture of this republicanism is the 'democratic spirit ... which

[23] *Ibid.* p. 69.
[24] *Ibid.* pp. 145–6.
[25] *Ibid.* pp. 154–5. In a striking sentence Hegel brings out the integral nature of life in the classical polis when he says (p. 147) that 'anyone who did not know the history of the city, the culture, and the laws of Athens could almost have learned them from the festivals if he had lived a year within its gates.'

gives an individual a greater measure of independence and makes it impossible for any tolerably good head to depend wholly and absolutely on one person'.[26] Popular military service made every citizen into a soldier who would thus identify his own cause with that of the commonwealth.[27] Kantian moral self-determination can work only in a republican, Herderian context of political self-government.

This seemingly unlimited enthusiasm for the classical world and its folk religion is, however, balanced by Hegel's awareness of the historicity of the phenomenon: the classical polis turned into an *imperium*. We shall later see how Hegel realizes the inner necessity of the changes wrought by imperial Rome – changes that were to culminate in the acceptance of Christianity. Despite the brilliance of the classical world, Hegel ultimately realizes that it cannot be resuscicated, and it is this realization that somewhat sets Hegel apart from the classicist humanism of his age.

This appears very clearly in the main theme of a fragment called *Is Judea, then, the Teutons' Fatherland?*, from which several of the passages about the classical *Volksgeist* quoted above have been taken. The fragment deals with the problem of authenticity in the German culture of Hegel's own age and in its relationship to the Christian heritage; it thus dwells upon the topical and social, rather than the theological and soul-searching, nature of the problem of religious attachment. The title of the manuscript follows a theme raised by the proto-Romantic poet Klopstock. Following him, Hegel remarks that it is the imagery of the Judaic tradition that lives in the mind of eighteenth-century Germans since Christianity put an end to the old Germanic folk-culture:

Christianity has emptied Valhalla, felled the sacred groves, extirpated the national imagery as a shameful superstition, as a devilish poison, and given us instead the imagery of a nation whose climate, laws, culture and interests are strange to us and whose history has no connection whatever with our own. A David or a Solomon lives in our popular imagination, but our country's own heroes slumber in learned history books ... Except perhaps for Luther in the eyes of the Protestants, what heroes could we have had, we who were never a nation? Who could be our Theseus, who founded a state and was its legislator? Where are our Hermodius and Aristogiton to whom we could sing scolia as the liberators of our land?[28]

This tension between a people's history and its present popular imagery brought about, according to Hegel, the attempt to sever the

[26] *Ibid.* p. 82.   [27] *Ibid.* pp. 164–5.   [28] *Ibid.* p. 146.

popular imagination from this foreign, Judaic tradition and to substitute it, via classicism, with the heritage of the Graeco-Roman
world: this was the fashionable trend of the eighteenth-century
German Enlightenment. But Hellas was as remote from the reality
of German life as Israel, and ultimately an attempt was made,
notably by Klopstock, to revive the old Teutonic mythology. While
following Klopstock's Herderian criticism of the dichotomy between
imagery and reality in contemporary Germany, Hegel sees as utterly
nonsensical the Romantic attempt to revive the old Germanic
imagery. The quest for an integral culture is foremost in Hegel's
discussion, but he seems fully aware that one cannot step twice into
the same stream. It is this strong resistance to any Romantic notion
about the ability to revive the past that appears time and again in
Hegel's writings. Not for him the facile answers of the attempt to
revive the pristine Germanic *Ur-Volk*:

But this [Teutonic] imagery is not that of Germans today. The project of
restoring to a nation an imagery once lost was always doomed to failure; and
on the whole it was bound to be even less fortunate than Julian's [the Apostate]
attempt... The old German mythology has nothing in our day to connect or
adapt itself to; it stands as cut off from the whole circle of our ideas, opinions,
and beliefs, and is as strange to us as the imagery of Ossian or of India.[29]

The manuscript *Is Judea, then, the Teutons' Fatherland?* thus
leaves the question open, after discarding the alternatives of Hellas,
Israel and the woods of ancient Germany. It is significant that the
question has been raised without being answered, for the whole
tenor of Hegel's investigations at this period is critical rather than
constructive. The polis was a noble experience, as was its paganism,
but it corresponded to a phase in the development of human society
that has now been superseded. If one may use a turn of phrase
from one of Hegel's later writings, it can be only understood, not
rejuvenated.

This realization is also evident in another of Hegel's historical
fragments from the Frankfurt period, where Hegel praises the
virtues of the classical republic. In the classical city-state people
could say 'we' and be identified and associated with the state. But
'in larger republics people are far more restricted'. The 'we' is
more foreign to those who express it 'to the extent that the number
of their co-citizens grows ... [In large republics] the whole domin-

---

[29] *Ibid.* p. 149; cf. p. 203: 'When the genius of a nation has fled, inspiration
cannot conjure it back.' Hegel passed an almost identical verdict on Klopstock
in his Berlin lectures on aesthetics in the 1820s.

ates the individual, and he finds himself under it. A free large nation is therefore a contradiction in itself . . .'[30] The immediate, non-alienated identity with the whole is impossible outside the small city-state; we shall later see that Hegel will maintain this view and in his theory of modern society attach extreme importance to the intermediate stages of social integration that would now come instead of the direct, immediate and total integration of the classical polis.

There is in the manuscripts dealing with Christianity at least one instance where an element appears which should probably not be over-emphasized, but which is of some interest when related to what is now known about Hegel's economic enquiries. Hegel's description of ancient Greece and of Judea makes it clear that to him they represent two extreme poles of historical entities: Hellas the culture of freedom and beauty, Israel the culture of fear, serfdom and 'positivity'. Yet there is, surprisingly, one problematic aspect which according to Hegel they do have in common, and both tried to solve it with the same aim in view, though their concrete solutions differed from one another. In both Greece and Israel property relations were regulated by and subsumed under the state; the sphere of economic activity did not have any autonomy of its own. The reason for this regulation of property relations by the state derived in both cases from the fear of the impact that poverty and the inequality of property would have upon the integration of the political structure:

In reference to the subordination of civil rights to the law of the land, an institution of the Mosaic state has a striking resemblance to the situation created in [Athens and Sparta] . . . In order to avert from their state the danger threatening to freedom from the inequality of wealth, Solon and Lycurgus restricted property rights in numerous ways and set various barriers to the freedom of choice, which might have led to unequal wealth. In the Mosaic state, similarly, a family's property was consolidated in the family for all time.[31]

---

[30] *Dokumente*, p. 263. The parallel with Rousseau is tantalizing, yet it only tends to bring out the differences between the two. For in his dedicatory epistle to the 'Discourse on the Origins of Inequality' (*The First and Second Discourses*, ed. R. D. Masters (New York, 1964), pp. 77–90), Rousseau still believes it possible to try and legislate for small republics, trying to limit his efforts as far as modern, large states are concerned to the teaching of individuals how to live a virtuous life in a kind of society which is not attuned to such a life on the collective level. Rousseau utterly despaired of trying to face modern society in its entirety, while all of Hegel's efforts were aimed at finding an answer to the problems of modern, large-scale and complex societies. See Roger D. Masters, *The Political Philosophy of Rousseau* (Princeton, 1968).   [31] *Early Theological Writings*, p. 197.

Positivity and freedom

Contrary to the prevalent notions about the classical polis, Hegel points here to an issue and a political solution that were usually sidetracked by the eighteenth-century romanticization of antiquity; namely, that the social problem was central to the life of the polis, that the state had to step in directly, and that, even so, social cleavages remained a sore point in the politics of the ancient city-states. The same applies, according to Hegel, to the Mosaic regulations about *shmita* and *yovel* which make land inalienable. The nature of these regulations was restrictive, aiming at preserving a preordained social *status quo*. As such, Hegel would have little use for them, but in this striking analysis of social legislation in the ancient world Hegel brings out a hidden similarity between two societies which he otherwise views as diametrically opposed. Consequently, different *Volksgeister* may work out different solutions, but the problem is universal. In his later studies on the philosophy of history Hegel would express this element of the ancient regulation of property relationships in a language that would refer to the lack of differentiation of civil society from the state among ancient Greeks and Hebrews alike. Bearing in mind Hegel's other earlier references to the problem of property in various societies – Berne, Vaud, the *sansculottes*, his study of Steuart – there can be little doubt that one sees here an awareness on Hegel's part of an aspect of social life which begins to figure quite prominently in his attempts, during this very early stage, at an historical understanding.

IMPERIAL ROME AND THE SPREAD OF CHRISTIANITY

The apparent paradox of Christianity, which began as a *Tugendreligion* and became just another 'positive' religion, can be explained, according to Hegel, only within the context of the post-classical world which embraced Christianity because it supplied answers to certain of its felt needs. In order to be accepted Christianity had also to undergo a number of changes and it is these which Hegel sets out to describe in detail.

Hegel himself heightens the tension between original, primitive Christianity and the institutionalized, later Church by presenting Jesus time and again as a teacher of autonomous, individual morality: 'He undertook to raise religion and virtue to morality and restore to morality the freedom which is its essence . . . Jesus recalled to the memory of his people the moral principles in their sacred books.'[32] If this was the foundation of Jesus' teaching, 'how could we have expected a teacher like Jesus to afford any inducement to the creation of a positive religion, i.e. a religion which is grounded in authority and puts man's worth not at all, or at least not wholly, in morals?'[33] To explain this, Hegel has to turn to the conditions in the Roman Empire which led to the transformation of Christianity, in the same way as he had earlier explained the emergence of Jesus as a Messiah within the context of the Jewish polity under Roman rule. Here as elsewhere, religion is treated by Hegel as an aspect of a larger social context, which is being explained by showing the political element to be of primary importance.

Imperial Rome put an end, according to Hegel, to the free republican spirit of classical antiquity:

> The picture of the state as a product of his own energies disappeared from the citizen's soul. The care and oversight of the whole rested on the soul of one man or a few. Each individual had his own allotted place, a place more or less restricted and different from his neighbour's. The administration of the state machine was entrusted to a small number of citizens, and these served only as single cogs deriving their worth solely from their connection with others.[34]

Under the Empire, the readiness to work for the whole disappeared and the citizen became a private person, not recognizing anything transcending his particularity. If in the polis the citizen was ready to go to war for the commonwealth, under the Empire the only thing he could defend would be his property, and for *this* no one was ready to sacrifice life and limb. Hence the citizen's militia of the polis was replaced by a standing army, which for its part added a further aspect of repression to the political structure.[35]

This reduction of the person to his own individual, atomistic self, unconnected through any social nexus with his fellow-men, aroused

---

[32] *Ibid.* p. 69. This seems to make it difficult to accept Kaufmann's view (in his article, quoted in n. 4 above) that Hegel's attitude is basically *anti*-theological: despite Hegel's criticism of the established, institutionalized and 'positive' Church, his attitude to Jesus is one of deep veneration for his spiritual qualities and mission.

[33] *Early Theological Writings*, p. 71.

[34] *Ibid.* p. 156. The image of state bureaucracy as a 'machine' appears again in 'The German Constitution' (*Hegel's Political Writings*, p. 163), and is, of course, reminiscent of Hegel's referring to the state as a 'machine' in the *Systemprogramm*. But these epitaphs still refer to the traditional view of the state – and its servants – as related to property; Hegel's later construction of the modern state as transcending these 'civil society' aspects would entail also a change of view with regard to the bureaucracy.

[35] *Early Theological Writings*, pp. 164–5. This is one of Hegel's earliest references to war and military service. See ch. 10.

the fear of death as the central notion of human consciousness. Whereas in the polis the citizen could see in the political culture around him an extension of his self, could envisage himself immortalized in the work of the polis, its edifices and institutions and thus reflect that *non omnis moriar*, under the Emperors individual life remained the only reality in a situation in which the individual became totally alienated from any participation in the political system:

Activity was no longer for the sake of a whole or an ideal. Either everyone worked for himself or else he was compelled to work for some other individual . . . All political freedom vanished also; the citizen's right gave him only a right to a security of that property which now filled his entire world. Death . . . must have become something terrifying, since nothing survived him. But the republican's whole soul was in the republic; the republic survived him, and there hovered before his mind the thought of his own immortality.[36]

It was this depravity of life which became a fertile soil for the seed of Christianity:

Thus the despotism of the Roman emperors had chased the human spirit from the earth and spread a misery which compelled men to seek and expect happiness in heaven; robbed of freedom, their spirit, their eternal and absolute element, was forced to take flight to the deity. [The doctrine of] God's objectivity is a counter-part to the corruption and slavery of man, and it is strictly only a revelation, only a manifestation of the spirit of the age.[37]

This is, of course, a radical departure from any Church-oriented explanation about the causes for the triumph of Christianity, and Hegel is well aware of it. He goes into some detail to show that traditional Christian apologetics, in attempting to explain the Church's victory over paganism in terms of its moral superiority or superior rationality, is more or less the reverse of truth. Anticipating his later theory of the *List der Vernunft*, the cunning of reason, Hegel shows that very mixed motives were operative in making Christianity the dominant religion of the late Empire and that the motives for the acceptance of Christianity have been at variance with its contents. The implication here is that the proselytizing techniques used by Christianity could not but have affected the religious doctrine itself:

[36] *Ibid.* p. 157. The description of the Roman Empire as a system of total subjection, leaving to the individual only his (now meaningless) individual life and property, reappears again in Hegel's Berlin lectures on the *Philosophy of History*. The historical fragments of the Frankfurt period contain a similar assessment (*Dokumente*, p. 265).
[37] *Early Theological Writings*, pp. 162–3.

26

Imperial Rome and the spread of Christianity

Even in the original reception of Christianity what was operative was not simply a pure love of truth, but at least to some extent very mixed motives, very unholy considerations, impure passions, and spiritual needs often grounded solely in superstition . . .

Christianity has been quickly and widely spread as a result of miracles, the steadfast courage of its adherents and martyrs, and the pious prudence of its more recent leaders who have sometimes been forced to use a pious fraud for the furtherance of their good work.[38]

This plurality of motives leads Hegel to a discussion of a number of devices used by Christianity in order to make its message acceptable and meaningful to the masses. Hegel points out that some of these devices had already been used, albeit sparingly, by Jesus himself for similar reasons, but that they became standard practices only in the later Church. It was these devices which turned Christianity into a 'positive' religion, and one can hear an echo of anti-Constantinian arguments in Hegel's indictment of the *ecclesia triumphans*. The list of these devices enumerated by Hegel is long and detailed: miracles; the use of the dramatic elements in the Crucifixion; the divinity of Jesus' person; the messianic Judaic tradition; the institutionalization of the disciples into an apostolic college; the command to propagate the faith even through pandering to popular superstition (which Hegel points out flies in the face of Jesus' own words in Matthew 7:22); and the hypostasis of the Last Supper into 'a substitute for the Jewish and Roman sacrificial feasts'.[39] Furthermore, some of the social traits associated with the primitive, apostolic Church had to be abandoned if the Christian sect was to become a universal Church. These were equality and common ownership of goods.

Equality, according to Hegel, 'was a principle with early Christians; the slave was the brother of his owner'. This, of course, could not be fitted into the political society into which Christianity became transformed. A subtle change thus infiltrated the theory: equality 'has been retained, to be sure, in all its comprehensiveness, but with the clever addition that it is in the eyes of Heaven that all men are equal in this sense'.[40] A similar fate overcame the early communism of the Church. In a world where a man's only tangible reality had become, as Hegel himself observed of the late Roman Empire, his property, Christianity could have hardly achieved success if it had preached the community of property. So the Church accommodated its teaching to the *status quo* on this point as well

[38] *Ibid.* pp. 72–3, 94.   [39] *Ibid.* pp. 71–91.   [40] *Ibid.* p. 88.

27

and community of property 'was abandoned, whether by dire necessity or from prudential considerations'.[41]

This is the way Hegel saw the Church's transformation from a voluntary community of believers into a 'positive' political organization. In a second version of the preface to 'The Positivity of the Christian Religion', written probably around 1800–1, Hegel points out that the change in Christianity towards 'positivity' was due not so much to any inherent elements in Christianity or to its own development, but has to be attributed to an immanent process all religions are undergoing: it is part of the success of every religious creed that it becomes institutionalized and hence 'positive'.[42] Such an interpretation removes much of the edge of Hegel's strictures against the later developments of Christianity. What had appeared earlier as a degeneration and emasculation of the original message of Jesus becomes a law of historical development. It is in a tone of resignation and acceptance of immutable patterns of history that Hegel thus cancels much of his earlier criticism against the Church as established and institutionalized. It is precisely at this point in Hegel's development that the idea of 'fate' makes its appearance, superseding to a degree his earlier notion of 'positivity'. For Hegel fate is the ultimate inability of man to become fully autonomous in his moral decisions; whence his need for the mediation of love, which at this stage comes to occupy a central place in Hegel's manuscripts.[43]

The problem of 'positivity' had yet another aspect and this had a direct bearing on the political sphere. 'Positivity' in religion, according to Hegel, entails the curtailment of freedom in the political sphere.

'POSITIVITY' AND POLITICAL LIFE: CHURCH AND STATE

Neither in the polis, nor in ancient Israel, did the problem of the separation of church and state arise. As Hegel points out, the classical city-state and the Israelite commonwealth had this in common: that political allegiance and religious affiliation were both directly integrated, though in different modes, into the political structure. Being an Athenian involved both citizenship in the state

41 *Ibid.*
42 *Ibid.* pp. 167–81.
43 See the fragment on 'Love' in *Early Theological Writings*, pp. 302–9; Rosenkranz, *Hegels Leben*, pp. 46 ff.

and participation in a religious cult, and the same was the case with the ancient Hebrews.

In his description of the development of Christianity from a sect into the religion of the Empire, Hegel brings his analysis to bear upon the dualism inherent in Christianity once it became a state religion. While classical paganism and Judaism alike were political religions from the start, the combination of Christianity and political power was purely historical and accidental and gave rise to a set of problems which were wholly alien to the unmediated folk-religion of antiquity. The actual transition from a voluntary sect to an established church changed the very nature of a number of religious precepts: 'Institutions and laws of a small society, where each citizen retains the freedom to be, or not to be, a member, are in no way admissible when extended to a large civil society, and cannot co-exist with liberty.'[44] What may be devotion in a small sect, appears as oppression in a state-church. Thus, Hegel argues, Christianity became in a way more 'positive' than Judaism. While in Judaism only actions were commanded and controlled, the Church went even further and commanded feelings; even thought came under its surveillance.[45] After all its tribulations, Hegel contends, Christianity did not succeed in emancipating itself from the harsh, statutory commandments which have been a characteristic of Judaism:

Our public religion, like many of our customs, appeals ... in the fasts and mourning of Lent and the finery and feasting of Easter Day, to rules for feelings ... This is why there is so much hollowness, so much spiritlessness in our usage; feeling has gone out of them ...

[The Church] has also directly prescribed laws for our mode of thinking, feeling, and willing, and Christians have thus reverted to the position of the Jews. The special character of Jewish religion – that of bondage to law from which Christians so heartily congratulate themselves on being free – turns up once more in the Christian church.[46]

Religious education, Hegel points out, became the instrument through which a person's free choice was made impossible for him

---

[44] 'Folk-religion and Christianity', Nohl, *Hegels theologische Jugendschriften*, p. 44. See also *Early Theological Writings*, p. 87: 'Purely as a result of the fact that the number of Christians increased and finally comprised all citizens in the state, ordinances and institutions, which hurt no one's right while the society was still small, were made political and civil obligations which they could never in fact become.' Also p. 135: 'What was a private affair became a state affair and what was and is by nature a free choice became a duty.'
[45] *Ibid.* pp. 143, 140, 104–5.
[46] *Ibid.* p. 139.

by conditioning the young to accept without reserve the teachings of the Church. Censorship was imposed to prevent deviant opinions from getting hold of people's imaginations. And, finally, the Church has become an instrument in the hands of political power, and though Hegel's criticism of the Church usually has a strong anti-Catholic bent, on this particular point he criticizes Protestant states even more than Catholic ones.[47] In the end, Christianity was able to accommodate itself to any and every form of political structure. The religious content of Christianity became totally neutral as far as the political system was concerned. In what must be one of the harshest accusations ever to have been levelled against the Church, Hegel says:

[Christianity] was the religion of the Italian states in the finest period of their licentious freedom in the Middle Ages; of the grave and free Swiss republics; of the more or less moderate monarchies of modern Europe; alike of the most heavily oppressed serfs and their overlords; both attended one church. Headed by the Cross, the Spaniards murdered whole generations in America; over the conquest of India the English sang Christian thanksgivings. Christianity was the mother of the finest blossoms of the plastic arts; it gave rise to the tall edifice of the sciences. Yet in its honor too all fine art was banned, and the development of the sciences was reckoned an impiety. In all climates the tree of the Cross has grown, taken root, and fructified. Every joy in life has been linked with this faith, while the most miserable gloom has found in it its nourishment and its justification.[48]

Yet Hegel is far from just presenting the Church as a culprit and leaving it at that. The problem posed by the Church as vested with political power is due to the most basic dilemma of how to objectify subjective belief: 'By love's extension over a whole community its character changes; it ceases to be a living union of individualities and instead its enjoyment is restricted to the consciousness of their mutual love.'[49] Through considerations of this kind Hegel is led to state as a point of principle that religion must remain a private affair, free from the interference of political power, while political life must be emancipated from the influence of religious institutions. This is a view Hegel would continue to hold all of his life.

Hegel's point is bluntly stated when he says that 'a state, as a civil state, should have no faith at all; nor should its legislators and rulers, in their capacity as such'.[50] Following Moses Mendelssohn's *Jerusalem* Hegel argues that the civil power can impose on a person only those duties which arise out of another's right, and a religious

[47] *Ibid.* pp. 115, 133–4, 138, 108–9.   [48] *Ibid.* pp. 168–9.   [49] *Ibid.* p. 289.
[50] *Ibid.* p. 112.

30

obligation is obviously not one of them.[51] The state can demand
morality of its citizens, but only in an exhortative and non-coercive
way, and on a voluntary basis; hence political rights should not be
dependent upon religious conviction, and Hegel deplores the fact
that in most countries, 'Catholic and Protestant alike', a dissenter is
debarred from civil rights. It is contrary to the rationale of political
power as well as of religious belief that dissenters from the state
religion 'cannot acquire real estate of any sort, cannot hold any
public office and [are] subject to differential treatment in the matter
of taxation'.[52] Since to Hegel religion is in the realm of subjectivity
and free choice, 'in matters of faith there is in strictness no social
contract', and a political establishment of the Church is a contradiction in terms.[53]

Hegel's view of the necessity for the separation of church and
state is thus bolstered by the traditional arguments advanced in its
favour. Hegel also lays the duty to guarantee religious freedom and
tolerance at the door of every ruler:

> To be true to one's faith and to be free in the practice of one's religion is a
> right in which the individual must be protected, not primarily as a church
> member, but as a citizen; and a prince in his capacity as such has a duty to
> secure this right to his subjects.[54]

Yet this liberal solution, though advocated by Hegel as forcefully
as possible, does not altogether satisfy him; and contrary to
orthodox liberal opinion, Hegel perceives in this separation of
church and state not an ultimate solution but the roots for further
tension. In the same fragments in which he calls for the separation
of church and state, Hegel also praises the ancient polis for its
integration of the religious and the political into one totality.
It would be facile to take him to task for contradicting himself;
a more subtle issue is involved – a quest for an integrated social
ethic, which can on the one hand praise the classical *virtus*, yet
know at the same time that it cannot be re-established, since

---

[51] *Ibid.* p. 97. It should be noted that Hegel's usage here of the term 'civil
society' (*bürgerliche Gesellschaft*) is in line with the customary meaning
attached to it at that period, which equated 'civil society' and 'state'. Only
at a later stage, with the evolution of his own theory about the modern state,
would Hegel introduce the distinction between the two terms which would
then become the corner-stone of his political theory.

[52] *Ibid.* pp. 108–9; also p. 93. Cf. Hegel's similar advocacy of the removal of
civil disabilities from Jews and members of Christian dissenting sects in
§ 270 of his *Philosophy of Right*.

[53] *Early Theological Writings*, p. 123.

[54] *Ibid.* p. 127; also p. 129.

Christian dualism makes a return to such an immediate, non-reflective integration impossible.

This quest is evident in 'The Spirit of Christianity and Its Fate', in which Hegel goes beyond the advocacy of Kantian morality and its expression, as he saw it, in the teachings of Jesus. This level of morality now appears to Hegel only as one aspect of a more comprehensive field of ethics, and what he is looking for is a social ethic, based not merely on the individual's own free choice, but connected with and oriented towards sets of relationships with other human beings, when these relationships are not by themselves a product of free will. The family relationship, for example, cannot, according to Hegel, be relegated to the kind of individual morality based on free choice, since one is born into a family and one's duties are thus in a way predetermined. In a dim and yet uncertain way Hegel sketches in this manuscript for the first time the contours of his later distinction between individual *Moralität* and social *Sittlichkeit*. At this stage, it is love which Hegel sees as presenting a link between the individual person and the others to whom he is thus related, and the Church's dilemma is that in trying to fulfill this role on a universal basis, it turns, against its initial intention, 'positive'.

To a person holding such a view, the separation of church and state, desirable as it may be, cannot be the ultimate solution. Only if one holds an extremely individualistic view of the nature of political life can one be satisfied with such a separation. In a fragment from the Frankfurt period, Hegel points to the duality and bifurcation of human consciousness caused by the separation of church and state. After pointing out that any attempt to subordinate the church to the state is bound to culminate in tyranny, Hegel says:

But if the principle of the state is a complete whole, then church and state cannot be separate ... The whole of the church is a mere fragment only when man in his wholeness is broken up into a political man and a church man.[55]

So, necessary as the separation of church and state is as a way of avoiding oppression and the power of 'positivity', its very necessity is a testimony to an internal lack of unity and integration. For Hegel the ancient polis did possess this cohesion and unity. Some observers conclude from this that at this stage of his development Hegel was looking to the polis as a paradigm, hoping for its resurrection.[56]

[55] *Dokumente*, pp. 281–2.
[56] Cf. Jürgen Habermas' *Nachwort* to his edition of Hegel's *Politische Schriften* (Frankfurt, 1966), p. 358.

'Positivity' and political life: church and state

Yet for all of Hegel's praise for the polis, he always remained fully conscious of the reasons for its decline and there is never any intimation in his writings that he might consider a renascence of ancient republicanism possible. Such Romantic wishful thinking is criticized by him repeatedly. Nevertheless, the dream of a kind of political structure that would cater not only to man as an individual but also to man as a social being always remained with Hegel. The problem for him was how to reach such a synthesis within the conditions of the modern world.

Even while Hegel was slowly evolving towards such a solution, his awareness of the duality and inner split in post-classical life continuously characterized his gropings. 'The Spirit of Christianity and Its Fate' is therefore also one of the most obscure of Hegel's writings, because his attempts there to overcome this split only place him in ever more seemingly insoluble predicaments. It is therefore not surprising that he ends this set of manuscript notes with an evocative passage, indicative of the mood of inner split which he was yet unable to mend: 'And it is its fate that church and state, worship and life, piety and virtue, spiritual and worldly action, can never dissolve into one.'[57] Neither traditional Christianity, nor its critique, was successful in providing a solution.

[57] *Early Theological Writings*, p. 301.

Chapter Three

THE MODERNIZATION OF GERMANY

In 1893 Georg Mollat published a manuscript by Hegel which dealt with political conditions in Germany. The original manuscript had no title, but following a remark by Hegel's disciple and first biographer, Karl Rosenkranz, Mollat entitled it *Kritik der Verfassung Deutschlands*. Later editors of the essay shortened the title to *Die Verfassung Deutschlands*, and the Knox–Pelczynski English edition of Hegel's political writings follows this usage, calling it *The German Constitution*.[1]

It is now firmly established that Hegel composed the final draft of the essay in 1802 at Jena, though an earlier version of the introduction dates back to 1799, when he was still in Frankfurt.[2] Rosenkranz, however, mistakenly attributed it to 1806–8, the period immediately following the French victory over the Prussians at Jena, and tried to see in it a patriotic reaction by Hegel to German humiliation and political impotence, similar to Fichet's *Addresses to the German Nation* of 1808.[3] Rosenkranz later accepted that the essay was written in 1801–2 and thus could not be attributed to the traumatic impact of the Battle of Jena;[4] but the circumstances of Mollat's publication of the essay, as well as his introduction to it, helped to sustain the image that the pamphlet expressed Hegel's concern for the unification of Germany. It was as such that it was interpreted in numerous discussions of Hegel's politics around 1870, when only partial quotes, based on Rosenkranz's biography, were known; and the coincidence of the centenary of Hegel's birth with the high tide of German nationalism helped to sustain this image.[5]

---

[1] G. W. F. Hegel, *Kritik der Verfassung Deutschlands*, ed. G. Mollat (Kassel, 1893).

[2] Rosenzweig, *Hegel und der Staat*, I, 231ff. See also Pelczynski's introductory essay to *Hegel's Political Writings*, pp. 13–14.

[3] Rosenkranz, *Hegels Leben*, pp. 235–6.

[4] See his *Hegel als deutscher Nationalphilosoph* (Leipzig, 1870), p. 62.

[5] Cf. Karl Köstlin, *Hegel in philosophischer, politischer und nationaler Beziehung* (Tübingen, 1870). See also Lasson's introduction to his edition of the essay in *Hegels Schriften zur Politik und Rechtsphilosophie* (Leipzig, 1913),

The modernization of Germany

Though there is no doubt that the total disintegration of the old
Holy Roman Empire of the German Nation in its confrontation with
republican France is at the root of Hegel's treatise, it would be a
mistake to see it as an appeal to nationalism or to classify Hegel as
'an ardent nationalist', as Sidney Hook would like to see him on the
evidence of this essay.[6] As we shall see, the essay makes clear that
ethnic, linguistic or national elements are totally alien to Hegel's
deliberations. Furthermore, in 1814 Hegel warmly welcomed the
decision of the Congress of Vienna not to set up a unified Germany;
in an 'ardent nationalist' such an attitude would certainly be incomprehensible. As we shall also see later, from 1806 to 1813 Hegel
adopted a line of wholehearted support of the French and violently
opposed the German nationalist movement as well as the anti-
French insurrection of 1813 so feverishly advocated by Fichte.[7]

Hegel's concern in his essay on *The German Constitution* is turned
in another direction. The blows dealt by the French revolutionary
army to the antiquated system of the historical Reich were not
viewed by him in terms of a clash of two nations or two national
movements but as a clash between two kinds of states and political
systems. The victory of French arms was evidence of the strength
and cohesion of the modern state, as forged in France by the combination of absolutist centralism and revolutionary transformation.
Against this social force, the medieval and particularist petty
princely *liberum veto* of the disintegrating old German Empire
proved totally helpless. The essay is thus not a call for German
nationalism but for the modernization of the German political system.
When later in 1814–17 Hegel contemplated the modernized, reformed states of Bavaria, Württemberg and Prussia, he saw in them
the modern political structures which in 1802 he envisaged could be
brought about only by political unification. Since not the problem
of unification as such but that of the modernization of the political
system in Germany was his aim, he welcomed these new German states and, because he saw them as having now achieved

Under the Nazis a new printing of Mollat's edition of Hegel's essay was
published, with the title subtly changed to *Die Verfassung des Deutschen
Reiches* (Stuttgart, 1935).

[6] Sidney Hook, 'Hegel Rehabilitated' and 'Hegel and His Apologists' in
W. Kaufmann (ed.), *Hegel's Political Philosophy*, pp. 55–70, 87–105.

[7] The documentary evidence for this is conveniently overlooked by Hook. See
my 'Hegel and Nationalism', in Kaufmann's volume, pp. 109–16; cf.
Herbert Marcuse, *Reason and Revolution*, new ed. (Boston, 1960), pp. 177–
80, 409–19.

his initial purpose, he did not call for any attempt to create a unified political state in Germany. For a nationalist, this would be nonsensical behaviour; for one looking for the modernization of the political system in Germany, the radical transformation of the structure of the German states during 1806–15 meant the realization of what Hegel had been pleading for in his 1802 essay.

We have seen in a previous chapter how Hegel has been groping in his earliest writings for an understanding of the structure of the modern state. Like his commentary on Cart's tract on the Pays de Vaud, the essay on Germany is not, by itself, a theoretical piece of writing. But in trying to wrestle with the realities of political life in Germany, Hegel develops some of his crucial ideas about the emergence and the specific nature of the modern state. It is in this context that the essay on Germany is not only an example of high-quality political writing, but an important step in the development of Hegel's political theory.

THE STATE AS UNIVERSAL POWER AND THE DISSOLUTION OF THE OLD ORDER

The old German Empire at the turn of the eighteenth century was a hodge-podge of kingdoms, principalities, duchies, markgraviates, landgraviates, bishoprics and free imperial cities, all held together by the tenuous semblance of the imperial crown, now firmly established for a couple of centuries in the Habsburg dynasty, bolstered up by legalistic fictions, pious religious humbug about the Universal Empire, and conflicting interests which viewed such an incongruous anomaly as an excellent and convenient arrangement.[8]

Hegel's first confrontation with one segment of this kaleidoscope is a fragment written in 1798 entitled 'On the Recent Domestic Affairs of Württemberg'. It was at this time that Hegel prepared the German translation of Cart's *Confidential Letters*, and the two pieces have in common an attitude of extreme criticism towards the existing oligarchical order in Berne and Württemberg respectively (Hegel's essay on Württemberg was originally entitled by him 'That Magistrates should be elected by the citizens'). Hegel's obvious interest in Württemberg, his homeland, will show itself again after 1815; this is significant not only for purely biographical

[8] For an excellent resumé of political thinking in the late eighteenth-century Old Reich, see Arnold Bernay, 'Reichstradition und Nationalstaatsgedanke 1789–1815', *Historische Zeitschrift* CXL (1929), 55–86.

reasons, but also because Württemberg was the only German *Land* where there existed a strong Diet, traditionally curbing ducal power and actively participating in administration. Württemberg was sometimes called the England of Germany, but at the close of the eighteenth century the Diet, originally a bastion against ducal absolutism, became a stronghold of oligarchical privileges, corrupt practices and entrenched 'positive' rights, jealously guarded by an army of lawyers, clerks and place-men and defended by a fossilized procedure, making any reform in the socio-political structure impossible.

Hegel's essay on Württemberg is very short and incomplete, and the existing fragment is nothing more than a mere sketch for an introduction to the essay proper which probably never got written. Nonetheless, it echoes quite unmistakably a more comprehensive view of contemporary conditions:

Calm satisfaction with the present, hopelessness, patient acquiescence in a fate that is all too great and powerful have changed into hope, expectation, and a resolution for something different. The picture of better and juster times has become lively in the souls of men, and a longing, a sighing for purer and freer conditions has moved all hearts and set them at variance with the actuality [of the present].[9]

The view that institutions have to adapt themselves to changes in human needs and consciousness, already encountered in Hegel's discussions about the transition from paganism to Christianity, is again expressed here most forcefully, this time in relation to the *Zeitgeist* of the French revolutionary era:

General and deep is the feeling that the fabric of the state in its present condition is untenable . . .

How blind they are who may hope that institutions, constitutions, laws which no longer correspond to human manners, needs, and opinions, from which the spirit has flown, can subsist any longer; or that forms in which intellect and feeling now take no interest are powerful enough to be any longer the bond of a nation![10]

Since the fragment breaks off shortly afterward, there is no intimation about Hegel's concrete suggestions for reform. But in another fragment, attributed by Haym to the same period, Hegel advances strong criticism against the Standing Committee of the Württemberg Diet. He points out that the reform has to be based

[9] *Hegel's Political Writings*, p. 243.   [10] *Ibid.* p. 244.

on the Diet itself, not on the Standing Committee which abrogated to itself the power which should reside in the elected assembly. But even this second fragment breaks off at this stage.[11]

Hegel's attempt to discuss conditions in Germany as a whole rests on similar premisses. In an early draft of the introduction to *The German Constitution*, Hegel again stresses that consciousness cannot be happy with the old order. It is a moving and penetrating description of the pettiness of life under the *ancien régime* in Germany, where as a result of the lack of real public life, a person was reduced to his mere individual existence and his property:

All phenomena of this age show that satisfaction cannot be found any more in the old life; this life meant being restricted to an orderly disposition over one's property, a contemplation and enjoyment of one's totally subservient little world; consequently also a self-destruction and exultation in spirit unto heaven, aiming at beautifying this restriction. The needs of the age have, on the one hand, attacked this property; on the other, they have transformed this restriction into luxury. In both cases, man has been made into the master, and his power over actuality has become supreme. Under circumstances of this tough life governed by understanding (*Verstandesleben*), his bad consciousness increases, trying to make his property, things, into the absolute, increasing all the while human misery. And a whiff of a better life has touched this age.[12]

Life in Germany has been reduced to particularism, and what is lacking is the universal power of the state:

In the German Empire there disappeared the power-wielding universality (*die machthabende Allgemeinheit*) as the source of all law; it isolated itself, turned itself into particularity. Hence universality exists only as thought, not as actuality.[13]

These preliminary thoughts in his first draft enable Hegel to begin his final version of *The German Constitution* with the radical statement that 'Germany is no longer a state'.[14] The critique of the *ancien régime* in Germany has a double edge: though the balance of the argument in the essay deals with matters of political institu-

---

[11] See *Schriften zur Politik und Rechtsphilosophie*, pp. 153–4.

[12] *Ibid.* p. 140. This early parallel draft is left out in the English translation.

[13] *Ibid.* p. 141. There are a number of expressions of similar sentiments in Hegel's other writings of that period. In an aphorism from the Jena period, he writes (*Dokumente*, p. 358): 'Balls, public places, the theatre, are not frequented any longer. *On s'assemble en famille* ... [One becomes] bored by the public [sphere].' And in a letter to Zellman written in 1807, he says that in Germany 'the leaders are separated from the people, both do not understand each other'. (Hegel to Zellman, 23 January 1807, *Briefe von und an Hegel*, I, 138).

[14] *Political Writings*, p. 143.

tions and processes, the inadequacies of the political system in Germany are always related to the broader spheres of social relationships and cultural consciousness. Although Hegel very seldom refers directly to Herder, a strong Herderian legacy of viewing historical phenomena within their integral socio-cultural perspective is always present.

At the outset Hegel's essay begins with a methodological criticism of two prevalent schools of constitutional law in Germany: the normative school, which limits itself to enunciating the lofty norms of wished-for behaviour, and the positivist one (today we would probably call it 'behavioural') which 'no longer treats constitutional law as a science (*Wissenschaft*) but only as a description of what exists empirically and not conformably with a rational idea'.[15] In a way already prefiguring his mature thought, Hegel rejects both approaches and reveals his own which would attempt to understand the inner rationale of the actual and its causes:

> The thoughts contained in this essay can have no other aim or effect, when published, save that of promoting the understanding of what is ... For it is not what is that makes us irascible and resentful, but the fact that it is not as it ought to be. But if we recognize that it is as it must be, i.e. that it is not arbitrariness and chance that make it what it is, then we recognize that it is as it ought to be.[16]

It would be a misunderstanding of Hegel's position to interpret this understanding 'of what is' as acquiescence or quietism. We have already seen Hegel's critique of the *ancien régime*, and the whole essay tries to present an alternative – but not through merely opposing existing actuality, but on the basis of understanding its causes, and removing them. Hegel's argument is that only the acceptance of actuality as necessary, given the existing circumstances, can become a starting point for a new departure. As he clearly points out, this method is not an acquiesence in what is, but a critical understanding of it with a view to its transformation. Knowing the causes of things, *rerum cognoscere causas*, implies setting up a system of causal relations which is the prerequisite for purposeful action and eventual change. The *status quo*, which is always open to being understood by rational criteria, is never for Hegel a moral norm. The critical, anti-conservative strain in Hegel comes out very

---

[15] *Ibid.*
[16] *Ibid.* p. 145. The practical intensity of Hegel's preoccupation with 'that which is' can be gauged by his remark that reading the daily paper is 'the morning prayer of the realist' (*Dokumente*, p. 360).

clearly when he states, 'It is generally fashionable everywhere to make into a *moral* power the mode of political existence which the individual states possess, and so to implant its sacrosanctity in men's hearts as to make it something no less fixed and inviolable than the generally accepted morals and religion of a nation.'[17]

Hegel's statement that Germany is no longer a state presupposes a definition of what is a state and an explanation of why the present system in Germany falls short of these requirements. It is during this discussion that the theoretical dimension of Hegel's essay stands out most sharply. It is also on this level that the problematical nature of Hegel's groping for an adequate understanding of what the state is in modern conditions is most evident.

Hegel's definition of a state brings into focus the two poles between which his quest for an appropriate expression for the specificity of political life was trying to find its rest. We have already seen that Hegel views as incomplete the conventional theory of the state which satisfies itself with the preservation of property. Property, however, still figures in his own definition of the state in *The German Constitution*, though it is tempered by solidarity, a readiness for common action:

A multitude of human beings can only call itself a state if it be united for the common defence of the entirety of its property. What is self-explanatory in this proposition must none the less be stated, namely that this union has not merely the intention of defending itself; the point is that it defends itself by actual arms, be its power and its success what they may.[18]

The corollary of this is that 'if a multitude is to form a state, then it must form a common military and public authority'.[19] Despite appearances, this is not a view that sees the state as a mere instrument for the preservation of property. Following Hegel's later language, one can say that his definition here hovers somewhat uncertainly between 'civil society' and 'state'. For though the defence of property is postulated here as the central core of the state, it is significant that Hegel does not refer in his definition to the private property of the individual members of the state, but talks about *its* property – the property of the group. Furthermore, in a language somewhat reminiscent of Rousseau, Hegel refers to the state thus defined as a 'union', thus transcending mere aggregation. Nor is the criterion for the existence or non-existence of such a union as straightforward as it might look. On the one hand Hegel

[17] *Political Writings*, pp. 206–7.
[18] *Ibid.* p. 153. [19] *Ibid.* p. 154; cf. also p. 173.

makes it clear that a state does not exist where there is 'merely the *intention* of defending itself'; the intention has to be actualized 'by actual arms'. Yet, on the other hand, he significantly adds that success in that venture is by itself immaterial. Not the success of arms is significant, but the actual recourse to them for defence. It is on a highly anti-Hobbesian note that Hegel rounds off his definition by saying that it is enough that the state 'defend[s] itself by actual arms, be its power and its success what they may'. Not power, but common will, is the foundation of the state.

It is the existence of this actual readiness for common action and common defence which is the crux of Hegel's definition of the state. This solidarity is tested in times of war rather than in times of peace, and hence 'the health of the state is generally revealed not so much in the calm of peace as in the stir of war. Peace is the state of enjoyment and activity in seclusion, when government is a prudent paternalism, making only ordinary demands on its subjects. But in war the power of association of all with the whole is in evidence.'[20]

The old German Empire is not a state not just because it failed in its military confrontation with republican France; to Hegel failure as such in an enterprise of this sort is by itself irrelevant. What is relevant is not the failure of the Empire but the fact that it is not at all 'united for the defence of the entirety of its property', i.e. that it possesses no machinery for defence, and this is a proof for the lack of the element of will to common action which is at the root of political life. Not the failure of German arms makes Germany into a non-state, but the virtual non-existence of such a common organ for defence.

The impotence of political life in Germany, according to Hegel, lies in the fact that instead of a common universality there is in Germany nothing but an aggregate of particular interests: 'The German political edifice is nothing but the sum of rights which the individual parts have wrested from the whole.'[21] What happened in Germany was that the commonwealth, the *res publica*, became *res privata* and, according to a parallel draft of the essay, 'this attempt to make public power into private property is nothing else than the dissolution of the state'.[22]

[20] *Ibid.* pp. 143–4. This can very easily be misconstrued as if meant to glorify war, which it evidently does not imply. Hegel does not say that war is the health of states, but that in war this health is put to the test – a very different statement. On the complex and seminal question of war in Hegel, see ch. 10.
[21] *Ibid.* pp. 150–1.
[22] *Schriften zur Politik*, p. 13.

Here Hegel brings out one of the characteristics of the late German Reich, derived from its feudal past, viz., that political rights were viewed under the rubric of private rights, and public and private law became indistinguishable. To Hegel, this distinction between private right and the public sphere is crucial to the understanding of the differentiated modern state. Hegel points out that 'one very important instance is the distinction between political power and an object of right; an object of right is private property, [but] political power cannot be private property, it flows from the state . . . What private property acquires is a matter of chance and caprice (*Willkür*); political power must relate most closely to the whole.'[23]

In the final draft of the essay, this universality of political power is defined even more pointedly:

An act issued by the public authority is a general act and in virtue of its genuine generality it carries in itself the rule for its application. The matter it affects is general, homogeneous. The act of the public authority carries in itself a free and general determinacy and its execution is at the same time its application.[24]

In Germany this universality does not exist, hence Germany is only a *Gedankenstaat*, a state which exists in thought and imagination alone, not in actuality. Germany is nothing other than a plethora of conflicting jurisdictions, claims, rights and interests; German constitutional law is to Hegel 'but a register of the most varied constitutional rights acquired in the manner of private rights'.[25] This, Hegel goes on to explain, was brought about by the historical development in Germany, where pristine German freedom has not been transformed into a politically coherent public order:

This form of German constitutional law is deeply grounded in what has been the chief fame of the Germans, namely their desire for freedom. This drive it is which never allowed the Germans to become a people subjecting itself to a common public authority, even after every other European people had become subject to the domination of a state of its own making. The stubbornness of the German character has held out against being subdued to the point where the individual [parts of Germany] would have sacrificed their particular [interests] to society, uniting themselves together into a universal whole, and found freedom in a common, free subjection to a supreme public authority.[26]

23 *Ibid.* p. 63.
24 *Political Writings*, p. 181.
25 *Ibid.* p. 149.
26 *Ibid.* pp. 146–7. In an earlier draft (*Dokumente*, p. 285), Hegel says: 'So a political structure came about, whose particular parts – each principality, each estate, each city, each guild, everyone who possessed any right – acquired these rights by himself, had not been given them by a universal

42

The state as universal power

This dissolution of political power into mere private rights is at the root of German impotence and is the basis for Hegel's statement that Germany is no longer a state. The general internal paralysis resultant from such a lack of political power is illustrated by Hegel when he enters into procedural details:

The paralysis ... may occur at each one of the stages. A general regulation is made; it is now to be carried into effect and in case of resistance legal procedure is necessary. If the resistance offered is not made by legal process, the execution of the regulation remains dormant; but if it is legally made, a decision can be hindered; if decision issues, no consequences may follow. But this *ens rationis* of a judgement is meant to be executed and a penalty should accompany [non-compliance]; therefore an order issues to compel the full execution of the judgement. This order in turn is not carried out, so a judgement follows.[27]

The state, according to Hegel, requires 'a universal center, a monarch, and estates, wherein the various powers, foreign affairs, the armed forces, finances relevant thereto, etc., would be united, a center which would not merely direct but would have in addition the power necessary for asserting itself and its decrees, and for keeping the individual parts dependent on itself.'[28] Such a center does not exist in Germany, where everyone of the 300-odd principalities, duchies and cities feels itself wholly independent of the imperial authority.

This being the case, the question could be asked why Hegel does not consider these particular political entities – some of them kingdoms of considerable power – into which the Reich had become divided, as states in their own right and thus recognize that what exists in Germany is not one state but a plurality of states. Hegel is very explicit on this: throughout the essay he refers to the individual

by a state, as a whole. Instead of each power and right in the constitution deriving from the whole, in Germany each member . . . has to thank himself for his political power. The principles of the system of German public law therefore are not derived from premises grounded in rational concepts, but are, as far as they are active, abstractions of actualities. Possession came before law, and it did not spring forth from laws, but was achieved by itself . . . German public law is therefore basically private law, and political rights are legal possession, property.'

[27] *Political Writings*, p. 183. It would be intriguing to speculate how much this could be said to be an adequate description of what passes for judicial and political procedure in the United States, whose constitution is, after all, one of the crowning achievements of the eighteenth century. Surely political rights are viewed in the U.S. under the rubric of private right, and a political right is ultimately treated as property. That Hegel himself did not consider America as a state, merely a 'civil society', see his *Vernunft in der Geschichte*, ed. J. Hoffmeister (Hamburg, 1955), p. 207.

[28] *Political Writings*, p. 150.

43

entities as 'estates' (*Stände*), not as states (*Staaten*). The reason for this distinction must lie in the fact that Hegel considers them as based on private right and acquisition, their legitimacy and boundaries resting on personal inheritance, marriage contracts and dynastic idiosyncracies. The authority whose writ runs in these territories is the personal authority of their rulers, not a universal political power. They are patrimonies, private estates magnified into quasi-political entities; they have succeeded in reducing the state power of the Empire to naught, but have not established an alternative focus for political power. True, they are similar to what passed for political entities in Europe several centuries earlier; but European states emerged from the private, embryonic stage to base themselves on universal political ties. In Germany, this stage has not yet been attained:

The power of these individual states has inhibited the growth of a state-power in Germany, and their aggrandisement has made such a power ever more impossible. The German character's stubborn insistence on independence has reduced to a pure formality everything that might serve towards the erection of a state-power and the union of society in a state.[29]

This critique applies not only to the specific conditions in Germany. Hegel's dissatisfaction with German circumstances is an application of a general critique of the old patrimonial state which viewed political power as nothing more than an expression and extension of personal property rights. It is the same criticism which he waged, following Cart, against the old Bernese system and which he would wage later once again when polemicizing during the Restoration against the Historical School of Jurisprudence and Ludwig von Haller's idea of a patrimonial state,[30] when he claimed that property is not the base of the state.

AGAINST UNIFORMITY

Hegel's definition of the state as a union for the defence of what is common to the members of a society is accompanied by a discussion of those traits of social life that are to him indifferent to the existence of the body politic. His insistence upon common defence as the basis of public authority is reinforced by stating that all other characteristics which are sometimes attributed to the state are

[29] *Ibid.* p. 196; also p. 188.
[30] See Hegel's long footnote, attacking von Haller, in *Philosophy of Right*, § 258.

irrelevant: they may or may not appear in certain individual instances, but their existence or non-existence is incidental to the nature of political power. Hegel proceeds to enumerate and catalogue these immaterial characteristics. For other political thinkers, some of these would have to appear as crucial to the very existence of the state or to its proper functioning. Hence Hegel's catalogue is an extremely interesting polemic against those other political theorists who wished to place the locus of political power somewhere else and thus saddled the state with a lot of attributes and activities which, according to Hegel, are not part of the basic requirements of political life.

This is the list of the criteria which are to Hegel immaterial to the question whether a certain entity is or is not a state:

(a) Whether the holders of authority be one or many;

(b) Whether they be born to this distinction or elected to it;

(c) The uniformity or lack of uniformity of civil rights among individuals;

(d) To which power legislation belongs or in which proportion various estates or the citizens in general participate in the process of legislation;

(e) The form and structure of administration;

(f) Equality or inequality of taxation;

(g) Whether the different geographical parts of the state are differently taxed;

(h) The ties among members of the state in respect of manners, education and language;

(i) Existence or non-existence of identity in religious matters.[31]

The last two points are of special significance. Item (h) directly relates to Hegel's attitude towards modern theories of ethnic nationalism. It is most significant to note that it is precisely in the *modern* state that Hegel sees ethnic-linguistic ties as unnecessary. Any assessment of what Hegel's intention in writing the essay on Germany was cannot overlook the following straightforward statement, which makes it impossible to attribute to Hegel any views which are sympathetic to modern notions of nationalism:

In our day, the tie between members of a state in respect of manners, education, language may be rather loose or even non-existent. Identity in these matters, once the foundation of a people's union, is now to be reckoned amongst the accidents whose character does not hinder a mass from constituting a public

31 This is an itemized condensation of Hegel's argument on pp. 155–8 of *Political Writings*.

authority. Rome or Athens, like any small modern state, could not have subsisted if the numerous languages current in the Russian Empire had been spoken within their borders, or if amongst their citizens manners had been as different as they are in Russia or, for that matter, as manners and education are now in every big city in a large country. Differences in language and dialect ... and differences in manners and education in the different estates – such heterogeneous and at the same time most powerful factors the preponderating weight of the Roman Empire's power (once it had become great) was able to overcome and hold together, just as in modern states the same result is produced by the spirit and art of political institutions. The dissimilarity in culture and manners is a necessary product as well as a necessary condition of the stability of modern states.[32]

Language belongs, according to Hegel, to the realm of the accidental and naturalistic, hence it is immaterial in a modern state, based, as the latter is, on the rational allegiance of the citizen to the community as mediated 'by the spirit and art of political institutions'. This cultural pluralism and multi-lingualism go together with religious diversity. Under the specific conditions of Germany, Hegel sees the principle of *cuius regio, eius religio* as catastrophic to religion and state alike; though it was a way out of the religious strife of the Reformation, it imposed on the subject the religion of his prince and brought religion into the political realm. If the ancient polis needed religion as part of its integrating civic culture, the modern state, Hegel argues, has to learn to live with religious diversity and dissent. Religious rights should in no way whatsoever interfere with political rights and participation in political life:

Here in religion at least an identity might have been thought necessary, but this identity too is something which modern states have found that they can do without ...

Similarity of religion has no more prevented wars or united peoples into a state than dissimilarity of religion has in our day rent the state asunder.[33]

These considerations resolve what would otherwise have appeared as a paradox in Hegel's political thinking. Because the state is based,

[32] *Ibid.* p. 158. In the parallel draft, Hegel adds a few details (*Schriften zur Politik*, pp. 24–5): 'A small state, Rome in its origins, or Athens, could not have survived, if within its walls Greek, French, German, Russian, Kamtchat, Kirghiz, etc. had been spoken ... or if as varied manners had prevailed among its citizens as the manners of the Russian court aristocracy, rich burghers, Kossacks, etc. [vary from each other] ... [The] powerful Austrian or Russian monarchies; their monarchs reign over innumerable languages ... The language of many provinces of France or even England is utterly different from the common language which is considered as the official language; in Wales, in the Hebrides, one does not even speak English.'

[33] *Political Writings*, pp. 158–9. Cf. *Philosophy of Right*, § 209: 'A man counts as a man in virtue of his manhood alone, not because he is a Jew, Catholic, Protestant, German, Italian, etc.'

for Hegel, on the common readiness of its citizens to defend themselves collectively, all other spheres of life are left to the citizens'
free decision and choice. The form of political framework which
emerges out of Hegel's discussion of the nature of the modern state
is a highly sophisticated and differentiated pluralistic system, where
the state authority is basic and necessary – but minimal.

What in Hegel's later writings would appear as the intricate relationship between the universality of the state and the particularistic nature of civil society, is spelt out here most clearly, though
the distinctive terminology is not yet articulated:

This is not the place to argue at length that the center, as the public authority,
i.e. the government, must leave to the freedom of the citizens whatever is not
necessary for its appointed function of organizing and maintaining authority
and thus for its security at home and abroad ...

We also regard these people as fortunate to which the state gives a free hand
in subordinate general activities, just as we regard a public authority as infinitely strong if it can be supported by a free and unregimented spirit of its
people.[34]

If, however, the state does not follow this pluralistic line, the
dangers are very clear and evident: people may then confuse what is
necessary with what is arbitrary and accidental in their political
allegiance, and the whole political edifice may be put in jeopardy.
Furthermore, an authoritarian system that would attempt to cater
for the totality of its subjects' interests and needs would stultify
spontaneity by its subordination of every individual to the hierarchy
of benevolent petty despots:

A mechanical hierarchy, highly intellectual and devoted to noble ends, evinces
no confidence whatever in its citizens and can expect nothing from them. It has
no assurance in any action not ordered, carried out, and arranged by itself;
thus it bans freewill gifts and sacrifices; it displays to its subjects its conviction
of their lack of intellect, its contempt for their capacity to assess and do what
is compatible with their private interests, and its belief in general profligacy.
Thus it cannot hope for any vital action, any support from its subjects' self-
respect.[35]

Hegel's language alludes that his argument here is aimed both at
political theorists, like Fichte, who would like to achieve a total
regimentation of social life by the state, as well as against the radical

---

[34] *Political Writings*, pp. 161, 164. Cf. p. 159: 'The example of almost all
European states could teach us this, since the more powerful of the genuine
states ... have laws that are through and through the reverse of uniform.'
[35] *Ibid.* p. 163.

47

attempts of the French Revolution which began from abstract principles of human rights and culminated with the reign of terror:

> Of course on the political theories of our day, partly propounded by would-be philosophers and teachers of the rights of man and partly realized in tremendous political experiments, everything we have excluded from the necessary concept of public authority . . . is subjected to the immediate activity of the supreme public authority, and in such a way that it is settled by that authority itself and driven by it down to the last detail.[36]

In an outspoken attack on the centralism of republican France which made almost every sphere of life dependent upon central decision, Hegel's view of what the state should not be becomes most evident:

> However, in recent theories, carried partly into effect, the fundamental presupposition is that a state is a machine with a single spring which imparts movement to all the rest of the infinite wheelwork . . .
>
> The pedantic craving to determine every detail, the illiberal jealousy of [any arrangement whereby] an estate, a corporation, etc., adjusts and manages its own affair, this mean carping at any independent action by the citizens . . . is clothed in the garb of rational principles. On these principles not a shilling of the public expenditure on poor relief in a country of 20 or 30 million inhabitants may be incurred unless it has first been not merely allowed but actually ordered, controlled, and audited by the supreme government. The appointment of every village schoolmaster, the expenditure of every penny for a pane of glass in a school, church or a village hall, the appointment of every toll-clerk or court officer or local justice of the peace is to be an immediate emanation and effect of the highest authority.[37]

Hegel is thus able to combine a critique of the centralizing, authoritarian consequences inherent in the principles of the French Revolution with a recognition of its liberating effects. Yet this critique is aimed not only at the centralism of republican France; in a way, republican centralism is nothing other to Hegel than the old, paternalistic state writ large and universalized. Frederickian Prussia and Jacobin France ultimately stand for the same principle: by invoking the idea of unlimited sovereignty they end up with a state as a machine 'with a single spring'. That the one bases its legitimacy on royal absolutism whereas the other sees itself legiti-

---

[36] *Ibid.* p. 159.
[37] *Ibid.* p. 161. This is incredibly similar to Marx's critique of French centralism in his *Eighteenth Brumaire:* 'Every common interest was . . . snatched from the activity of society's members themselves and made an object of government activity, from a bridge, a schoolhouse and the communal property of a village community to the railways, the national wealth and the national university of France.' Cf. Marx–Engels, *Selected Works* (Moscow, 1962), I, 333.

mized by popular sovereignty is immaterial to the common trait shared by both systems: the utter subordination of social activity to the power of the state, the attempt to stifle every and any voluntary form of association. Where most of Hegel's contemporaries saw only the external difference between them, Hegel achieved a rare insight into the common denominator underlying both Prussian absolutism and French radical republicanism. In a language one would find again only in Tocqueville, Hegel draws the harsh parallel between the old absolutism and the new republicanism:

> How dull and spiritless a life is engendered in a modern state where everything is regulated from the top downwards, where nothing with any general implications is left to the management and execution of interested parties of the people – in a state like what the French Republic has made itself – is to be experienced only in the future, if indeed this pitch of pedantry in domination can persist. But what life and what sterility reigns in another equally regulated state, in the Prussian, strikes anyone who sets foot in the first town there or sees its complete lack of scientific or artistic genius, or assesses its strength otherwise than by the ephemeral energy which a single genius has been able to generate in it for a time by pressure.[38]

There were very few people around 1800 who had the clarity of vision to see this and express their uneasiness about such tendencies in modern society. Hegel has given vent here to his apprehensions about what modern life may turn out to be in the political realm, and while advocating the modernization of Germany he also suggests the alternative, the state which would center on common defence while leaving all other spheres of social life to the free play of human interests, passions and inclinations. The institutionalized form of such an arrangement is not yet spelt out in this essay, yet it does contain Hegel's attempt to relate the growth of the modern state to the shift in the socio-cultural sphere which caused the emergence of these tendencies towards centralization and overall control. It was this awareness of the social forces at work which would later enable Hegel to set up the institutional guarantees aimed at taming and circumscribing the attempt of the state to subordinate everything to its power. To this discussion of the social forces involved in the emergence of the modern state we shall now turn our attention.

[38] *Political Writings*, pp. 163–4. Because of these considerations, Hegel would later in the essay disqualify Prussia from the role of uniting Germany and would rejoice in the Prussian defeat at Jena in 1806.

The modernization of Germany

In suggesting an historical explanation for the rise of the modern state, which created one political center of allegiance instead of the multitude of personal and particularistic relations characterizing feudalism, Hegel does not limit himself to changes in the political order alone. It is to the culture of the bourgeoisie (*Bürgerstand*) and its ethos that Hegel attributes the changes in the political realm. In an analysis which in its attempt to understand the connections between economics, politics and religion is similar to those to be found later in Marx and Weber, Hegel sees in bourgeois culture the roots of individualism, division of labour, diversity of religious beliefs and the emergence of the modern state.

In the old feudal order, especially as it appeared in Germany, 'there was no state power opposed to individuals and independent of them as there is in modern states. The state's power and the power and free will of individuals were one and the same.'[39] This simple, unmediated unity of the public sphere as subsumed under private life and particularism meant that no public power existed as distinguishable from the effective power of those free individuals who could coalesce to make their will into the law of the land. This unreflective unity in the secular sphere has as its corollary a unity in Church life as well: 'When religion was uniform, and when the still embryo *bourgeoisie* had not introduced a great heterogeneity into the whole, princes, dukes and lords could regard one another more easily as a whole and accordingly could act as a whole.'[40]

But the nascent burgher class introduced diversification and a division of labour:

But when through the growth of the Imperial cities, the *bourgeois* sense, which cares only for an individual and not self-subsistent end and has no regard for the whole, began to become a power, this individualization of dispositions would have demanded a more and more general and positive bond.[41]

This implied a necessary change in the conduct of public affairs. The public sphere began to differentiate itself as a consequence of the social division of labour introduced by the bourgeoisie. Under the old, feudal order, everyone dealt indiscriminately with things private and public; the emergence of the bourgeois class meant that each person began to concentrate more and more on his individual, private affairs. This individualism and privatization created the

[39] *Ibid.* p. 189.   [40] *Ibid.*   [41] *Ibid.* p. 190.

50

necessity for a differentiated public sphere, since otherwise public matters would not have been cared for by anybody at all. Private life and public activity became distinct from one another – and this, to Hegel, is the major characteristic of modern society:

> With the change in manners and the way of life each individual was more preoccupied with his own necessities and his own private affairs. By far the greater number of free men, i.e. the strictly bourgeois class (*Bürgerstand*), must have had to look exclusively for their own necessities and their own living. As states became larger, those people who must have had to concern themselves exclusively with their own affairs formed a class of their own. There was an increase in the mass of things needed by the free man and the noble, who had to maintain themselves in their social position respectively by industry or by work for the state. The foreign relations involved in the greater complexity of national affairs became stranger to every individual. As a result of all these changes the management of national affairs became more and more closely concentrated in a center consisting of a monarch and the estates.[42]

The political structure of the modern state derives its form from its history. The idea of representation derives from the feudal system and the subsequent development of the modern bourgeoisie. Representation is not, to Hegel, a novel idea introduced by theories of natural rights or the French Revolution, though the decay of the representative institutions of France made their reintroduction by the Revolution a necessity. Yet basic to Hegel's view is his historical understanding of the socio-cultural context which gave rise to representation in Western society:

> Representation is so deeply interwoven with the essence of the feudal constitution in its development along with the rise of the bourgeois that we may call it the silliest of notions to suppose it an invention of the most recent times. By the transformation of free men into masters, the feudal constitution, i.e. in modern countries, a state has been developed in which each individual no longer has a direct voice himself in any national affair; on the contrary all obey a whole founded by themselves, i.e. a state, and its branches and particularizations (the laws), an abiding fixed center to which each individual has a mediate relation derived from representation. All modern states subsist by representation, and its degeneration alone, i.e. the loss of its true essence, has destroyed France's constitution, though not France as a state.[43]

The political structure of the modern state Hegel has in mind is thus an integral outgrowth of European history, not an outcome of a cataclysmic event. The French Revolution ultimately only expressed in violent form the latent developments inherent in the European historical legacy. The idea of representation, integrally

[42] *Ibid.* p. 202.   [43] *Ibid.* p. 206.

developing out of the forests of Germany through feudalism and modern, bourgeois individualism, is turned by Hegel into a principle of world historical significance:

The system of representation is the system of all modern European states. It did not exist in the forests of Germany, but it did arise from them; it marks an epoch in world-history. The continuity of world-culture has led the human race beyond oriental despotisms, through a republic's world-domination, and then out of the fall of Rome into a middle term between these extremes . . .

This system did not exist in the forests of Germany, because each nation must on its own account have run through its own proper course of development before it encroaches on the universal course of world history.[44]

In this context Hegel also states quite explicitly that the modern state cannot succeed in emulating the participatory system of the direct democracy of the classical polis; the modern state needs mediation, and this is the function of representation: 'The size of the modern states makes it quite impossible to realize the ideal of giving every free individual a share in debating and deciding political affairs of universal concern.'[45]

The success of the modern states in Europe depended upon their ability to subordinate particular groups – warlike barons, estates, religious sects – to one sovereign authority. Richelieu is, to Hegel, the architect of modern France: it was he who smashed the Huguenots' 'state within a state', yet guaranteed their right to practice their religion in private; he thus confined religion to its proper place, that of a private affair, not a focus for political organ-ization. The modern state in France and England is a 'success in pacifying and uniting the elements which fermented within the state and threatened to wreck it'.[46] In Germany, however, the precise opposite occurred: the Treaty of Westphalia made religion dependent upon political suzerainty, and in so doing it severed completely any vestige of the old Imperial bond still existing, while at the same time instituting a system of religious coercion and persecution. Germany got the worst of both worlds: the decay of central authority coupled with petty religious intolerance – the precise opposite of what a modern state is for Hegel.[47]

A further aspect of modernization is, according to Hegel, a gradual disappearance of the distinction between the old nobility and the nascent bourgeoisie. Here again the French Revolution

---

[44] *Ibid.* p. 203. Some of the ideas of Hegel's later philosophy of history are already clearly evident in this passage.
[45] *Ibid.* p. 160. [46] *Ibid.* p. 217 [47] *Ibid.* pp. 198, 213, 232.

only intensified and legitimized a lengthy process of historical development. The universalistic principle of *carrière ouverte aux talents*, which would figure very prominently in Hegel's later writings, is here conceived as one of the striking traits of the new age.[48]

Germany and Italy are both mentioned several times by Hegel as two examples of countries where the emergence of the modern state has been thwarted by a combination of political and religious centrifugal forces. It is in this context that Hegel mentions, and praises, Machiavelli, and the passage in which this is done has been taken to suggest an affinity between the political thinking of Hegel and that of Machiavelli.[49] It is therefore of some interest to try and specify what it is that Hegel saw in Machiavelli as worthy of admiration. Moreover, since Hegel tries to place Machiavelli in a methodological perspective as well, the full measure of Hegel's assessment of Machiavelli is of utmost importance. Hegel bases his interpretation of *Il Principe* on the last chapter, in which Machiavelli calls for the liberation of Italy from the foreign barbarian invaders. He compares the Florentine secretary with Cato and sees his thoughts not as a general theory of politics but as a tract for his time, a *Gelegenheitsschrift*:

Profoundly moved by this situation of general distress, hatred, disorder, and blindness, an Italian statesman grasped with cool circumspection the necessary idea of the salvation of Italy through its unification on one state ...

Machiavelli's fundamental aim of erecting Italy into a state was misunderstood from the start by the blind who took his work as nothing but a foundation of tyranny or a golden mirror for an ambitious oppressor ... In this instance, however, there can be no question of any choice of means. Gangrenous limbs cannot be cured with lavender water. A situation in which poison and assassination are common weapons demands remedies of no gentle kind ...

It is utterly senseless to treat the execution of an idea directly created out of an insight into the Italian situation as a compendium of moral and political principles applicable indifferently to any and every situation, i.e. to none.

[48] *Ibid.* p. 205: 'This process whereby the difference [between nobility and bourgeoisie] is being diminished by nature and in most states (e.g. in Prussia, to some extent, in civil affairs; in England, Austria, and other states in military affairs), has been intensified to the extreme in France. There judicial positions and a military career are closed to birth, and the person as such is made into a principle.'

[49] Cassirer even saddled Hegel with the charge that 'he dreamed of becoming a second Machiavelli', whatever this may mean; see Ernst Cassirer, *The Myth of the State* (New Haven, 1946), p. 122. Cf. also Hermann Heller, *Hegel und der nationale Machtstaatsgedanke in Deutschland* (Leipzig and Berlin, 1921); and A. Elkan, 'Die Entdeckung Machiavellis in Deutschland zu begin des 19. Jahrhunderts', *Historische Zeitschrift* cxix (1919).

The modernization of Germany

You must come to the reading of *The Prince* immediately after being impressed by the history of the centuries before Machiavelli and the history of his own times. Then indeed it will appear as not merely justified but as an extremely great and true conception produced by a genuinely political head with an intellect of the highest and noblest kind.[50]

This purely instrumental view of Machiavelli's *Il Principe* within the historical context of its composition is heightened by Hegel's remark that in dedicating the book to Lorenzo de' Medici, Machiavelli was merely playing on this ruler's vanity in order to move him to put an end to a political situation in which 'assassination, poison and treachery' were the order of the day. One detects a glimpse of Hegel's *List der Vernunft* here, the notion which Hegel later used to explain how world historical leaders are led to great achievements while all the time motivated by base, trivial and self-serving causes. A similar aspect comes to light when, contrary to Machiavelli, Hegel remarks that Cesare Borgia's downfall was a necessity, and not – as Machiavelli would have it – just a piece of bad luck: 'We must descry in [Cesare's] fall a higher necessity which did not allow him to enjoy the fruit of his deeds or to exploit them to greater effectiveness, for nature, as it appears in his vices, seems to have intended him rather for ephemeral splendour and for being merely an instrument for the founding of a state.'[51]

It is in this mood that Hegel reads Machiavelli and comments upon him. One can certainly take exception to his way of reading Machiavelli; but it is a strictly historicized understanding of *The Prince*. To Hegel, Italy was in a situation in which political power disappeared and particularism reigned supreme; it was in such a context that Machiavelli appeared as a restorer of political power, not a counsellor to princes.

CAN GERMANY BE MODERNIZED? THESEUS AND RESIGNATION

In his essay Hegel comes back time and again to the problem of the incompatibility between political institutions and the actual contemporary conditions prevailing in Germany. It is his conclusion that social and political arrangements in Germany are hopelessly out of date which gives his criticism theoretical dimension; it is this con-

---

[50] *Political Writings*, pp. 219–20. This should be compared with the uncritical romanticization of Machiavelli in Fichte's *Machiavell*, which evoked an enthusiastic response from Carl von Clausewitz.
[51] *Political Writings*, p. 222.

viction which also makes explicit the difference between him and the Burkean frame of mind. Hegel's feeling for the traditional and the historical is strong and he explains everything, including representation, in historical, developmental terms. Yet his admiration for the historical is balanced by his critique of 'postivity' which he sees as an uncritical veneration of institutions just because they happen to exist or because they have functioned well in the past. It is as a reformer and modernizer, not as a traditionalist, that Hegel levels his radical critique of conditions in Germany, while at the same time remaining deeply conscious of the historical forces of the past:

The organization of this body called the German constitution was built up in a life totally different from the life it had later had and has now. The justice and power, the wisdom and courage of times past; the honour and blood, the well-being and distress of generations long dead; and the relationships and manners which have perished with them; all these are expressed in the forms of this body. But the course of time and of the civilization that has been meanwhile developing has sundered the fate of that past from the life of the present. The building in which that fate dwelt is no longer supported by the fate of the present generation.[52]

The dissolution which has thus overtaken Germany is fraught with dangers. The disappearance of the common bond uniting individuals in one body politic pushes men into an atomistic isolation which dehumanizes them. In a passage which may be seen to prefigure some of the dangers which were to bedevil German social and political life a century and more after Hegel's essay, he diagnoses tendencies in Germany which need to be checked in time:

The German people may be incapable of intensifying its obstinate adherence to particularism to that point of madness reached by the Jewish people – a people incapable of uniting in common life with any other. The German people may not be able to carry separatism to such a pitch of frenzy as to murder and be murdered until the state is wiped out. Nevertheless, particularism has prerogative and precedence in Germany.[53]

One of the main reasons which Hegel sees as contributing to this disintegration of political power in Germany is the peculiarity inherent in the fact that the old German Reich has been considered coeval and coexistent with the universal Empire. Hegel engages in a lengthy historical and legalistic argument, the aim of which is to show that the claim to universal Empire emptied the old German Reich of its effective political power. By claiming suzerainty over

[52] *Ibid.* p. 146.   [53] *Ibid.* p. 242; cf. *Early Theological Writings*, pp. 182–205.

foreign lands, the German Emperors turned political power into a fiction. They received fictitious expressions of allegiance from foreign monarchs, and this, in turn, gave foreign governments a say in the affairs of the Empire. Sweden, Denmark and England thus attained effective power within the Empire. Moreover, the Emperors embroiled the power of the Reich in the defence of territories that had nothing to do with the historical German state, and the real power of the Empire suffered further diminution due to such claims.

Hegel thus disposes of the historical claims of the Empire to Poland, Hungary, Naples and Lombardy; he limits the German Empire to areas which could constitute some sort of political unity. The scourge of Germany – and of Italy – has been the confusion between a state, which can wield effective political power based on common defence, and the chimera of a universal Empire which forever remained an abstraction and thus vitiated the achievement of actual political power. Germany would have to emancipate itself from the medieval, chivalrous, Christian romantic utopianism of a universal Empire, in the same way as it had disposed of the claim to universality of the Catholic Church. In its stead, a modern state would emerge, based on a central power and offering religious toleration to all.[54]

Hegel's discussion of the distinction between the German Reich and the universal Empire also refers to the problem of Prussia. Though the Mark of Brandenburg, the crucible of Prussia, was always unmistakably a part of the German Reich, Hegel entertains some doubts as to whether the area strictly called 'Prussia' (i.e. the old warrior state of the Teutonic Order, which passed on to the Hohenzollern dynasty at a later date) is really a part of the historical Reich.[55] This is, in a way, nothing more than a curiosity, just another example of the unique complexity confronting anyone who would like to disentangle the Gordian knot which has been woven for a thousand years since the days of Charlemagne, when the Frankish king became Roman Emperor. It does, however, make it clear once again that any simplistic view which would like to see Hegel's essay as an expression of German nationalism *tout court*, is plainly abstracting from historical realities and textual evidence.

Hegel comes back to the issue of Prussia towards the end of the essay, when he attempts to confront the question of how the

[54] *Political Writings*, pp. 174–8; cf. *Dokumente*, p. 359, where Hegel distinguishes between a state and an 'empire', which he calls 'an empty concept'.
[55] *Political Writings*, pp. 174–5, 198.

reconstruction of political life in Germany can be accomplished. Two candidates, potentially capable of undertaking the task of political unification and modernization, present themselves to Hegel: Prussia and Austria. Hegel chooses Austria, out of considerations which derive from his views about the comparative political structures of the two entities involved.[56]

Prussia, as we have seen earlier, is to Hegel the epitome of a mechanistic, hierarchical, authoritarian political structure. In Prussia everything is in the hands of the state, regulated and regimented by it; 'sterility' reigns in the country and it is completely devoid of 'scientific or artistic genius'.[57] Furthermore, since Hegel sees representation as the mark of the modern state, Prussia has to be ruled out. While in the Habsburg crownlands of Austria and Bohemia the traditional representative Diets have been preserved, they have totally disappeared in the Prussian provinces:

> The interest of this German freedom naturally seeks protection from a state which itself rests on this system of freedom ... The true, abiding ... interest cannot now find any protection in Prussia. The estates of the Prussian provinces have lost their significance owing to the power of the King's authority.[58]

Finally, Hegel fears the drive for self-aggrandizement which he discerns in Prussia. If Prussia were to become the renovator of Germany, it would not unite the disparate members of the German polity into one body politic, but would rather simply Prussianize all of Germany. The dullness, spiritlessness and sterility of Prussia would become the common norm for all of Germany. In a curious passage Hegel likens Prussia to a *nouveau riche*, and Hegel's fear that a Prussianized Germany would be nothing other than a mere cloak for the brutal interests of 'civil society' adds a fascinating dimension not only to Hegel's own perspicacity of vision, but possibly also to the perspective of later developments in Germany which, after all, were so very different from what Hegel would have liked them to be:

> Prussia's modern politics have not proceeded from the principle of royalty or majesty, but from the *bourgeoisie*, and now, e.g. in contrast to the Austrian power, are in a position of a *bourgeois* who has built up his resources tiresomely penny by penny through his labour in contrast to the free nobleman who has inherited wealth.[59]

Though the choice of Austria is complicated because of the

[56] Cf. Haym, *Hegel und seine Zeit*, p. 74; Habermas, *Nachwort* to *Politische Schriften*, p. 348.
[57] *Political Writings*, p. 164.   [58] *Ibid.* p. 235.   [59] *Ibid.* p. 229.

identification of the Habsburgs with the claim to universal Empire, Hegel could point out that the latter members of the dynasty, especially Joseph II, stood for a kind of modernizing spirit which would be essential in a restorator of political power in Germany. The greatest achievements of the late eighteenth-century Habsburgs lay in their transformation of what originally amounted to a haphazard collection of dynastic domains, linked together only through personal ties of allegiance to the family, into rationally organized crownlands, measuring up to modern criteria of political organization. Compared with this enlightened attempt at modernization and reform, the Prussian achievement looked very bleak indeed. Austrian reformism went hand in hand with a liberalizing policy towards Protestants and Jews, an aspect which certainly did not escape Hegel's attention, since religious tolerance figured so strongly in his discussion of the modern state.

When approaching the concrete problem of how to modernize Germany, Hegel sees the focus of possible change and transformation in two aspects of public life – the organization of the army and the finance system. The decrepit old Reich no longer possesses any military structure, and the so-called levies are nothing more than contingents sent at will by the different particular estates, under the command of their own officers, owing allegiance to their duke or count rather than to the Emperor. In most wars in the preceding century, Germans fought each other, sometimes at the command of foreign rulers who had some standing in the Reich (the kings of England and Sweden, for example), and the individual princes pulled their armies out of the war the moment they managed to achieve a separate peace for their own particular principality. Likewise, there existed no system of imperial taxes; the Emperor lived off his dynastic domain like any other petty territorial prince and there was no authority which could impose taxation on the various estates. The transition from this medieval state of affairs to a modern one, which countries like England and France had undergone centuries earlier, never occurred in Germany.[60] Similarly, there was no legal system applicable to the whole territory of the Reich and in legal, as in military and financial matters, the various estates regarded their relationship to the Empire as belonging to the realm of private law and voluntary association: 'The estates do associate for the administration of justice but in this union they will not give up any of their existence in relation to one another and that

[60] *Ibid.* pp. 164–9, 179.

existence rests in separation and the negation of common action. They join together, but without the will for any common end.'[61]

A restoration of political power in Germany should begin, according to Hegel, with the re-assertion of the role of the common link in various spheres. The Imperial Supreme Court at Wetzlar should be given concrete legal functions, and it should be subdivided into a number of sections, according to the various branches of legal activity, so as to make it more efficient and effective. Its jurisdiction should be made binding upon the various estates, which should thus begin to view it as a court of law, not as an organ of voluntary arbitration.[62]

The central reform, however, should be that of the army. A German central army, under the command of the Emperor, should be established. As a concession to the present reality of the distribution of power in Germany, each prince should be allowed to command the contingent hailing from his territory. But these units should no longer be considered as the prince's own army; instead each should be a part of a unified army under the Emperor. A system of universal taxation, to defray the costs of this army, should be imposed on all territories of the Empire. This would necessitate the re-introduction of a representative system. Hegel would like to see the old Imperial Diet, the Reichstag, as the nucleus for this new representative assembly, but its outmoded feudal structure should be totally reformed and overhauled. The whole area of Germany should be divided into a number of provinces as the basis for representation. These representatives, thus elected on the basis of territorial divisions, should then join the members of the Third College of the old Reichstag (which comprised the representatives of the old Imperial cities) to form a 'third bench' which would function alongside the two other benches, made up of the electors and princes.[63] This system of representation would be at the root of the political modernization of Germany, since 'without such a representative body, freedom is no longer thinkable ... It is a fundamental principle in public opinion.'[64]

Yet this plan for radical reform, based as it was on existing institutions and their transformation, is accompanied in Hegel's essay by a deep sense of skepticism and a basic doubt about its

[61] *Ibid.* p. 185.   [62] *Ibid.* pp. 184–5.   [63] *Ibid.* p. 239.
[64] *Ibid.* pp. 234–5; also p. 234: 'The guarantee that the government will proceed in accordance with law and with the co-operation of the *general will* in the most important affairs of state which affect everyone, the people finds in the organization of a body of representation of the people' (my italics).

feasibility. Hegel fears that German insistence on legalistic formalism will make it very difficult to expect radical change in Germany.[65] Towards the end of the essay, he remarks that the Germans have never been successful in the transition from barbarism to civilization: 'The Germans have failed to find a middle way between subjection [and] despotism ... and complete disintegration.'[66] In another instance the gloom that overtakes Hegel seems to reach a tragic dimension:

[Representation] came out of Germany; but there is a higher law that the people from whom the world is given a new universal impulse, perishes in the end before all the others, while its principle, though not itself, persists.[67]

It is the bleak horizon of despair which moves Hegel to see redemption in the idea of a German Theseus, who might weld together the centrifugal forces in Germany into one political bond. Hegel is thus caught in a vicious circle: he has drawn up a plan for reform but he recognizes it as an empty chimera, since it runs contrary to the interests of all the powers that be in Germany. He thus turns to the Rousseauist idea of a legislator and founder of a state:

If all parts of Germany were to succeed by these means in making Germany into one state, an event of that sort has never been the fruit of deliberation, but only of force. This has been true even when the event has accorded with the general culture of the day and when the need for it has been deeply and distinctly felt. The common people in Germany ... to whom a national union is something totally alien, would have to be collected together into one mass by the power of a conqueror; they would have to be compelled to treat themselves as belonging to Germany.

This Theseus would have to have the magnanimity to grant to the people he would have had to fashion out of dispersed units, a share in matters that affected every one.[68]

There has been some speculation about the identity of this Hegelian Theseus. The most plausible candidate is Archduke Charles of Austria, though Napoleon has also been mentioned, especially since Hegel speaks of a 'conqueror'.[69] Yet the speculation is, in a way, besides the point. It is immaterial whom Hegel might have had in mind since it is the general principle of such a Theseus which concerns him. If Hegel had someone specific in mind, one would have expected him to mention names. He has been, after all, quite

[65] *Ibid.* p. 152.   [66] *Ibid.* p. 237.   [67] *Ibid.* p. 206.
[68] *Ibid.* p. 241; Rousseau himself uses the example of Theseus as founder of a state (cf. R. D. Masters, *The Political Philosophy of Rousseau* (Princeton, 1968), p. 270.   [69] See Knox's footnote to *Political Writings*, p. 241.

outspoken about a number of less important details in his plan for the reorganization of Germany, so that it would be illogical for him to leave the identity of the restorator of political power in Germany to guesswork. Since the essay is a draft manuscript, and not a printed version, considerations of censorship or fear of political complications could not have been the prime reason for the vagueness of Hegel's language.

In fact, Hegel must have been vague about this point because he had no one cast in the role of a German Theseus. His Theseus is not a real person; it is an *ens rationis*, a Rousseauist abstraction, a wished-for *deus ex machina*. Because of this, the passage which follows his forceful evocation of a Theseus, and with which Hegel's essay ends, is full of resignation and quietism, expressing his fear that because of their historical lack of ability for political action, the Germans may end up like the Jews – stateless.[70]

Hegel had opened his essay with an attempt at promoting the understanding of what is. His discourse was aimed at emancipating the German political system from the shackles of feudalism, medievalism and petty absolutism, and at helping bring about the modernization of political life in Germany. Though in the course of his essay Hegel manages to develop his own theories on the nature of the modern state, the project itself comes to naught, culminating with the utopian plea for the emergence of a Theseus and then plunging into despair. The understanding of what is has ultimately reached its final shore – that Germany is not a state any more, and cannot become one, given the conditions of its existence. It is only after conditions in Germany and in Europe have been radically changed by the events of 1806–15 that Hegel comes back again to the discussion of political reality in Germany. And though his conclusions about the *form* of the political system in Germany would be almost the exact opposite of the utopian programme of 1802, they would curiously bear out both his analysis of German conditions and his thoughts on the nature of the modern state. The shift in reality would thus enable Hegel's ideas to catch up with historical conditions. What remained a dream in 1802 would become an actuality in 1817, though in a different form. But because of this change in historical reality, Hegel's views would thus not be left hanging in the air, as they were towards the end of his essay on *The German Constitution.*

[70] *Ibid.* p. 242.

Chapter Four

THE NEW ERA

Hegel moved to Jena in 1801 and stayed there as a *Privatdozent* at the University until 1807. It was during these years that Germany became ever more engulfed in the political consequences of the French Revolution; this was the period in which the Holy Roman Empire was finally dissolved and Prussian military might suffered the humiliating defeat at the Battle of Jena.

The political events at the turn of the eighteenth century had somehow dimmed the lustre of Jena as the capital of the German Enlightenment; but the tiny duchy of Saxe-Weimar, with Goethe as the ducal chief minister, still stood for all that was best in the tradition of German intellectual life. In the 1790s the University of Jena was famous for the scope of its academic freedom. Fichte's lectures there symbolized the intellectual reception of the French Revolution in Germany; its theological faculty was imbued with critical rationalism; and it was there that the empirical sciences were first introduced into German academic life. Inspired by Goethe, Duke Carl August did not join in the repressive measures introduced by other German potentates after the outbreak of the French Revolution, and Jena thus remained relatively free from the restrictions which were imposed upon the other German universities at the time of the wars against France.[1]

It was in this atmosphere that, together with Schelling, Hegel edited in Jena the *Kritisches Journal der Philosophie*. It was a fighting journal, which sought to combat accepted opinions and to use critical faculties against obscurantism and traditionalism.[2] This

---

[1] Cf. Kaufmann, *Hegel*, pp. 71–119; Rosenkranz, *Hegels Leben*, pp. 147ff.; Heinz Kimmerle, 'Dokumente zu Hegels Jenaer Dozententätigkeit (1801–1807)', *Hegel Studien* IV (1967), 22ff.

[2] Hegel to Hufnagel, 30 December 1801 (*Briefe von und an Hegel*, I, 65). See Hegel's programmatic introduction to the *Journal*, in *Gesammelte Werke*, ed. H. Buchner and O. Pöggeler (Hamburg, 1968), IV, 117–28.

belief in the liberating force of philosophical speculation was expressed, albeit in somewhat hyperbolic language, in one of Hegel's letters of that period in which he writes that a nation will remain barbarian until it can give voice to its cultural heritage in its own language; he, Hegel, 'will teach philosophy to speak German'.[3]

The period of Hegel's stay in Jena saw the fiercest battles between the French army and various coalitions of German states ranged against it. What characterized Hegel's political attitude during this period, as well as during his subsequent periods in Bamberg (1807–8) and Nuremberg (1808–16), was his firm support for the French, his rejoicing at the Prussian defeat at Jena, his opposition to the German nationalist anti-French upsurge in 1813 and, above all, his admiration for Napoleon, the great modernizer of Europe and of Germany.[4] Much more than mere infatuation with Napoleon, which was quite common among intellectuals at the time, was involved here, and Hegel's correspondence of that period provides ample textual evidence to support the contention that his political views were related to a fundamental theory about the historical significance of what was happening in Germany.

On the eve of the Battle of Jena, Hegel wrote to his friend Niethammer that 'all wish the French army luck', and commented that the Prussian army can expect nothing but defeat.[5] While fearing that the manuscript of the *Phenomenology*, which had been sent to the printer in Bamberg, might have been lost due to the havoc wrought by the French army, he reported on his first-hand impression of seeing Napoleon:

This morning I saw the Emperor [Napoleon] – this world-soul (*diese Weltseele*) – ride through the town ... It is a marvellous feeling to see such a personality, concentrated in one point, dominating the entire world from horseback ... It is impossible not to admire him.[6]

The Prussian defeat at Jena put an end to the old Prussian army, shattered the fabric of the old military-dynastic Prussian system,

---

[3] Hegel to Voss, 1804 (*Briefe von und an Hegel*, I, 99–100).
[4] All this was too embarrassing for Rosenkranz, who conveniently glossed over Hegel's political orientation at that time (*Hegels Leben*, p. 227).
[5] Hegel to Niethammer, 13 October 1806 (*Briefe von und an Hegel*, I, 121).
[6] *Ibid.* p. 120. It should be remarked that Hegel called Napoleon a 'world soul', a slightly romantic notion different from that of 'world spirit' which he uses in his philosophy of history and which cannot, of course, be identified with any particular person. Hegel's pro-French attitude in Jena was described in some detail in 1840 by one of his erstwhile students there, Georg Andreas Gabler, who later succeeded to Hegel's chair in Berlin (see *Hegel-Studien* IV, 65–73).

and paved the way for the reforms inaugurated by vom Stein and for the emergence of a modernized and liberalized Prussian state. Though his own house was burned down by the French, the University was closed down and he was left without employment, Hegel saw the Battle of Jena as an event of world historical importance:

Philosophy is something lonely; it does not belong on the streets and in the market-place, yet it is not alien to man's actions ... As a matter of fact, there is no better proof [than contemporary events] that education *(Bildung)* is triumphing over rudeness *(Roheit)* and spirit over spiritless understanding and mere cleverness *(Klügelei)*. Science *(Wissenschaft)* alone is the theodicy.[7]

This link between philosophy and the actual world, this postulate of philosophical principles being realized in the political and historical realm, also appears in a fragment from the Jena period in which Hegel states that:

Through consciousness spirit intervenes in the way the world is ruled. This is its infinite tool – then there are bayonets, cannon, bodies. But the banner [of philosophy] and the soul of its commander is spirit. Neither bayonets, nor money, neither this trick nor that, are the ruler. They are necessary like the cogs and wheels in a clock, but their soul is time and spirit that subordinates matter to its laws. An *Iliad* is not thrown together at random, neither is a great deed composed of bayonets and cannon: it is spirit that is the composer.[8]

Hegel ended his lectures at the University in September 1806 on a similar note of restless anticipation of the new world, heralded by philosophy and ushered in by the handmaids of political change and upheaval:

We stand at the gates of an important epoch, a time of ferment, when spirit moves forward in a leap, transcends its previous shape and takes on a new one. All the mass of previous representations, concepts, and bonds linking our world together, are dissolving and collapsing like a dream picture. A new phase of the spirit is preparing itself. Philosophy especially has to welcome its appearance and acknowledge it, while others, who oppose it impotently, cling to the past.[9]

These thoughts are at the center of the *Phenomenology of Spirit*, finished by Hegel at about the same time. The *Phenomenology* is Hegel's first major attempt at a comprehensive philosophical system. Though much was to be remodelled and refined in his later writings, the basic structure of his argument here is, in a way, simple. While Kant maintained that ultimate reality is opaque to human

---

[7] Hegel to Zellmann, 23 January 1807 *(Briefe von und an Hegel, i, 137)*. This description of Prussia is very similar to the one contained in 'The German Constitution' *(Political Writings, pp. 163–4; see above, p. 49)*.
[8] Printed by Nicolin in *Hegel-Studien* iv, 14.
[9] Lecture of 18 September 1806 *(Dokumente, p. 352)*.

knowledge, Hegel returns to the classical Aristotelian position that reality is intelligible. Kant's *Ding-an-sich* ultimately left human knowledge knocking, to no avail, at a closed door. Hegel, however, tried to do away with the Kantian distinction between the nouomenal and the phenomenal. Hence the title *Phenomenology of Spirit*, which implies that ultimate reality, *Geist*, is manifest in its phenomenological appearances and intelligible through them. Yet while the classical Greek tradition viewed the *logos* as given, Hegel sees it as unfolding in the procession of human manifestations – in history. Reason does not exist *a priori*; its potentiality has to be actualized in practice, it develops in human consciousness. History is thus not a meaningless calendar of senseless events but a hieroglyph of reason, and an adequate philosophical understanding has to look for the keys to its meaning. The *Phenomenology* is Hegel's first systematic attempt to write this philosophical history of the human spirit. This biography of the spirit is thus, for Hegel, the philosophical history of man.[10]

It is in the context of this development of consciousness that Hegel maintains that his own epoch stands at the beginning of a new dawn. In his preface to the *Phenomenology*, he writes:

It is not difficult to see that our epoch is a birth-time, and a period of transition. The spirit of man has broken with the old order of things hitherto prevailing, and with the old way of thinking, and is in the mind to let them all sink into the depths of the past ... It is here as in the case of the birth of a child; after a long period of nutrition in silence, the continuity of gradual growth in size, of quantitative change, is suddenly cut short by the first breath drawn – there is a break in the process, a qualitative change – and the child is born. In like manner, the spirit of the time, growing slowly and quietly ripe for the new form it is to assume, disintegrates one fragment after another of the structure of its previous world . . . This gradual crumbling to pieces which did not alter the general look and aspect of the whole, is interrupted by the sunrise, which in a flash and a single stroke, begins to view the form and structure of the new world.[11]

[10] A detailed analysis of the *Phenomenology* cannot be given here. The reader will find illuminating attempts to decipher it in Alexandre Kojève, *Introduction to the Reading of Hegel*, ed. A. Bloom (New York, 1969); Jean Hyppolite, *Genèse et structure de la Phénoménologie de l'Esprit* (Paris, 1946); Manfred Riedel, *Theorie und Praxis im Denken Hegels* (Stuttgart, 1965); and Judith N. Shklar, 'Hegel's *Phenomenology*: an elegy for Hellas', in Pelczynski's *Hegel's Political Philosophy*, pp. 73–89. Though Baillie translates the title as *Phenomenology of Mind*, it seems that *Spirit* is a more adequate rendering of Hegel's *Geist*.

[11] *Phenomenology* (Baillie's translation), p. 75. For an excellent commentary on the preface to the *Phenomenology*, as well as a new translation of it, see Kaufmann's *Hegel*, pp. 363–459; cf. Jean Hyppolite, *Studies on Marx and Hegel*, trans. J. O'Neill (London, 1969), pp. 35–69.

Yet the birth of the new world is, despite this dramatic description, a lengthy process. The new world makes its first appearance
'merely in general outline', and it is the task of the philosopher to
be midwife to this new consciousness.[12] The new world is initially
as little fully realized as a new-born child is at first a mature
person: 'A building is not finished when its foundation is laid.'[13]
The work of intellectual discovery is as yet hard and arduous. What
the *Phenomenology* seeks to show is how out of the Enlightenment,
through the birthpangs of the French Revolution and reign of terror,
a new form and mode of experience arises, that of 'the moral life of
the Spirit', about to be realized in post-revolutionary Europe.[14]

Since Hegel thus saw that the principles arrived at through
modern philosophy were about to manifest themselves in historical
actuality, his political attitude became a corollary of these considerations. And the major political factor of this period was the
transformation and modernization of the German political system as
a consequence of Napoleonic victories. Through annexations in
the Rhineland, the establishment of the Kingdom of Westphalia
and the introduction of French-inspired reforms in pro-French
German states such as Bavaria, the principles annunciated by the
French Revolution were being adopted in Germany. 'The French
nation,' Hegel writes, 'has managed to free itself, through a blood-
bath, from many arrangements which human spirit had to overcome like baby-shoes . . . and spiritless fetters.'[15]

Hegel comments frequently on the introduction of new, French-
inspired social and political institutions. Remarking on the political
changes in Germany, Hegel calls Napoleon 'the great constitutional
lawyer in Paris', who teaches the German princes the meaning 'of
the concept of a free monarchy'.[16] It is a lengthy process, Hegel
notes: 'It is, though, quite a lot what Germany has learned from
France, and the slow nature of the *Allemands* will profit over time
from this. One cannot demand everything at once.'[17] Yet Hegel is

[12] *Phenomenology*, p. 76.   [13] *Ibid*. p. 75.
[14] *Ibid*. p. 610. One of the Enlightenment's main achievements has been, to
Hegel, the overcoming of the dualism between the secular and the divine:
'Both worlds are reconciled, and heaven is transplanted to the earth below'
(*ibid*. p. 598). Hegel's contemporaries saw in the *Phenomenology* 'a basic
book of the liberation of man, a key to the new gospel of which Lessing had
prophesied' (Windischmann to Hegel, 27 April 1810, quoted in Kaufmann,
Hegel, p. 324).
[15] Hegel to Zellmann, 23 January 1807 (*Briefe von und an Hegel*, I, 138).
[16] Hegel to Niethammer, 29 August 1807 (*ibid*. I, 185).
[17] Hegel to Niethammer, November 1807 (*ibid*. I, 198).

also aware of the ambiguous nature of Napoleonic rule – the combination of immense personal authority superimposed on the principles of the French Revolution. And he fears lest only the external element of Napoleonic rule be taken over from the French:

> Until now our emulation of the French has limited itself only to one half of it while neglecting the other. It is the other half which is the most noble one – the liberty of the people, its participation in elections and decisions, or at least presentation of governmental regulations before the opinion of the people.[18]

It is at this time that Hegel accepted the editorship of a pro-French newspaper in Bamberg in Bavaria. To his friend Niethammer, who found this position for him after the closing of the University of Jena had left Hegel stranded without employment, he writes that he would welcome such an opportunity, since 'as you know, I follow world affairs with curiosity'.[19]

What Hegel finds essential for the making of a modern form of government is its accountability to the public for public expenses and the public debt, as well as its tolerance of the freedom of the press. He calls this freedom 'this conversation of the government with the people [which is] . . . one of the greatest elements of strength of the French and English people'.[20] As a resident now of Bavaria, Hegel was able to witness at first hand the transformation of this feudal patrimony into a modern state. He expected representative institutions to be introduced into Bavaria, and when the Napoleonic Code was adopted as the law of the land to supersede the archaic traditional customary law, Hegel greeted it with the remark: 'The importance of the Code does not compare, however, with the importance of the hope that can now be surmised that the further parts of the French and Westphalian constitution will also be introduced [in Bavaria].'[21]

Later, in 1808, Hegel was summoned to become the Rector of the Gymnasium in Nuremberg. Under the reforms in Bavaria, Hegel's friend Niethammer became head of the educational system in the new government, and it was he who offered this position of Rector to Hegel. The school in question was a very distinguished institution, the oldest humanistic Gymnasium in Germany, founded by Philip

---

[18] *Ibid.* I, 197.
[19] Hegel to Niethammer, 20 February 1807 (*ibid.* I, 145). To another friend he confides that 'as you know, I always had an infatuation with politics' (Hegel to Knebel, 30 August 1807, *ibid.* I, 186). Hegel did, however, run into numerous problems with the censors (*ibid.* I, 240ff.).
[20] Hegel to Niethammer, 22 January 1808 (*ibid.* I, 209).
[21] Hegel to Niethammer, 11 February 1808 (*ibid.* I, 218).

Melanchthon. A Protestant like Niethammer, Hegel found himself ranged against the old Catholic hierarchy of Bavaria, which tried to ensure its traditional hold over education and prevent the introduction of an open-minded, humanistic curriculum into the school system. Using the French system as a model, Niethammer's educational reform was part of an overall effort at modernization in highly conservative and Catholic Bavaria, and Hegel's position thus placed him for a number of years in the middle of one of the most important political battles of early nineteenth-century Germany.

Hegel put great hopes in what was being done: 'A new world may arise in Bavaria; one has hoped for this for a long time.'[22] In an eloquent letter to Niethammer, he goes back to his earlier notions about the relationship between philosophy and actuality, expressing the belief that it is the realm of ideas that revolutionizes the world:

Daily do I get more and more convinced that theoretical work achieves more in the world than practical. Once the realm of ideas is revolutionized, actuality does not hold out (*Ist erst das Reich der Vorstellung revolutioniert, so hällt die Wirklichkeit nicht aus*).[23]

Hegel threw himself with all his zeal into this attempt to revolutionize the realm of ideas. He himself took over the teaching of philosophy in all forms at the Gymnasium, and even wrote a philosophical propaedeutic. His rectorial addresses, given at the end of each school year, preserve some of the direction of his thought and educational policy.

In one of these addresses, he sets up the development of the judicial system and the state of the educational system as two criteria for judging the nature of any society.[24] On another occasion, when military training was being introduced into the highest form at the Gymnasium, Hegel extols this introduction of a citizens' army

---

[22] Hegel to Fromann, 9 July 1808 (*ibid.* I, 235). Haym points out that due to the reforms, Bavaria came to be considered a model *Intelligenzstaat* and attracted to its service some of the best intellectual minds in Germany (*Hegel und seine Zeit*, pp. 261–4).

[23] Hegel to Niethammer, 28 October 1808 (*Briefe von und an Hegel*, I, 253–4). On Hegel's skirmishes with the local Catholic reaction in Nuremberg, see his letters to Niethammer of 3 November 1808 and 10 October 1816 (*ibid.* I, 337, and II, 141, respectively). See also his letter to Schelling of 23 February 1807 (*ibid.* I, 149), in which he discusses the struggle for educational reform in Bavaria.

[24] Rectorial address of 1809, in G. W. F. Hegel, *Nürnberger Schriften*, ed. J. Hoffmeister (Leipzig, 1938), p. 303. The main theme of this address is that educational reform in Bavaria is to be praised for not creating a hiatus with the past, but building on its foundations.

which, he points out, has always been, ever since the Greek polis, at the root of the popular identification with the political structure; a standing, professional army, on the other hand, usually goes hand in hand with a growing estrangement between the government and its citizens.[25]

In 1811, the expected platitudes about school preparing young people for life are followed by remarks about the way in which the individual can find himself integrated into the real world only if he is integrated into the universality of the state. These two forces, the individual and the claims of society, are the two poles around which adult life centers, and one has to attain integration in both.[26] The educational function of the new state is stressed time and again: 'What is being done for the education of the young in modern times . . . is only one single aspect of the newly constituted life of the state.'[27] Conversely, the role of the educational system is expressed by Hegel in terms taken from the modernized French experience – to prepare civil servants for the state.[28]

This impact of immediate political events is even more evident in Hegel's rectorial address of 1813, delivered at the height of the popular German agitation against the French. As we shall see later, Hegel opposed this first fervent expression of German nationalism, and in his address of that year he carefully warns against an uncritical and too-easy infatuation with the new fashionable ideas. The state and social life have been most carefully modernized and transformed in the last decade in Germany, he says, and one should be most careful to preserve these achievements and not undercut such real progress by rocking the boat: 'When laws and institutions, which should be the solid ground for that which is ever-changing, are themselves made changeable, on what then can the ever-changing base itself?'[29]

Here, for the first time, a new tone begins to be heard in Hegel: the voice that called for change and modernization, for scrapping the old order lock, stock and barrel, is now undergoing transformation into a voice calling for moderation, for a careful preservation of the existing scheme of things. This has sometimes been viewed as if Hegel had changed from a fiery young critic to an accommodating moderate, if not a staid conservative. The point, however, is that

25 Rectorial address of 1810 (*ibid.* p. 321).
26 Rectorial address of 1811 (*ibid.* p. 341).
27 Rectorial address of 1815 (*ibid.* p. 370).
28 *Ibid.* p. 360.   29 Rectorial address of 1813 (*ibid.* p. 359).

in the meantime the socio-political order has been completely
transformed. The order Hegel is now beginning to defend is not the
old order he had so radically attacked in 1801. It is not Hegel's
views which have changed in the crucial decade between 1805
and 1815, but the whole fabric of German social and political
life which has been transformed under the tremendous jolt it had
received from the Napoleonic wars. The German system Hegel
appears to be defending around 1815 is precisely the system he
wished to see established in 1802. Dialectically, however, the new
system emerged not through an internal transformation of German
conditions out of their own accord, but as an outcome of the impact of French victories. This transformation of German political
life thus came about either through defensive modernization, as in
Prussia, or through direct French intervention in local conditions,
as in the Rhineland, Westphalia, Bavaria and Württemberg. The
old order of 1802 disappeared totally, and it was the new, French-
inspired, modern, anti-feudal, order which Hegel now felt had to
be defended against the dubious attacks of nationalists and romantics.

All through the last years of Napoleon's rule Hegel stood by his
support of the French. In 1809, he congratulates Niethammer on the
French victory over the Austrians at Regensburg.[30] In 1813, with
the beginning of German resistance to the French, he opposes in the
strongest terms these first expressions of vehement German nationalism. A few days before the battle of Grossgörschen, Hegel comments icily on 'Cossacks, Bashkirs, Prussian patriots and all sorts of
liberators'.[31] A year later he adversely refers to the illusion of the
public and the 'rabble' (*Pöbel*) about 'freedom'; his wife, he reports,
dreams of 'a camp full of wild soldiers, Cossacks, Prussians'.[32] In
another letter, commenting on the younger generation's enthusiasm
for the 'liberators', Hegel says: 'I am ready to fall down on my
knees if I see one liberated person';[33] and the attempt to revive the
traditional German dress as an expression of nationalist anti-French
feelings, supplied Hegel with an occasion for a few more caustic
remarks. The free-wheeling enthusiasm and subjective romanticism

---

[30] Hegel to Niethammer, 7 May 1809 (*Briefe von und an Hegel*, I, 283). Hegel's
only brother, Georg Ludwig, died in Russia while serving with the Württemberg contingent in Napoleon's army.

[31] Hegel to Niethammer, 21 May 1813 (*ibid.* II, 6).

[32] Hegel to Niethammer, 29 April 1814 (*ibid.* II, 27).

[33] Hegel to Niethammer, 23 December 1813 (*ibid.* II. 14).

associated with the national uprising of 1813 runs contrary to all of Hegel's conceptions about the nature of politics.[34]

Napoleon's defeat and abdication come as a great shock to Hegel. Sarcastically commenting on 'our yet-to-be-achieved freedom', he writes to his friend Paulus: 'What do you say to our great Napoleon?'[35] In a letter to Niethammer he tries to console himself that Napoleon's ultimate defeat has actually been implied by him in his *Phenomenology*, and continues:

Great things are happening around us. It is an immense spectacle to see an enormous genius destroy himself. This is the most tragic thing that exists. The whole mass of mediocrities presses incessantly with all the absolute iron of its gravity until it lowers the heights down to its own *niveau*, or crushes them.[36]

When Napoleon returns from Elba, Hegel entertains no hope for a comeback: he knows that all is lost. Yet in an introspective letter he says that if he had harboured any hopes for a possible Napoleonic victory, he would have 'put a rifle on his shoulder' and gone to join him.[37]

Der Kaiser, der Kaiser gefangen. The dream of a new world seems to have collapsed. But the world-historical individual, Hegel would later remark in his *Philosophy of History*, referring directly to the Napoleonic experience, is not distinguished by his personal fate but by the objective outcome of his acts.[38] *Si monumentum vis, circumspicere.* And Napoleon's actions, whatever his personal fate, have helped to pave the way for a new world; and the point was to defend it even if its creator has himself disappeared. Indeed, in Bavaria Hegel was immediately confronted with the attempt of the old Bavarian ultra-montane party to dismantle the reforms of the past decade. In the most political of his rectorial addresses Hegel warns against this attempt to resurrect the past or to turn the clock backwards:

We must oppose this mood which always uselessly misses the past and yearns for it. That which is old is not to be deemed excellent just because it is old, and from the fact that it was useful and meaningful under different circumstances, it does not follow that its preservation is commendable under changed conditions – quite the contrary ... The world has given birth to a great epoch.[39]

[34] Hegel to Paulus, 9 October 1814 (*ibid.* II, 42–3).
[35] Hegel to Paulus, 18 April 1814 (*ibid.* II, 23).
[36] Hegel to Niethammer, 29 April 1814 (*ibid.* II, 28). In yet another letter, of 1 July 1814 (p. 29), he calls the Prussians 'liberation beasts' (*Befreiungsbestien*).
[37] Hegel to Niethammer, 19 March 1815 (*ibid.* II, 50).
[38] G. W. F. Hegel, *Reason in History*, trans. R. S. Hartman (New York, 1953), p. 41.   [39] Rectorial address of 1815 (*Nürnberger Schriften*, pp. 370–3).

This belief in ultimate progress, though mediated through what sometimes appears as meaningless skirmishes, is most vividly expressed in an almost poetic passage in which Hegel wishes to assure the beleaguered Niethammer that their common attempt to withstand the post-Napoleonic reaction will ultimately prevail. In a language whose images strangely evoke Tolstoy and Stendhal, and which must have been influenced by the traumatic impact of the gigantic Napoleonic battles, Hegel writes:

I stand by my belief that the world spirit has given [our] time the order to advance. This order is being obeyed. This advance goes on, through thick and thin, like an inscrutable, armoured, closed phalanx, its movement as imperceptible as that of the sun. Innumerable light troops, fighting for and against it, flank it on both sides, most of them not even knowing what it is all about; they are being hit on the head as if by an invisible hand. All fibbing and wisecracking and yelling is helpless against it. It can perhaps read this colossus up to his shoelaces, put some shoe polish or dirt on them, but it cannot loosen them up ... The surest thing, both internally and externally, is to keep this advancing giant straight in sight.[40]

RATIONALISM VERSUS POSITIVE LAW AND THE NEW GERMAN STATE

In 1817, Hegel published in the *Heidelberger Jahrbücher* a long commentary on the proceedings of the Württemberg assembly of estates of 1815–16. This essay on *The Württemberg Estates* marks the second time that Hegel discusses conditions in his native homeland; but the conditions there had changed drastically since 1798, when he had written his draft notes for his unfinished first essay on Württemberg.[41]

The post-1815 Kingdom of Württemberg was a very different political animal from the much smaller duchy of pre-Napoleonic days. Through annexations of smaller neighbouring principalities and ecclesiastical lands, as well as through the mediatization of imperial knights who had previously been tenants-in-chief of the Empire (*Reichsunmittelbar*), the ancestral territory of ducal Würt-

---

[40] Hegel to Niethammer, 5 July 1816 (*Briefe von und an Hegel*, II, 85–6).
[41] See Pelczynski's introductory essay to *Hegel's Political Writings*, pp. 18–26; also Rosenkranz, *Hegels Leben*, pp. 308–12. Beyer has recently claimed that an anonymous article on Württemberg in the *Würtembergischer Volksfreund* was authored by Hegel, but this has been convincingly contested; see Wilhelm Beyer, 'Hegels Mitarbeit am *Würtembergischen Volksfreund*', *Deutsche Zeitschrift für Philosophie* XIV (1966), 709–17; Hartmut Buchner, 'Ein unbekannter politischer Text Hegels?', *Hegel-Studien*, IV (1967), 205–14.

temberg was almost doubled and its ruler elevated to royal dignity. An overall administrative and judicial reform, spurred on by the Napoleonic impact, had transformed the whole structure of the country, introducing a modern, rational civil service to replace the old, oligarchic, semi-independent and corrupt petty officialdom of the Standing Committee of the old Diet. In 1815, the King asked a newly elected Assembly of Estates to ratify a constitutional charter formalizing these changes, and it was around this issue that a major constitutional crisis developed in Württemberg. The traditional, conservative, aristocratic elements, and especially the erstwhile independent imperial knights, saw in the King's program an attempt to divest them of their old, prescriptive privileges and subject their autonomous status to the new concept of Württemberg's sovereignty and thus put an end to their virtual exemption from any effective political supervision. We have already noted that of all the German *Länder*, Württemberg had been the one whose old oligarchic constitution was the most similar to the system of *liberum veto* of the old Polish Commonwealth. Clinging to these pre-1789 arrangements, the conservatives hoped that by opposing the royal constitution, they would be able to undo the modernizing effects of the decade preceding 1815.

Hegel took the King's side, and his support for the royal program has sometimes been taken to represent support for royal absolutism against parliamentary liberalism; this, however, is a serious misunderstanding of the historical context involved, projecting as it does on 1817-Württemberg the images of later constitutional struggles.[42] Within the concrete historical context of the period, it was the *opposition* to royal power that represented the most conservative and reactionary element in Württemberg society; it was this aristocratic opposition that believed that a restoration of pre-1789 arrangements would now become possible, once Napoleon had been defeated. The King, on the other hand, stood for an attempt to uphold the social and political achievements reached under the liberalizing impact of French influence in South Germany.

The conservative opposition maintained that the old customary law regulating privileges and limiting the royal authority was still in force. The old imperial tenants-in-chief still saw themselves as independent lords, regulating their relations with the King of

---

[42] Haym, *Hegel und seine Zeit*, pp. 349–56. Haym, an 1848 vintage liberal-nationalist, could not but see the arguments of the Frankfurt National Assembly prefigured in the Württemberg debate.

Württemberg on a contractual basis. The only way a new constitution could be formulated, so they argued, was through a deal, freely arrived at, between the King and the estates, premissed on the assumption that the historical rights and privileges of the nobility remained inviolable so long as they had not been freely traded in for royal concessions.

It is against such a feudal conception of political rights as personal property that Hegel uses some of his strongest language in his essay; his argument here follows the one he had voiced fifteen years earlier in the essay on *The German Constitution*. This is the argument of rationalism versus prescription, Hegel states, adding:

'Old rights' and 'old constitutions' are such fine grand words that it sounds impious [to contemplate] robbing a people of its rights. But age has nothing to do with what 'old rights' and 'constitution' mean or with whether they are good or bad. Even the abolition of human sacrifice, slavery, feudal despotism, and countless [other] infamies was in every case the cancellation of something that was an 'old right'. It has often been repeated that rights cannot be lost, that a century cannot make wrong into right, but we should add: 'even if this century-old wrong has been called right all the time', and further that an actual positive right a hundred years old rightly perishes if the basis constituting its existence disappears.[43]

Hegel's old argument against 'positivity' reappears, this time in a specific political context: 'The fundamental error in the position adopted by the Württemberg estates lies in this, that they start from positive law.'[44] Recalling the experience of the French Revolution Hegel says that 'one must regard the start of the French Revolution as the struggle of rational constitutional law against the mass of positive law and privilege by which it had been stifled'. The Württemberg estates, however, Hegel adds, would like to disregard the history of the last 25 years:

One might say of the Württemberg Estates what has been said of the returned French emigrés: they have forgotten nothing and learnt nothing. They seem to have slept through the last twenty-five years, possibly the richest that world history has had, and for us the most instructive, because it is to them that our world and our ideas belong.[45]

The problem of traditional as against codified law Hegel sees as settled in favour of the latter because of the ultimate subjectivity of traditional, customary law. The 'Good Old Law of Württemberg',

---

[43] *Political Writings*, pp. 282–3. The strong anti-Burkean tone in this passage is most striking. Hegel's opposition to prescriptive, traditional law comes up again in his polemic against von Savigny, *Philosophy of Right*, §§ 258–9.
[44] *Political Writings*, p. 281.   [45] *Ibid.* p. 282.

which the conservative opposition would like to preserve, is, according to Hegel, conspicuous for its not being known: nobody really knows what it is, since it derives from a multitude of sources and authorities and not all of them are equally clear and explicit.[46] Furthermore, any attempt to judge present-day conditions by criteria derived from the past is anachronstic; the old feudal order of estates freely negotiating their 'pact' with a prince cannot be the foundation of a modern state. While the old order based itself on private law, the modern state is based on public law: 'The concepts concerning the matter at issue, which we must bring with us to this event, we may not cull from any remote age.'[47] The purely 'positive' nature of the claims of the conservative opposition is brought up by Hegel time and again:

> The Assembly did not reject the King's constitution on the ground that it was contrary to the rights that subjects could claim in a political constitution on the strength of the eternal rights of reason . . . On the contrary, it rejected it on the ground that it was not the old constitution of Württemberg . . . The dead, however, cannot be revived.[48]

Hegel then goes on to defend the constitutional charter proposed by the King. It is important to go into some of the details of Hegel's defence since his arguments against the conservative opposition in the Assembly may give rise to the mistaken impression that Hegel was opposed to representative assemblies in general. In fact, what he opposed was the traditional structure and conservative policy of the Württemberg Assembly. As for assemblies in general, in modern states they were 'the formation of a representative constitution, the rule of law, popular influence on legislation'.[49]

The royal constitutional charter proposed a unicameral assembly, made up both of *ex officio* members and elected ones. Crown officials, officers, clergymen and physicians were to be ineligible as elected members. Otherwise, every male member of a Christian

---

[46] *Ibid.* pp. 275, 284. In a lengthy passage, not included in the Knox–Pelczynski edition, Hegel enumerates a long catalogue of the possible sources for traditional law (*Schriften zur Politik*, p. 221), calling it a 'paper labyrinth'. Hegel had a similar view of the unreformed, pre-Peel English Common Law (*Berliner Schriften*, pp. 718–24).

[47] *Political Writings*, p. 247.

[48] *Ibid.* p. 274.

[49] *Ibid.* p. 250. The King's greatest achievement, according to Hegel, is that all his subjects are now equal before the law (p. 251). Hegel also supported the demands of his friends in Baden for an Assembly of Estates and condemned the government's harassment of *Justizrat* Martin of Heidelberg which followed the latter's demands for such an assembly; see Hegel's letter to Frommann of 20 December 1816 (*Briefe von und an Hegel*, II, 65).

denomination over thirty was to be eligible for election, with no property qualifications. Entitled to vote were Christian males of over twenty-five years possessing a net annual income of 200 guilders. One third of the members of the assembly would be elected once every three years. The powers of the assembly would include all fiscal and tax legislation and no new taxes could be levied, or existing ones increased, without its consent. The Crown would have to submit an annual report about expenditures; legislative initiative was to be in the hands of the Crown, yet Assembly members would also be able to propose legislation; and all laws regarding freedom, property and the constitution would have to be ratified by the Assembly. Given the context of 1817, Hegel justly remarks that this is the most liberal constitution ever given by a monarch to his subjects.[50]

Yet despite Hegel's basic support for the royal constitution, he also had a number of reservations, which he described in great detail, and this critique of the royal charter also shows that Hegel's tract was not a mere attempt to whitewash the royal position. Hegel's main objection to the royal charter concerns the injunction against the eligibility for the assembly of members of the professions. In a small country like Württemberg, Hegel notes, most members of the liberal professions would be in one way or another state employees; barring them from assembly membership will leave the assembly in need of members with the necessary intellectual qualities and would also push the assembly into the hands of the lawyers whom Hegel always sees as possessing a built-in conservative, prescriptive and 'positive' conception of what the law is. Hegel remarks that recent historical developments 'have imbued the youth in our universities with a higher interest than mere concentration on future bread-winning and income . . . Are they, along with the whole class of academically educated people, who generally expect the same destiny [to enter public service], to lose the capacity to become members of the estates, representatives of the people?'[51]

Hegel's major reservation about the proposed constitution deals, however, with its vision of direct, undifferentiated representation. To him, such a system of direct suffrage means that the individual has no real bond with the body politic, that as a consequence of this he feels estranged from the state and impotent *vis-à-vis* the political power confronting him:

[50] *Political Writings*, p. 254.   [51] *Ibid.* p. 259.

The electors appear otherwise in no bond or connexion with the civil order and the organization of the state. The citizens come on the scene as isolated atoms, and the electoral assemblies as unordered inorganic aggregates; the people as a whole is dissolved into a heap. This is the form in which the community should never have appeared at all in undertaking any enterprise; it is a form most unworthy of the community and most in contradiction with its concepts as a spiritual order. Age and property are qualities affecting only the individual himself, not characteristics constituting his worth in the civil order. Such worth he has only on the strength of his office, his position, his skill in craftsmanship which, recognized by his fellow citizens, entitles him accordingly to be described as a master of his craft, etc.[52]

This runs, of course, against the grain of what came to be identified with liberal principles, ever since both Rousseau and *The Federalist* argued, for different reasons, against 'factions' and the French Revolution disbanded all 'partial' organizations. To Hegel, such an abstract identification of the citizen-voter with the universality of the political structure is pure fantasy and wishful thinking; this identification with the state needs mediation. In a passage astonishing for its insights into much later problems of representative government, Hegel says:

It is as well to remember that the exercise of a wholly occasional calling, like that of being a voter, easily ceases to be of interest in a short time and in any case depends on an accidental attitude and a momentary preference. This calling is exhausted by a single action, an action occurring only once in a few years; when the number of voters is large, the individual may regard as very unimportant the influence of his own vote, all the more because the deputy whom he helps to elect is himself in turn only one member of a numerous assembly where only a small number ever give evidence of being of much importance, and where in any case the contribution made by *one* vote out of many is unimpressive. . .

But experience has shown that the excessive gap between the importance of the effect which is supposed to ensue, and the extremely small influence which the individual seems to himself to have, soon produces the result that the enfranchised become indifferent to this right of theirs.[53]

A system of representation based on mere property qualifications gives rise, according to Hegel, to the atomization and privatization

[52] *Ibid.* p. 262. Hegel is afraid lest such an estrangement should cause people to be 'brought up to a sense of merely private concerns . . . gripped by the spirit of narrow-mindedness and private self-seeking' (p. 268).

[53] *Ibid.* p. 264. The reader who might consequently see Hegel as a forerunner of the 'corporative state' should bear in mind that it is precisely this mediating role that modern political parties and other voluntary organizations, nonexistent in Hegel's days, play in the modern representative system. See esp. Robert A. Dahl's theory of 'polyarchy' in his *Preface to a Democratic Theory* (Chicago, 1956), pp. 63–89.

of life and encourages the voters to view political concerns solely
in terms of their economic interests. Hegel would prefer an alternative in which representation would articulate legitimate group
interests, thus integrating every citizen, through his peers, into the
political structure:

A living interrelationship exists only in an articulated whole whose parts
themselves form particular subordinate spheres. But, if this is to be achieved,
the French abstractions of mere numbers and quanta of property must be finally
discarded, or at any rate must be no longer made the dominant qualification or,
all over again, the sole condition for exercising one of the most important
political functions. Atomistic principles of that sort spell, in science as in
politics, death to every rational concept, organization, and life.[54]

It is this vision of a modern, differentiated state that Hegel proposes as against the feudal, pre-revolutionary notion of the Württemberg nobility as well as against the more acceptable, yet still
slightly mechanistic, form suggested by the royal constitution. The
legal bent of the Württemberg opposition clung, in Hegel's view,
to another fiction, namely, that the Holy Roman Empire of the
German Nation had never ceased to exist. The nobility 'has never
accepted the abdication of the Roman Emperor . . . and [maintained
that] after the dissolution of the Confederacy of the Rhine it has
come again into the legal possession of all its former rights'.[55] To
Hegal this is pure fiction and make-believe. Just as in his essay on
The German Constitution he wished to do away with the legal fictions
surrounding the historical Reich and to understand that which is, so
here his prime object is to comprehend reality, while the people of
the opposition in Württemberg 'declare themselves indeed to be
Estates of another world, of a time long past . . . The entire Assembly
thus takes up a position directly opposed to the actual world situation.'[56] But the dead cannot, to Hegel, be revived and the old world
of the crumbling Empire cannot be resuscitated. On the ruins of the
old Empire, which lacked the power to transform itself into a modern
state, new states have been established. The German phoenix rejuvenated itself out of the ashes of its own bonfire; but now it has
many forms rather than just one. Not one German state has
emerged from the debris of the old world, but a plurality of states.

[54] *Political Writings*, p. 263. While welcoming the demise of the old, restrictive
and coercive guild system, Hegel welcomes any attempt to set up voluntary
organizations that would 'bring the lower spheres back again into respect
and political significance and, purged of privileges and wrongs, to incorporate
them as an organic structure into the state'.
[55] *Ibid.* p. 272.   [56] *Ibid.* pp. 271–3.

Unlike the old patrimonial 'estates' of the old Empire, these entities are not purely personal domains, based on property and dynastic links. Under the impact of Napoleonic reform and the subsequent history of German politics, they have evolved into modern states, rationally organized, based on the modern principles of the universality of law and representation. The old dream of the Empire is dead; the reality of the new states in Germany is actual:

The age had produced a new task for Württemberg and the demands for its discharge, the task of erecting the provinces of Württemberg into a state. After the nonsensical arrangement called the German Empire . . . has reached the end it deserved, an ignominious end suited to it even in externals, the Württemberg of that time acquired an enlargement of territory up to more than double its previous size . . . [It] crossed the frontier into sovereignty, into the position of a state, i.e. into that of one of the actual German realms which are taking the place of the nonentity which had borne only the empty name of an 'Empire'.[57]

Hegel has thus come full circle: in 1802 he had hoped to create a focus for political power in the reform of the Empire; but he ended his essay on *The German Constitution* on a note of quiet despair. The Empire could not be rejuvenated; the plan for its reform had only brought into cruel relief the inner rationale of its ultimate demise. Now, Bavaria, Württemberg, Prussia – the new, sovereign modern German states emerging in post-1815 Germany – are the bearers of modernization and transformation: reformed, rationalized, incorporating the lessons of the French Revolution. The call for political unity has become superfluous and the individual states have become the subject of political power in Germany. The idea of the modern state has finally taken root in Germany: 'Twenty-five years of past and mostly terrible history have given us a sight of the numerous attempts to grasp this idea.'[58]

The program of 1802 has been realized, though with a dialectical twist. Political life in Germany has been modernized, though the old Reich has reached 'the end it deserved'. Any movement for political unity in Germany would *now* run the danger of undoing what has been accomplished. Moreover, since the foundations of a truly political system have already been established in the particular German states, overall political unity in Germany could be based now only on such subjective and arbitrary elements as language and historical memories; and as for such aspirations, we have already seen Hegel's opposition to any ideas of ethnic nationalism.

[57] *Ibid.* pp. 247–8. Haym uses this passage to show that Hegel had no 'national feelings whatsoever' (*Hegel und Seine Zeit*, p. 353).
[58] *Political Writings*, p. 249.

Hence Hegel's total opposition to any attempt during 1813–15 to create political unity in Germany is a vindication of the principles which governed his position in 1802. Thus it was that he opposed the anti-French nationalist sentiments of 1813 and the romantic nationalist attempt to revive the German Empire. The modern German state does exist, and the dead cannot be revived.

Chapter Five

MODERN LIFE AND SOCIAL REALITY

We have seen how Hegel's political writings present a consistent and progressively unfolding panorama of the way in which his political theory evolved through constant confrontation with historical reality. His systematic writings, on the other hand, reflect an attempt to develop the general theoretical framework within which his theory of the modern state could be defended.

Of all Hegel's systematic writings relating to political philosophy, the *Philosophy of Right* (1821) is the best known; it is also the only one which has been translated into English. Yet before his thought found its definitive expression in this work, Hegel had already attempted several times to systematize his thinking on political theory. It is these earlier versions of his mature political philosophy which show a remarkable continuity in the kind of questions Hegel was asking as well as in the general direction of his enquiry. Some of these earlier attempts also include detailed studies of issues which later would be merely summarized, or just hinted at, in the mature *Philosophy of Right*. These earlier attempts are thus indispensable for the understanding of Hegel's political philosophy both on their own merit and as the groundwork of his later thought.

Anyone going through these various attempts at a systematic treatment of political thought cannot but reach the conclusion that Hegel had not only been persistently preoccupied with the same set of problems, but that in a way he was also trying to write the same book all the time: we thus have before us early drafts, so to speak, of the *Philosophy of Right*.

Even the actual titles of the writings involved point in that direction. The *Philosophy of Right* is subtitled 'Natural Law and Political Science'; Hegel's first systematic essay on political thought, published in 1802, is entitled *On the Scientific Modes of Treatment of Natural Law – Its Place in Practical Philosophy and Its Relationship to the Positive Science of Law*. The two other earlier attempts are the *System der Sittlichkeit* ('System of Ethics') and the two

81

versions of the *Jenaer Realphilosophie,* both never published in Hegel's lifetime. Their structure, as well as their content, are clearly a prefiguration of what ultimately became Hegel's mature *Philosophy of Right.*

FROM NATURAL LAW TO SOCIAL COHESION

The essay on Natural Law was published in the *Kritisches Journal der Philosophie,* which had been jointly edited by Hegel and Schelling. Both of them saw it as the main weapon in their fight against the old philosophy. In 1801, a year before the publication of the essay, Hegel had published in Jena the first printed work bearing his name, an essay on the difference between the philosophical systems of Fichte and Schelling.[1] Whereas this first essay is still very much within the horizon of Schelling's *Naturphilosophie* and is heavily indebted to it, the essay on Natural Law consciously tries to place spirit above nature and shows an attempt by Hegel to evolve an independent philosophical position, although the terminology is still sometimes exasperatingly Schellingian.[2]

Despite its title, the essay is wider in scope than a mere treatment of Natural Law. In it Hegel attempts a radical critique of both Kant's formal rationalism and British empiricism. He looks for a valid foundation for legislation that would succeed in preserving the partial truth which, after all, Hegel admits both *a priori* rationalism and empiricism contain.

According to Hegel, the main weakness of the empiricists was their attempt to derive and define the context of such social institutions as marriage and punishment from the empirical characteristics of the historical arrangements bearing these names. Hegel maintains that drawing up such a list or catalogue of empirical functions cannot teach us anything about the essence and nature of these institutions.[3] Furthermore, when the empiricists talk about 'coercion' or 'necessity' they are using abstract categories just like the traditional metaphysicists. Despite their disclaimers, the empiricists have recourse to a number of hidden premises; ultimately, their

---

[1] 'Differenz des Fichte'schen und Schelling'schen Systems der Philosophie', in G. W. F. Hegel, *Gesammelte Werke* (Hamburg, 1966), IV, 5–92. It was with this essay, Rosenkranz says (p. 149), that Hegel sought to make his impact on intellectual life in Jena.

[2] Ibid. IV, 432; cf. Kaufmann, *Hegel,* pp. 69–108; Lasson's introduction to his edition of Hegel's *Schriften zur Politik und Rechtsphilosophie,* pp. xxxiv–vi.

[3] *Gesammelte Werke,* IV, 421–2.

views relate only to 'understanding' (*Verstand*), which perceives only particular aspects and not the totality involved.[4]

It is, however, in the political sphere proper that Hegel sees the breakdown of traditional Natural Law theories. In Rousseau, the general will is postulated as the ultimate legitimacy of the political order; the problem, however, is how 'this general will becomes necessarily real in the subjects'.[5] Natural Law theories tend to solve this dilemma by postulating, besides the government, a second repository of legitimacy in the form of supervisory organs, curbing and controlling the government. But this, to Hegel, creates a dichotomy which causes more problems than are solved. For the problem is twofold: firstly, how does one prevent the government, which claims to stand for the general will, from imposing itself on the citizens; and, secondly, how does one prevent the people from directly imposing their unstructured control over the government. To Hegel, Natural Law theories failed to find a middle way between Hobbes and Robespierre.

Hegel criticizes in detail some of the attempts to solve this problem. He criticizes, for example, Fichte's idea of an Ephorate, a board of control, which would supervise the actions of the government. Hegel points out that Fichte's Ephorate is really dependent upon the government's good will, and thus cannot effectively control it. On the other hand, were the Ephorate to be given real political power and made truly independent of the government, it would then become itself a parallel government and the consequences would be a virtual standstill leading to political paralysis.[6]

As against an impotent Ephorate, Hegel envisages the other possibility inherent in Natural Law theories, i.e. making the popular representative body into an effective political organ of supreme control. The dangers Hegel sees in this are clearly an echo of the political turmoil associated with the more violent phases of the French Revolution:

Lastly, however, when the supreme holders of power freely allow this second representative of the general will to convene the community, so that it would judge between them and the controllers – what can one begin to do with such a rabble (*Pöbel*) . . . which does not lead a public life and which has not been

---

[4] *Ibid.* IV, 428–30. It is of some interest to note that in this context Hegel uses the term 'anti-socialist' to denote those natural law theories which start with 'the being of the individual as the primary and highest [fact]' (p. 431).
[5] *Ibid.* IV, 443.
[6] *Ibid.* IV, 445.

educated (*gebildet*) to the consciousness of the common will and to action in the spirit of the whole.[7]

Here Hegel clearly realizes how much Rousseau's advice to force people to be free only begs the question. What Hegel is searching for is something not much different from that which, in his theological writings, he had found in the ancient polis: the consciousness of belonging to a community, that feeling which would not view the community in merely instrumental terms. Belonging to such a community, to a people, is for Hegel 'absolute ethical life' (*absolute Sittlichkeit*) not because the people represents as such any absolute ethical idea, but because this membership is absolute rather than relative, it is its own end rather than a mere means towards an end determined by self-interest, security or the like.[8]

It is the classical *virtus* that emerges here again. Nevertheless, though Hegel is most eloquent about it, it is obvious that he does not expect it to be resurrected, as some of his asides in the direction of Rousseau clearly indicate. Here, too, the historical context of the disappearance of classical virtue is brought up by Hegel: in later Rome people still possessed *individual* courage, but it was *public* courage that disappeared; personal status came to replace public standing, and this sinking into privacy characterized the decline and fall of the Roman Empire.[9]

It is this privatization of life, of which Hegel saw a contemporary parallel in the conditions of the old German Reich, that Hegel considers as the greatest danger to absolute *Sittlichkeit*, to political *virtus*. Though agreeing with Plato that the proliferation of laws and litigation is harmful, he has his own reasons for such a view: the more law-suits you have in society, the more this proves that its members pursue their own, individual private interests and neglect the *res publica*. The danger is that under such conditions the state becomes a mere executor of the economic interests of its citizens. This danger has to be avoided:

It is not enough that . . . complete security and facility of business be guaranteed . . . The ethical whole has rather to keep [property] within the

[7] *Ibid.*
[8] *Ibid.* iv, 449.
[9] *Ibid.* iv, 456–7. It is here that Hegel also suggests a fascinating explanation for the disappearance of slavery in antiquity: 'That relationship of slavery disappeared by itself into the empirical manifestations of the universality of the Roman Empire: with the loss of absolute ethical life, with the humiliation of the noble class, both formerly distinct classes became equal to each other, and with the disappearance of freedom, slavery necessarily disappeared as well.'

feeling of its own nullity . . . and prevent its development (which is natural to it) in the direction of ever-increasing differentiation and inequality. This happens more or less unconsciously in every state, appearing as an external natural necessity . . . in the form of ever-growing state expenses. Consequently, taxation rises, property is diminished and business is curtailed, mostly through war.[10]

The antinomy to classical Natural Law theories could not be more explicit: under no condition should the state be conceived as an instrument for the preservation and defence of property. But Hegel goes one step further in this passage: he does not leave it as a mere postulate; he argues that this *is* the inner rationale of the state, that by its very nature the state infringes upon property rather than protects it. The more wealth there is in society, the more the state taxes it. Taxation and war are, as a matter of fact, the great equalizers and each in its own way is a guarantor against the state becoming a front for economic interests. Hegel thus sees the hidden hand of the immanent universality of the state clearly at work, though (as he puts it) 'unconsciously' and appearing as 'external natural necessity', within each given historical society.

The point for Hegel, however, is to make this esoteric reason explicit, to raise this hidden universality to the level of consciousness. This constructive aspect of Hegel's thought is far less well expressed, mainly because the essay was conceived as a critique of Natural Law theories rather than as an independent exposition of Hegel's own views. Some hints are however there: the old *virtus* cannot be revived, mainly because life has reached a stage where economic interests do play a crucial role and have to be legitimized. Social differentiation, which we have seen Hegel deplore, he nonetheless sees as a natural necessity of this state of affairs: it could, though, be utilized to integrate economic interests into the universality of the state.

It is here that Hegel arrives at his theory of social classes, which will later appear in a much more explicit and sophisticated form in the *System der Sittlichkeit*, the *Jenaer Realphilosophie* and the *Philosophy of Right*. At its roots it is an attempt to integrate classical *virtus* into modern, differentiated social life through the mediation of the system of needs. Not everyone can live a public life, but not all life should be thrown wide open to the laws of the market-place. Society should therefore have two classes (*Stände*), one devoted to public life, the 'absolute' class, and the other engaged in economic activity.

[10] *Ibid.* IV, 450–1.

The absolute class possesses the 'real consciousness of ethical life'; its freedom consists in absolutely abstracting from the immediate material conditions of life. This is symbolized in its readiness not only to serve the whole rather than engage in its own particularistic pursuits, but ultimately also in its readiness to die for the community; this is the height of its absolute identification with the community.[11]

What Hegel says about the commercial class is of significant interest since in it he relates the emergence of the modern world to the appearance of *bourgeois* man:

> The power of this estate is thus so determined that it consists in possession generally and in a system of law relating to possession. It constitutes an interrelated system, and . . . the relationships of possession are integrated into a formal unity. Everyone, who is thus capable of holding possession, relates to all as a universal – as a burgher, in the sense of *bourgeois*. As a compensation for the political nullity [in which members of this estate find themselves] since they are private persons, they enjoy the fruits of peace and business and find in their enjoyment their complete security.[12]

Hegel's attempt to transcend the limits of Natural Law theories is however severely handicapped by his inability, or reluctance, to go into detail about the nature of the relationship between these two classes. Nor is his theory of social classes related in any way whatsoever to a theoretical foundation or to general philosophical principles. It is as if it were introduced as an afterthought; and it has the appearance of a diluted Platonic device. Only at a later stage, when he related his views on labour and the economic process, which had been implied in his early writings ever since his acquaintance with political economy, to a general theory of man's place in the universe, did Hegel develop the theoretical dimension of this class-system. This is to be seen in his manuscript on *System der Sittlichkeit* and the two sets of lectures known as *Realphilosophie I* and *Realphilosophie II*. To these we must now turn.

[11] *Ibid.* IV, 462. That Hegel's idea about an 'absolute' (or, later, 'universal') class has Platonic affinities is obvious. But its philosophical justification is very different from Plato's philosophical anthropology, and it is utterly free of Plato's racist overtones. Hence Hegel could, despite the parallel, condemn the closed nature of Plato's 'caste system'. See M. B. Foster, *The Political Philosophies of Plato and Hegel* (Oxford, 1935), who, however, limits himself only to the *Philosophy of Right* and disregards the Jena manuscripts.

[12] *Gesammelte Werke*, IV, 458.

Modern life and social reality

In the *System der Sittlichkeit* and the two versions of the *Realphilosophie* Hegel introduces for the first time his theory of what he would later call 'objective spirit', though the *Realphilosophie* contains also much else.[13] Both sets of texts remained unpublished in Hegel's own lifetime. The *System der Sittlichkeit*, composed around 1802–3, was published in its entirety for the first time by Lasson in 1913, though an earlier incomplete version was published by Mollat in 1893. The two versions of lectures known as *Realphilosophie I* and *II*, delivered by Hegel at Jena University in 1803–4 and 1805–6 respectively, were published by Hoffmeister for the first time in the early 1930s.

A careful analysis of these two sets of texts, unknown to most of Hegel's traditional commentators, shows that while Hegel's main concern was always the attempt to achieve a comprehensive system of general philosophical speculation, his preoccupation with problems of a social and political nature consistently remained as the focus of his theoretical interest. These texts also point to a remarkable continuity in his political thought and clearly show that the political philosophy of the *Philosophy of Right* cannot be understood in terms of a mere justification of the Restoration of 1815, since most of its themes and ideas go back to Hegel's thought during the Jena period.[14] Though the *System der Sittlichkeit* and the *Realphilosophie* differ on a number of issues, they will be treated jointly here.

The *System der Sittlichkeit* tries to delineate the context within which a philosophy of social relationships can be justified. *Sittlichkeit*, ethical life, is defined by Hegel as the identification of the individual with the totality of his social life.[15] What Hegel sets out to do is to describe the series of mediations necessary for individual consciousness to find itself in this totality.

Hegel's point of departure is nature; consciousness' first moment

---

[13] Rosenzweig, *Hegel und der Staat*, pp. 130ff. That *Realphilosophie I* is an earlier attempt at a comprehensive system has recently been challenged: see the editor's remark to the new edition of *Realphilosophie II* (Hamburg, 1967). We shall, however, follow the traditional way of referring to the two works involved as *Realphilosophie I* and *II*.

[14] Cf. Marcuse, *Reason and Revolution*, pp. 73–90; Lukács, *Der junge Hegel*, pp. 407–31; Mihailo Marković, 'Economism or the Humanization of Economics', *Praxis* v (1969), 460–1.

[15] 'System der Sittlichkeit', in *Schriften zur Politik und Rechtsphilosophie*, p. 419.

is the realization of its apartness and separateness from nature. This realization gives rise to the impulse to overcome this separation, to integrate nature into oneself. Consciousness seeks its own recognition in its objects. This is the notion of need, in which the human subject relates to objects of nature and seeks to subsume them under his subjectivity and thus restore the primeval identity of subject and object. Man wants to devour the object, and Hegel projects this process in three stages: (a) need; (b) the overcoming and fulfilment of need; and (c) satisfaction.[16] Through satisfaction the individual achieves this transcendence of separation, but only on an immediate level: this satisfaction, in which the object is being destroyed, is purely sensuous and negative. It is limited to a particular object and cannot be generalized. The consciousness of separation remains after each individual act of subsumption.

The emergence of property is seen by Hegel as another attempt by man to appropriate nature to himself, but this time on a higher level. No longer is the natural object appropriated in order to be negated and destroyed; on the contrary, now it is being preserved. But the significance of this appropriated object now no longer lies in its relationship to the appropriating subject, but rather in the fact that other subjects recognize it as belonging exclusively to this one particular subject:

The right of possession relates immediately to things, not to a third party. Man has a right to take into possession as much as he can as an individual. He has this right, it is implied in the concept of being himself: through this he asserts himself over all things. But his taking into possession implies also that he excludes a third. What is it which from this aspect binds the other? What may I take into my possession without doing injury to a third party?[17]

It is from these considerations that Hegel derives the transsubjective, non-individual nature of property: *property pertains to the person as recognized by others*, it can never be an intrinsic quality of the individual prior to his recognition by others. While possession relates to the individual, property relates to society: since possession becomes property through the others' recognition of it as such, property is a social attribute. Thus not an individualistic but a social premise is at the root of Hegel's concept of property, and property will never be able to achieve an independent

[16] *Ibid.* p. 422.
[17] *Realphilosophie II*, 207; cf. *Realphilosophie I*, 240, on the transition from possession to property: 'The security of my possession [becomes] the security of the possessions of all; in my property, all have their property. My possession has achieved the form of consciousness.'

stature in his system. This is significant because though Hegel's description of the economic process is taken, as we have already noted, from classical political economy, he holds a totally different view about the basic nature of property. Property always remains premissed on social consensus, on consciousness, not on the mere fact of possession.

Property is thus to Hegel a moment in man's struggle for recognition.[18] It does not derive from merely physical needs, and has thus an anthropological significance which it was always to retain in Hegel's philosophy. Yet there still remains an accidental element in possession, even when turned into property, since the objects of property relate to this or that individual in a wholly arbitrary way.

It is at this stage in his philosophical anthropology that Hegel introduces labour into his system. Only through labour, Hegel maintains, 'is the accidentality of coming into possession being transcended (*aufgehoben*)'.[19] Labour, to Hegel, is the sublimation of primitive enjoyment; in labour 'one abstracts from enjoyment, i.e. one does not achieve it . . . The object, as an object, is not annihilated, but another is posited in its stead'.[20]

Labour is thus a mediated transcendence of the feeling of separation from the object; moreover, by its very nature, it is the locus of a synthesis of the subjective and the objective. The instrument of labour facilitates this mediation, and it is through labour that man becomes recognized by others. Labour is the universal link among men, 'labour is the universal interaction and education (*Bildung*) of man . . . a recognition which is mutual, or the highest individuality'.[21] In labour, man becomes 'a universal for the other, but so does the other'.[22]

Labour appears then as the transformation of the appetites from their initial annihilative character to a constructive one: whereas primitive man, like the animals, consumes nature and destroys the object, labour holds up to man an object to be desired not through negation but through re-creation. While the goal of production is thus explained as recognition through the other, its motive is still need. Consciousness, by desiring an object, moves man to create it, to transform need from a subjective craving and appetite into an external, objective force. Labour is therefore always intentional, not instinctual for it represents man's power to create his own

[18] *Schriften zur Politik*, p. 439.   [19] *Realphilosophie II*, 217.
[20] *Schriften zur Politik*, p. 424.   [21] *Ibid.* p. 430.   [22] *Ibid.* p. 428.

world. Production is a vehicle of reason's actualization of itself in the world. In a passage which prefigures his later dictum about the rational and the actual, Hegel remarks that 'Reason, after all, can exist only in its work; it comes into being only in its product, apprehends itself immediately as another as well as itself'.[23]

But Hegel's views on labour as the instrumentality through which man acquaints himself with his world and thus develops both this world as well as himself is accompanied by a realization that the conditions of labour postulate not only an actualization of man but also his possible emasculation. To Hegel labour as practised in history has a double aspect. On the one hand, it is the externalization and objectification of man's capacities and potentialities: through labour, nature becomes part of the natural history of man: 'I have done something; I have externalized myself; this negation is position; externalization (*Entäusserung*) is appropriation.'[24] But labour also brings forth conditions which frustrate man's attempt to integrate himself into his world. This element of alienation in the process of labour is, to Hegel, not a marginal aspect of labour which can be rectified or reformed: it is fundamental and immanent to the structure of human society, and it is one of the characteristics of modern society that this element is being continually intensified. What we have in Hegel's discussion of this issue is one of the first most radical realizations that the development of modern society – much as it is welcomed by Hegel – adds a further burden to the traditional predicaments of human life.

This vision of the workings of modern society does not come to Hegel through any empirical study of the social or economic conditions in his contemporary Germany. His account of these conditions in *The German Constitution* certainly does not describe a vital, let alone active and productive society. Nor does he refer to other, more developed societies: Hegel's views here are rather a distillation of the model of society presented by modern political economy raised to the level of a philosophical paradigm.[25]

---

[23] *Realphilosophie I*, 233.   [24] *Realphilosophie II*, 218.

[25] That this was Hegel's point of departure was clearly realized by Marx, who wrote in his *Economic-Philosophical Manuscripts*: 'Hegel's standpoint is that of modern political economy. He conceives *labour* as the essence, the self-confirming essence of man.' But since Marx was not acquainted with the unpublished texts of the *System der Sittlichkeit* and the *Realphilosophie*, he was not aware that Hegel did realize that labour entails alienation. Hence he mistakenly concludes that Hegel 'observes only the positive side of labour, not its negative side'. See K. Marx, *Early Writings*, trans. T. B. Bottomore (London, 1963), p. 203.

Labour, alienation and the power of the market

The problematic aspect of labour is bound up with its social nature, and is hence inescapable. We have seen that to Hegel labour is the mediation through which man is related to his fellow beings. Now Hegel adds a further dimension: in production, man produces not for himself, but, on a reciprocal basis, for others as well. Labour becomes social labour, and men's aims in the process of labour are not only their individual aims, but broader, trans-individual ones: 'Labour for all and the satisfaction of all. Everyone serves the other and sustains him, only here has the individual for the first time an individuated being; before that it has been only abstract and untrue.'[26]

Contrary to the atomistic, individualistic view of labour, which sees labour as primary and exchange as secondary and derivative, based on surplus, for Hegel labour is always premissed on a reciprocal relationship, subsuming exchange under its cognitive aspects. No one produces for himself, and all production presupposes the other – hence a basic element of recognition is always immanent in labour.

Yet this reciprocity gives rise to a problem: though every human need is concrete, the totality of needs for which the totality of production is undertaken is abstract and cannot be concretely expressed until the whole process of production and distribution has been completed. Production thus becomes abstract and the division of labour appears related to the needs of production and not to the needs of the producers. Man produces not the objects of his own specific needs, but a general product which he can then exchange for the concrete object or objects of his needs. He produces *commodities,* and the more refined his tastes become, the more objects he desires which he cannot produce himself but can attain only through the production of more objects which he then exchanges. There thus appears a universal dependence of each human being on the universality of the producers and the character of labour undergoes a basic change:

Because work is being done for the need as an abstract being-for-itself, one also works in an abstract way ... General labour is thus division of labour, saving ... Every individual, as an individual, works for *a* need. The content of his labour [however] transcends *his* need; he works for the satisfaction of many, and so [does] everyone. Everyone satisfies thus the needs of many, and the satisfaction of his many particular needs is the labour of many others. Since his labour is thus this abstraction, he behaves as an abstract self, or according to the way

26 *Realphilosophie II*, 213.

of thingness, not as a comprehensive, rich, all-encompassing spirit, who rules over a wide range and masters it. He has no concrete work: his power is in analysis, in abstraction, in the breaking up of the concrete into many abstract aspects.[27]

The dialectical nature of social labour is thus evident: on the one hand, by creating sociability, a universal dependence of each on all, it makes man into a universal being. On the other hand, this reciprocal satisfaction of needs creates a hiatus between the concrete individual and his particular and concrete needs. By working for all, the individual does not work for himself any more; an element of distance and a need for mediation is consequently thrust between his work and the satisfaction of his needs. Social labour necessarily entails alienation:

Man thus satisfies his needs, but not through the object which is being worked upon by him; by satisfying his needs, it becomes something else. Man does not produce anymore that which he needs, nor does he need anymore that which he produces. Instead of this, the actuality of the satisfaction of his needs becomes merely the possibility of this satisfaction. His work becomes a general, formal, abstract one, single; he limits himself to one of his needs and exchanges this for the other necessities.[28]

This universal dependence of man on man, while bringing out man's universal nature, also creates a power over man which grows beyond his control; what men produce under these conditions are not the objects of their immediate desire, but commodities:

This system of needs is, however, formally conceived as the system of universal reciprocal physical inter-dependence. Nobody is for himself [regarding] the totality of his needs. His work, or any method whatsoever of his ability to satisfy his needs, does not satisfy it. It is an alien power (*eine fremde Macht*), over which he has no control and on which it depends whether the surplus, which he possesses, constitutes for him the totality of his satisfaction.[29]

The more labour becomes thus divided and specialized, the more commodities can be produced; the more labour becomes removed from the immediate satisfaction of the producers, the more productive it becomes. Man thus achieves ever greater comfort at the price of ever greater abstraction and alienation in the process of production itself:

His labour and his possessions are not what they are for him, but what they are for all. The satisfaction of needs is a universal dependence of all on all; there disappears for everyone the security and the knowledge that his work is immediately adequate to his particular needs; *his* particular need becomes universal.[30]

[27] *Ibid. II*, 214–15.
[28] *Realphilosophie I*, 237–8.
[29] *Schriften zur Politik*, p. 492.
[30] *Realphilosophie I*, 238.

Labour alienation and the power of the market

The process of labour – originally man's recognition through the other, intended to create for each his own objective world – becomes a process over which man loses all control and direction. Man is far from being integrated into the objective world through creative consciousness, i.e. labour; the abstract nature of labour, together with the division of labour, makes him totally alien to this objective world. Hence Hegel comes to be troubled by the real conditions of factory labour, and his general anthropology of labour becomes social analysis. Quoting Adam Smith, Hegel says:

The particularization of labour multiplies the mass of production; in an English manufacture, 18 people work at the production of a needle; each has a particular and exclusive side of the work to perform; a single person could probably not produce 120 needles, even not one ... But the value of labour decreases in the same proportion as the productivity of labour increases. Work becomes thus absolutely more and more dead, it becomes machine-labour, the individual's own skill becomes infinitely limited, and the consciousness of the factory worker is degraded to the utmost level of dullness. The connection between the particular sort of labour and the infinite mass of needs becomes wholly imperceptible, turns into a blind dependence. It thus happens that a far-away operation often affects a whole class of people who have hitherto satisfied their needs through it; all of a sudden it limits [their work], makes it redundant and useless.[31]

This analysis undoubtedly reveals Hegel as one of the earliest radical critics of the modern industrial system. Hegel goes on to point out the necessary link between the emergence of machinery and the intensification of alienation, and here again he takes a middle position between the idealizers of the machine and the machine-smashers: while recognizing the alienation caused by the introduction of the machine, he sees it as a necessary element in the anthropological determination of modern society based on ever-increasing production. Originally, Hegel contends, tools were nothelse than the mediation between man and his external world; as such, they always remained a passive object in the hands of the producer. But,

In the same way, [the worker] becomes through the work of the machine more and more machine-like, dull, spiritless. The spiritual element, the self-conscious plenitude of life, becomes an empty activity. The power of the self resides in rich comprehension: this is being lost. He can leave some work to the machine; his own doing thus becomes even more formal. His dull work limits him to one point, and labour is the more perfect, the more one-sided it is ... In the machine man abolishes his own formal activity and makes it work for him. But this deception, which he perpetrates upon nature ... takes vengeance on him.

[31] *Ibid. I*, 239.

The more he takes away from nature, the more he subjugates her, the baser he becomes himself. By processing nature through a multitude of machines, he does not abolish the necessity of his own labour; he only pushes it further on, removes it away from nature and ceases to relate to it in a live way. Instead, he flees from this negative livingness, and that work which is left to him becomes itself machine-like. The amount of labour decreases only for the whole, not for the individual: on the contrary, it is being increased, since the more mechanized labour becomes, the less value it possesses, and the more must the individual toil.[32]

The immanent link between division of labour, mechanization and the alienating nature of labour becomes more and more the center of Hegel's argument:

Labour, which is oriented towards the object as a whole, is (being) divided and becomes particular labour; and this particular labour becomes more and more mechanical because its manifold nature is (being) excluded ... It becomes alien to totality. This method of working, which is thus divided, presupposes that the remainder of the needs were to be achieved through another fashion, since they have also to be worked out – through the labour of other men. In this emasculation (*Abstumpfung*) of mechanical labour there directly lies the possibility of separating oneself completely from it: because labour is wholly quantitative, without variety . . . something completely external ... It only depends upon it to find an equally dead principle of movement for it, a self-differentiating power of nature, like the movement of water, of the wind, of steam, etc., and the instrument turns into a machine.[33]

We thus have here, in one of the more speculative documents of German idealist philosophy, one of the most acute insights into the working of modern, industrial society: from an *a priori* philosophical anthropology, Hegel moves on to incorporate the results of political economy into a philosophical system – an attempt almost identical in its systematic structure with Marx's program forty years later. How many of Marx's later conclusions are already to be found, explicitly or implicitly, in Hegel's earlier texts would however require a separate discussion.[34]

[32] *Ibid.* I, 232, 237. The parallels with Marx's description in the *Economic-Philosophical Manuscripts* are, of course, striking (see *Early Writings*, pp. 120–34). The major difference has, however, already been pointed out by Lukács: while Hegel sees alienation as a necessary aspect of objectification, Marx maintains that alienation does not reside immanently in the process of production itself, but only in its concrete historical conditions. For Marx, therefore, there exists the possibility of ultimate salvation, whereas for Hegel one will never be able to dissociate the cross from the rose of the present.

[33] *Schriften zur Politik*, p. 437.

[34] In discussing Marx's views on the alienation of the worker in my *The Social and Political Thought of Karl Marx* (Cambridge, 1968) I referred, on pp. 55–56, to Adam Müller's and Franz von Baader's writings to show that the

Labour, alienation and the power of the market

Commodity-producing society, according to Hegel, needs also a universal, abstract criterion which can mediate between labour and the subject. This is money:

Those multiple labours of the needs as things must also realize their concept, their abstraction: their universal concept must also be a thing just like them, but [it must be] a universal, which represents all. *Money* is this materially existing concept, the form of the unity of the potentiality of all the things relating to needs. Need and labour are thus elevated into this universality, and this creates in a great nation an immense system of communality (*Gemeinschaftlichkeit*) and mutual dependence, a life of death moving within itself (*ein sich in sich bewegendes Leben des Toten*). This system moves hither and thither in a blind and elemental way, and like a wild animal calls for strong permanent control and curbing.[35]

The ultimate power in commodity-producing society is the power of the market: 'In this system the ruling [element] is the unconscious blind totality of needs and the methods of their satisfaction.'[36] The power of the market is connected with the transformation of the use value of objects into the exchange value of commodities.[37] Man's labour, which had been aimed at achieving both recognition through the other and power over objects, thus ultimately places man in a diametrically opposed condition of utter dependence and total impotence *vis-à-vis* the powers which were created by him and his own subjectivity – but over which he had now lost all control.

Hegel's account of commodity-producing society abounds with explicit references to the sociological structure of this society.

social consequences of industrial society were grasped by German thinkers well before Marx and the advent of industrialization in Germany itself. At that time I was unaware of the extent to which Hegel dealt with these problems. In fact, his treatment not only antedates both Müller and von Baader, but is carried out in much greater detail and occupies a central position in the formation of his social philosophy – something that cannot be said for two other thinkers quoted by me. There is one further difference, of course: while Müller's and von Baader's writings were published, Hegel's discussions of this problem remained in manuscript, and were unknown to his contemporaries.

[35] *Realphilosophie I*, 239–40. In later years, Hegel coined the following aphorism about money: 'Money is the abbreviation of all external necessity' (*Berliner Schriften*, p. 731). Again, the parallel with Marx's fragment 'On Money' (*Early Writings*, pp. 189–94), as well as with Moses Hess' tract on the same subject, is very close.

[36] *Schriften zur Politik*, p. 493. Cf. p. 492: 'This value depends upon the totality of needs and the totality of surplus; and this totality is a power little known, unseen and incalculable.'

[37] *Ibid.* p. 438: 'So this possession has lost its meaning for the practical feeling of the subject, is not anymore a need for him, but [becomes] surplus; its relation to use is therefore a universal one.'

Aspects of class-domination appear in a very prominent way in Hegel's description when he expresses his awareness of the fact that the wealth of nations can be built only at the expense of the poverty of whole classes: 'Factories and manufacturers base their existence on the misery (*Elend*) of a class', he remarks.[38] And, in another context, his description is no less brutal in its candour: '[This power] condemns a multitude to a raw life and to dullness in labour and poverty, so that others could amass fortunes.'[39]

The condition of poverty, in which this mass finds itself, is endemic to commodity-producing society: 'This inequality of wealth is in and for itself necessary', because wealth has the necessary, immanent tendency to accumulate and multiply itself.[40] The power driving men to act in the market is infinite and knows no bounds:

Though it appears that enjoyment has to be something definite and limited, its infinity is its ideality, and in it it is infinite ... Cultured enjoyment, in overcoming the roughness of needs, must look to the noblest and most refined and adapt it, and the more differentiated its lustre, the greater the labour that is necessary for its production.[41]

From this Hegel draws the conclusion that wealth and poverty are interdependent and constitute two aspects of the Janus-like immanent forces of the market. The rapid expansion of the market necessitates ever-expanding and continually-changing needs. Again, in a rare insight into the dialectics of ever-changing demand creating pressure for ever-increasing production, Hegel says: 'Needs are thus multiplied; each need is subdivided into many; tastes become refined and differentiated. One demands a level of finish which carries the object ever nearer to its use.'[42]

Fashion becomes the determinant of production, and Hegel is

---

[38] *Realphilosophie II*, 257. Cf. p. 232: 'A mass of the population is condemned to stupefying, unhealthy, and precarious labour in factories, manufactures, mines, etc.'

[39] *Ibid.* II, 238.

[40] *Schriften zur Politik*, p. 495. In these paragraphs Hegel speaks explicitly about 'the working class' (*die arbeitende Klasse*,' p. 498). It should be noted that only in referring to workers does Hegel use the modern term *Klasse*, rather that the traditional *Stand*, which he uses when otherwise discussing social classes.

[41] *Ibid.* pp. 494–5. Cf. p. 496: 'High wealth is ... likewise connected with the deepest poverty ... Labour becomes ... on one side ideal universality, on the other really mechanical.'

[42] *Realphilosophie II*, 231–2. The slightly censorious tone evokes echoes of Rousseau; but never does Hegel suggest that a recourse to a more simple, less differentiated society is feasible. The yearning for pristine simplicity, evident in both Plato and Rousseau, is totally absent in Hegel.

thus one of the first thinkers who has grasped the internal logic of constantly-changing fashions and fads and its function within the productive process. The constant disquiet of concrete life in industrial society is here described from the consumer's point of view as well:

> But this plurality creates *fashion*, the versatility and freedom in the use of these things. The cut of clothes, the style of furnishing one's home, are nothing permanent. This constant change is essential and rational, far more rational than sticking to one fashion, imagining to find something permanent in such particular forms. The beautiful is not ordered by one fashion; but here we have to do not with free beauty, but with luxury that attracts . . . Hence it has accidentality in it.[43]

These fluctuations in taste have a bearing on the basic lack of security which characterizes modern society. Whole sectors of the population live by the whim of a changing mode. Hegel's description of the conditions of life of these classes sinking into poverty is truly amazing when one reflects that Hegel reaches his conclusions through an immanent development of the consequences of the theories of political economy:

> Whole branches of industry which supported a large class of people suddenly fold up because of a change in fashion or because the value of their products fell due to new inventions in other countries. Whole masses are abandoned to poverty which cannot help itself. There appears the contrast between vast wealth and vast poverty – a poverty that cannot do anything for itself . . .
>
> Wealth, like any other mass, makes itself into a power. Accumulation of wealth takes place partly by chance, partly through the universal mode of production and distribution. Wealth is a point of attraction . . . It collects everything around itself – just like a large mass attracts to itself the smaller one. To them that have, shall be given. Acquisition becomes a many-sided system which develops into areas from which smaller businesses cannot profit. The highest abstraction of labour reaches into the most particular types of labour and thus receives an ever-widening scope. This inequality of wealth and poverty, this need and necessity, turn into the utmost tearing up (*Zerrissenheit*) of the will, an inner indignation (*Empörung*) and hatred.[44]

The ultimate consequences of these conditions then push the helpless mass of the poor into personal dependence upon the

[43] *Ibid. II*, 232.
[44] *Ibid. II*, 232–3. It is extremely interesting to note that the term 'inner indignation' (*Empörung*) used here by Hegel, is the same he uses in the addition to § 244 of the *Philosophy of Right* where he says that 'poverty in itself does not make men into rabble; a rabble is created only when there is joined to poverty a disposition of mind, an inner indignation against the rich, against society, against the government, etc.' Moreover, the only oblique reference in Marx to Hegel's discussion of poverty in the *Philosophy of Right* is a fleeting hint that *Empörung* is not enough; see K. Marx/F. Engels, *The Holy Family*, trans. R. Dixon (Moscow, 1956), p. 51.

wealthy, who are their employers. Economic inequality calls for a situation of domination, and out of economic relations there emerges a dangerous pattern of inequality and power:

This necessary inequality ... causes through its quantitative constitution ... a relationship of domination. The enormously rich individual becomes a power, he transcends the continuing physical dependence [which meant that one] depended upon a universal, not a particular [power].[45]

Man's Promethean attempt has ended in shambles: the forces unleashed by his creative consciousness have become fetters, and the generality of human beings becomes enslaved by its own needs and by the modes of satisfying them.

THE STATE AND SOCIAL CLASSES

Hegel has thus painted a most detailed and, for his period, quite astonishing picture of the system of needs which he would later call 'civil society'. Because the Jena manuscripts were left unpublished for more than a century, Hegel's radical critique of industrial society remained virtually unknown. Only some dim echoes of it found their way into the *Philosophy of Right*, where they always stood out as posing some disturbing questions to all of Hegel's political philosophy; yet there they were nothing more than a marginal phenomenon.[46] When writing the *Philosophy of Right* Hegel thought that he had already found an answer to his problem, and hence the criticism appeared as secondary, while the proposed solution came to occupy the center of his argument. In his Jena manuscripts, on the other hand, he was still seeking a solution, and the problem was only beginning to present itself with all its force. Hence its salience and prominence in these earlier writings.

To anyone who has followed Hegel's argument about the nature of modern commodity-producing society, it would appear natural that Hegel would now proceed to argue for a radical transformation of this society. Yet it is precisely at the point where Hegel shows how modern society abandons whole masses to poverty and destitution, that the possibility of a radical transformation of society presents itself to Hegel – only to be discarded. Ultimately, this possibility, in Hegel's language, remains an 'inner indignation', not an act to be externalized. At the height of his critical awareness of

---

[45] *Schriften zur Politik*, p. 495.
[46] Cf. Eric Weil, *Hegel et l'État* (Paris, 1950), pp. 93–7.

the horrors of industrial society, Hegel ultimately remains quietistic, searching for a solution that would incorporate this horrifying reality into a system that could integrate and accommodate it. Philosophy can only interpret the world, not change it.

It is in this context that Hegel looks at the political structure proper and introduces the state as a system of integration aimed at overcoming the atomistic individualism of the economic sphere. A state that would merely express the dominant economic interests is to Hegel, as we have already seen, an abomination. Hegel's emerging political theory is an attempt to achieve a universality (a 'general will') that would not be, on the one hand, an aggregate of individual wills yet would not appear, on the other, as a merely external, coercive antithesis to the individual wills. To achieve this, Hegel has to find a moment of mediation, and this he sets out to do.

Thus the state appears in the *Realphilosophie* at the moment when the critical analysis of modern society reaches its zenith. The state is shown as a force regulating and integrating economic activity, transcending by its very universality the centrifugal forces of the market. In the course of developing this idea, Hegel adds some further touches to his picture of industrial society when he points out that the state may initiate economic expansion abroad in order to preserve internal stability and prosperity:

Government comes onto the scene and has to see to it that every sphere be preserved ... [It has to look for] ways out, for channels to sell the product abroad, though this makes it more difficult, since it is to the detriment of the others. [But] freedom of commerce remains necessary, interference must be as inconspicuous as possible, for this is the sphere of arbitrariness (*Willkür*). The appearance of power must be prevented, and one should not try to save that which cannot be saved, but try to employ the remaining classes in another way. Government is the universal overseer; the individual is buried in the particular. The [particular] occupation will admittedly be abandoned by itself, but with the sacrifice of this generation and an increase in poverty. Poor taxes and institutions are required.[47]

The state becomes necessary at the moment when society seems to be heading for disruption and chaos: it is the re-integration of the self into itself as a universal being after economic life has particularized, atomized and made its activity into an abstraction. The basic scenario of Hobbes is, in a way, being re-enacted here within a context presenting a synthesis of speculative philosophy and political economy: the abstraction of *bellum omnium contra omnes* becomes concrete in terms of human activity and consciousness.

[47] *Realphilosophie II*, 233.

Hence while stressing the minimalist function of the state in those of its activities impinging upon economic life ('freedom of commerce remains necessary, interference must be as inconspicuous as possible . . . The appearance of power must be prevented'), Hegel can at the same time point to the immanence of political life: 'The individual has his supposed right only in the universal. The state is the existence, the power of right, the keeping of contracts and . . . the existing unity of the word.'[48]

The state has to be above the contending interests of the sphere of needs, it has to be 'indifferent to the various parts' of society.[49] Thus, the state has to intervene in the free play of the forces of the market in order to guarantee a minimum standard of living to which every individual is entitled; if the automatic regulating forces of the market will not guarantee this, the state has to step in and regulate this through taxation and price control:

Out of this totality it must be determined what are the necessary needs of a man, and this can be conceived partly through rough nature according to the various climates, and partly through cultivated nature, i.e. what in a given nation is considered necessary for existence. It happens naturally that this right balance is (being) preserved either through insignificant fluctuations or is (being) restored by greater fluctuations if it be disturbed by external circumstances. But in the latter case . . . caused either by the appearance of the same kind of labour in other regions, or by a fall in prices [of the products], etc. . . . – government must restore nature to its balance.[50]

Hegel also specifies that government has to mitigate extreme economic inequality – though, again, he makes clear that the existence of inequality as such is necessary, since it is immanent in the process of commodity production:

Government has the foremost task of acting against this inequality and the general destruction consequent upon it. This can be done directly through making it difficult to achieve high profits; and when [the government] abandons a part of this class to mechanical labour and factory work (*Fabrikarbeit*) and leaves it in its rough state, it must however preserve this whole class in some kind of viable condition.[51]

[48] *Ibid. II*, 234.
[49] *Schriften zur Politik*, p. 494.
[50] *Ibid.* p. 493. During the Jena period Hegel explicitly supported the imposition of maximum prices by the government, arguing that under conditions of war and scarcity, prices would otherwise soar and make many products inaccessible to the broad public; see *Dokumente*, pp. 372–3.
[51] *Schriften zur Politik*, p. 496. Hegel is also careful to point out that taxation should be so arranged that it would not impoverish 'the working class' (p. 498).

The state and social classes

The state is the protector of the weaker classes in society. Being one of the first to perceive the alienating and pauperizing effects of industrial society, Hegel is also one of the first to propose something which has, despite all the differences in terminology, many of the characteristics of the modern welfare state. Time and again, Hegel mentions taxation as the great equalizer and instrument for income redistribution; in one instance, he argues that dialectically 'the inequality of property is accepted on the condition that high taxes are imposed'.[52]

In developing his theory, Hegel endows the state with a dual quality which accentuates the dialectical nature of his whole attitude: on the purely subjective level, the state is merely instrumental; people view it as a convenient device to secure their ends, to smooth the functioning of economic institutions, to alleviate some of the glaring tensions created by the system of commodity production. But on a higher plane, the state embodies man's basic universal nature, the immanent necessity of man to transcend individualistic interests and reach a sphere which Hegel would later call 'objective spirit'.

This has a number of consequences. The ambivalent status of the state will later enable Hegel to construct the realms of art, religion and philosophy as spheres transcending the state yet functioning within its context. The state, while incorporating the individual in a universal unity, does not subsume his activities under its existence. Because on the one hand the individual uses the state as an instrument for his own particular ends while on the other the state is the individual's true being, the classical means/end relationship between individual and state comes to be transcended:

This unity of individuality and universality exists then in a double way; in the extreme of the universal, which is itself an individuality – as government. This is not an abstraction of the state, but an individuality which has the universal as such as an end, while the other extreme has the individual person as an end.[53]

The general will thus appear in Hegel's system in a radically different way from that of Rousseau. Hegel points out in several instances that any social contract theory is a *petitio principi* since it takes consensus, the readiness to abide by the terms of the contract,

---

[52] *Realphilosophie II*, 238. Hegel mentions also individual charity, but this is left here, as in the *Philosophy of Right* later, to subjective feeling, and should not become a substitute or alibi for the need for universally oriented state regulations concerning poverty (*Schriften zur Politik*, p. 472).

[53] *Realphilosophie II*, 248–9.

for granted. In the same way as there could be no right in the state of nature, the general will could not be perceived as the constitutive aspect of the body politic.[54] The general will for Hegel is not the premise on which the state is founded, historically or logically, but the emergent outcome of the lengthy process of *Bildung*, which created through differentiation and opposition the political consciousness out of the diverse elements of man's struggle for recognition. The general will is the will of the individuals made into an object within the institutions of the state:

> The general will is the will of all and each ... It has first of all to constitute itself as general out of the will of the individuals so that it will appear as the principle and element, but on the other hand it is first and essential. The individuals have to make themselves into a universal through negation of themselves, through externalization and education *(Entäusserung und Bildung)*.[55]

This objectification of the individual will as it appears in the general will, in the state, entails the recognition by the individual that what appears as something alien and external – political power – is nothing else than the externalization of his own will. The system of law is this objectification of the subjective will:

> The rule of law is not meant to be an act of legislating as if the others did not exist: they are there. The relation is the movement of the person educated to obey towards the commonwealth ... The second element is the trust that appears, i.e. that the individual knows himself to be in it as his own presence, that he finds himself preserved in it.[56]

This need for the external limitations of the individual's will is the essence of what Hegel calls *Polizei*. The possible misunderstandings connected with its present usage can be at least partly cleared up when we recall that for Hegel *Polizei* comes 'from Politeia, public life and rule, the action of the whole itself'.[57] This public authority is needed, since in caring for himself alone and enjoying the quiet bliss of his property rights, the individual may hurt another by simply disregarding the impact his own actions may have on the life of another. An element of *List der Vernunft* comes into the picture when Hegel describes how the state is willed by the individuals for their own self-preservation and better

---

[54] *Ibid.* II, 205, 245–7. Cf. Hegel's insistence in an article in the *Kritischer Journal der Philosophie* that the 'subordinate form' of a contract could never be adequate to 'the total majesty' of the political order (quoted by Rosenkranz, *Hegels Leben*, p. 176).

[55] *Realphilosophie II*, 244–5.

[56] *Ibid.* II, 248.

[57] *Ibid.* II, 259.

protection while also representing an actuality transcending this interest:

The general *form* is this turning of the individual into a universal and the becoming of the universal. But it is not a blind necessity, but one mediated through knowing. In other words, each is an end to himself, i.e. the end is the motive, each individual is immediately the cause. It is his interest that drives him [to the state], but it is likewise the universal which has validity, is the middle, allies him with his particularity and actuality.[58]

In the *System der Sittlichkeit* Hegel distinguishes between two kinds of ethics: relative ethics, which denotes man's relationship to other human beings taken from an individualistic standpoint, and absolute ethics, which is his relationship to the community of human beings;[59] the terms roughly correspond to Hegel's later usage of *Moralität* and *Sittlichkeit*. 'Absolute' in this context means that this form of ethical behaviour is self-referring and that its criteria are immanent, whereas 'relative' ethics refers to external criteria and hence their 'relative' nature. Political life is thus characterized by the relationship to the whole, to the *Volk* – not in any ethnic sense, but in the Rousseauan sense of *peuple*:

[Absolute ethical life] appears not as love for the fatherland and people and law, but as absolute life in the fatherland and for the people ... It is absolute selflessness, since in the eternal nothing is one's own. It, and all its movements, are the highest beauty and freedom.[60]

Since political life is this mediated identity of the individual with the universal nature of himself, it is in it that 'the individual perceives himself in every other individual' – not as an abstract concept but in concrete life. Hence Hegel's presumption to name this unity 'divine', since it transcends the individual interests and ultimately also the boundaries between one individual and another, 'reaching into higher subject-objectivity'.[61]

Yet this is not an immediate identity, like the one presented in the past by the polis: in modern society, this identity has to be mediated. This is achieved dialectically through the double aspect of Hegel's state, which is both instrumental and immanent. This

---

[58] *Ibid. II*, 243.
[59] *Schriften zur Politik*, pp. 469–72.
[60] *Ibid.* p. 469. Cf. p. 468: 'The concept of ethical life is in its objectivity the transcendence *(Aufhebung)* of particularity. This destruction of the subjective in the objective is the absolute reception of the particular in the universal.'
[61] *Ibid.* pp. 466–7. It is precisely this which Marx sought to achieve in communism; see *Early Writings*, pp. 154–5.

ambivalence is represented in the individual in his dual role as a particular as well as a universal being. In one of the most pointed passages, which prefigures both his own mature thought as well as Marx's later quarrel with it, Hegel says that man is both a member of civil society and a citizen of the state and has to strike a balance between these two aspects of his existence:

> Both individualities are the same. The same [individual] takes care of himself and his family, works, signs contracts, etc., and at the same time he also works for the universal and has it as an end. From the first viewpoint he is called *bourgeois*, from the second *citoyen*.[62]

These two aspects of human activity lead to Hegel's discussion of social classes. The crucial point is, of course, that Hegel does not see the antinomy between man as *bourgeois* and as *citoyen* as something to be overcome in a total, new unity; it is part of the dialectical progress of man towards his self-recognition. This should be kept in mind, since one of the common errors in discussing this problem in Hegel arises from being carried away by the apparent similarity between Hegel's discussion of civil society and some aspects of Marx's analysis. The truth of the matter is that Hegel's point of departure is the exact opposite of Marx's. For Marx, classes are aggregates formed by types of social labour, linked together by the common relationship of their members to the means of production, seeking a political articulation for their socio-economic interests. The class nature of political power is to Marx a sin against the state's presumed claim to express the universal as against the particularism and egotism of civil society. For Hegel, the institutionalization of class relationships into the political structure is the way through which the atomism of civil society becomes integrated into a comprehensive totality. The different classes represent to Hegel not only modes of production, but modes of consciousness which are relevant to a society differentiated in its structure according to the criteria of Hegel's general system. While for Marx classes represent a division of labour that has to be overcome, for Hegel they stand for the integration of this regrettable yet necessary division into a meaningful whole. Classes reflect the various stages of consciousness, just

---

[62] *Realphilosophie II*, 249. The French terms appear in Hegel's original text – as they do, for that matter, in Marx's 'On the Jewish Question' (*Early Writings*, pp. 13–31). For Marx, however, this split of man into *bourgeois* and *citoyen* is the measure of his alienation in modern society, whereas for Hegel it is the basis of his integration into it.

as do periods in history.[63] For Hegel, classes always remain *estates*, in the sense that they represent a legitimized differentiation. Each estate stands for a different mode of consciousness: the principle of immediate trust and obedience is represented in the peasantry; the principle of law and order – in the middle classes; and the principle of universality – in the bureaucracy, the universal class. Though the principle of classification is similar to that of the *Philosophy of Right*, the internal division of each estate is more complex and represents a slightly more sophisticated awareness of class differentiation than the neat divisions Hegel would adopt later. Furthermore, in the *Realphilosophie* the form of labour performed by each class figures more prominently, and thus the connection between class and the anthropology of labour is brought out much more clearly.

Each estate, according to Hegel, is in itself an expression of universality, since it is based on what is common to its members. This universality does not lie outside it, nor is it just a figure of speech: it is through belonging to an estate that a person achieves his ties with other persons. Each estate 'recognizes itself in its equality and constitutes itself as a universal as against [another] universal, and the relationship of the different estates is not a relationship of particulars to particulars. Every individual, by virtue of his belonging to an estate, is a universal and thus a true individual, a person.'[64]

The main function of the estates is to mediate the physical dependence, inherent in the relationships of the system of needs, into an ethical relationship of mutual interdependence, in which the brute force of physical and economic power is sublimated into political organization:

The relationship of physical dependence is one of absolute isolation and of dependence upon something which is mere thought, an abstraction. The constitution [of the estates] predicates a living dependence and a relationship of individuals to individuals, another, internal, active connection which is not that of physical dependence. To say that this estate is constituted in itself means that within its limits it is a living universality. The rich man is required to mitigate the relationship of domination (*Herrschaftsverhältnis*) and even its semblance

---

[63] *Realphilosophie II*, 253. They also reflect various modes of ethical behaviour; thus each estate has a mode of ethics peculiar to it and adequate to its station in life (*Schriften zur Politik*, p. 475).
[64] *Ibid.* p. 475. Slaves, who cannot constitute a universal, are not an 'estate': 'the slave relates to his master as a particular'.

through universal participation in it, and external inequality is reduced externally . . . and the drive towards infinite wealth is wiped out *(ausgerottet)*.[65]

We now may proceed to the description of the estates themselves: the peasantry, the commercial class and the class of civil servants. The peasantry is distinguished by being the class of immediate labour, whose concrete work relates to a natural object (land) and not to a product. It thus represents a low level of consciousness, not yet differentiated from substantiality. On a social level this reflects itself in the peasantry accepting its work and role as they are, without much questioning; the peasantry is the class of immediate trust, of unreflective consciousness:

> The estate of immediate trust and raw concrete labour is the peasantry . . . The peasantry is thus this trust lacking in individuality, having its individuality in the unconscious individual, the earth. As for labour, [the peasant's] work does not have the form of abstract labour: he takes care, more or less, of almost all his needs . . . The inter-relationship between his purpose and its realization is unconscious, natural. He ploughs, sows, but it is God who orders that it will thrive; it is the seasons and his trust that [ensure] that it will become by itself what he had put into the ground. The activity is underground. He pays taxes and tributes because that's how it is; these fields and cottages have been situated in such a way from time immemorial; *that's how it is,* and that's all . . . Concrete labour is elemental, substantial subsistence. In war, this estate makes up the raw mass.[66]

In speaking of the next estate, the commercial class, Hegel distinguishes between the burghers *(Bürgerstand)* and the class of businessmen *(Kaufmannstand)*. The *Bürgerstand* is made up mainly of artisans, its labour being characterized by the adaptation of nature; the business class, on the other hand, is distinguished by its being engaged in exchange. Both the artisans and the businessmen see in law and order the principle of their existence; property, acquisitiveness and social mobility are the pillars of their being. In a striking description of the social ethos of the *Bürgerstand,* Hegel gets at the root of many of what are unmistakably middle class values:

> [The burgher] knows himself as a property owner, not only because he possesses it, but also because it is his right – so he assumes; he knows himself to be recognized by his particularity. Unlike the peasant, he does not enjoy his glass of beer or wine in a rough fashion, as a way of elevating himself out of his

[65] *Ibid.* p. 496. As an example, Hegel cites the Athenian law which imposed the financing of festivals on the wealthy residents of each quarter.
[66] *Realphilosophie II*, pp. 254–5. In the 'System der Sittlichkeit' Hegel adds that the peasantry is capable of a low form of courage, and hence is eligible to serve in the army in inferior positions (*Schriften zur Politik*, p. 480).

The state and social classes

dullness . . . but because [he wants] to show by his suit and the finery of his wife and children that he is as good as the other man and that he has really made it. In this he enjoys himself, his value and his righteousness; for this did he toil and this has he achieved. He enjoys not the pleasures of enjoyment but the joy of his self-esteem.[67]

Within the business class, on the other hand, a higher degree of abstraction is achieved:

The work of the businessman is pure exchange, neither natural nor artificial production or formation. Exchange is the movement, the spirit, the means, liberated from utility and need as well as from work, from immediacy . . .[68]

A member of the business class experiences a 'drowning in possessions and particularity', a 'serfdom' (*Knechtschaft*) to money, and it is this which makes him into 'a burgher, a *bourgeois*'.[69]

The mode of existence of the businessman calls forth the emergence of money as a commodity in itself:

The object itself is being divided into two: the particular thing, the object of commerce, and the abstract, money – a great invention. All needs are reduced to this unity. The object of need has become a mere image, unusable. The object is here something that has meaning purely according to its value, not for itself, not in relation to the need . . . A person is real to the extent that he has money . . . The formal principle of reason is to be found here – it is the abstraction from all particularity, character, historicity, etc. of the individual. The disposition [of the businessman] is this harshness of spirit, wherein the particular, now completely alienated, does not count anymore. [There exist] only strict rights. The bill of exchange must be honoured – he himself may be destroyed – his family, welfare, life, etc. may go to pieces – total lack of mercy.[70]

Once again, what stands out here is not so much the similarity with Marx as Hegel's diametrically opposed reconciliation with this state of affairs: for no radical call of action follows his harsh analysis. The nature of modern society is grasped with an amazing lucidity given the period in which these texts were written; but all is incorporated within the integrative functions of the state. There is neither rebellion nor deviation.

This integration is carried out through the mediation of the third, the universal, class: 'The public estate works for the state . . . Its disposition of mind is the fulfillment of its duty.'[71] The

---

[67] *Realphilosophie II*, 256.   [68] *Ibid.*

[69] *Schriften zur Politik*, p. 477. 'Righteousness' (*Rechtsschaffenheit*) is the mode of operation of this class, the law of property its vehicle.

[70] *Realphilosophie II*, 256–7. Cf. *Schriften zur Politik*, p. 478.

[71] *Realphilosophie II*, 259. In the 'System der Sittlichkeit' Hegel uses the term 'the absolute estate' for this class, and the accent is more on its function of defending the state than administering it (*Schriften zur Politik*, p. 476).

business class expresses already a sort of universality – the universality of the market – but it is still abstract. Universality becomes concrete only in the class of public servants who represent 'the intervention of the universal into all particularity'; the civil servant is likened to the arteries and the nerves that run through the body, though he is not, of course, identical with it.

The universal class is at the apex of the social pyramid not only because of its universal intentionality, but also because it is the only class of society whose objective is knowledge itself, not nature, artefact or abstraction, as is the case with all other classes. The specific academic background of the German bureaucratic tradition is very much in evidence in this concept of the universal class as an educated estate, including not only civil servants in the narrow sense but also teachers, doctors, lawyers:

This pure knowledge has to be realized, has to give a content to itself out of itself, a free content, which is at the same time also a disinterested object... This is science generally. Spirit has here an object with which it deals without relating to appetite and need. It is fulfilled thought, intelligence that knows itself.[72]

The system of estates thus enables Hegel to combine a differentiated social structure – whose roots he finds in the necessary working of modern society – with a highly integrated political system. The estates described by Hegel are not the old medieval guilds: there is nothing restrictive about them, and their principle of organization is functional and rational, based on social mobility, not on heredity or ascription. In an atomized society, they aim at mediating between the individual and the general body politic; and we have already seen how in his 1817 essay on Württemberg Hegel was to come out in favour of a system of representation based on occupational units rather than on a purely mechanistic and atomistic system of unmediated representation. For Hegel the modern state, in order to survive, cannot be based on the direct identification of its citizens with the totality of the political system: a series of mediations is needed, and this Hegel saw as institutionalized in the system of estates.

Yet Hegel's system, as expounded in the *System der Sittlichkeit* and the *Realphilosophie*, seems to have one serious flaw and it is one which appears when Hegel tries to solve this issue of mediation. We have seen Hegel's masterly account of the structure of modern society and have pointed to his grasp of the social prob-

[72] *Realphilosophie II*, 260.

lems brought forth by the advent of modern industry. Hegel's major achievement in this context is his analysis of the state of those individuals directly involved in production, in *Fabrikarbeit*. Yet it is this group, more than any other, whose needs call for integration and mediation – and one looks in vain for this class in Hegel's system of estates. Obviously the worker is not part of the peasantry nor does he belong to the civil service. But neither does the commercial estate, the class of businessmen, include him: in Hegel's account of this estate one finds the small, independent artisan, but as for the worker, he is conspicuous by his absence; and certainly Hegel's paradigm of the burgher spirit cannot, of course, relate to the worker.

It would be absurd to write off Hegel's tremendous intellectual achievement by pointing out that the whole edifice falls down simply because the worker, whose agony Hegel recognizes and describes most acutely, is left out; it would also amount to a blatant anachronism to judge Hegel in the light of later working class history and, on this basis, find him wanting. In fact, had Hegel himself not drawn our attention to the problematic nature of working class life in modern society, one would obviously not have been able to take him to task for not suggesting a remedy for it. But since he has raised the question himself, his failure to find a solution to it within his system seems to justify a gnawing doubt. We shall see that the same problem will arise again in the *Philosophy of Right*; but at least one can pay tribute to Hegel's intellectual integrity for not trying to suggest an easy solution in place of a real one.

GOVERNMENT AND ITS FORMS

Hegel's treatment of politics in his Jena manuscripts postulates a political structure that would be able to surmount the problems posed by the emergence of modern society. Hegel's state is thus faced with the challenge of integrating social and economic change into a developing political structure. After the violent transformations of the French Revolution, it would have to fulfill the dual task of innovation and preservation. To be receptive to change, sometimes even to introduce it, without however being swept away by its consequences, is the difficult task of government:

Today, one governs and lives differently in states whose constitution has remained nonetheless the same – and this constitution changes according to the times. Government must not come forward on the side of the past and defend it obstinately; but similarly it should always be the last one to be convinced of introducing changes.[73]

The delicate dialectics of controlled change leads Hegel to a discussion of the role of public opinion in the political process. Though government appears as the expression of the self's true identity, it does not direct public policy in a void. Government to Hegel interacts with public opinion in a way that points to the necessity for consensus, and here Hegel once again shows his awareness of a problem which is specifically modern:

One cannot do anything against informed public opinion ... From it proceed all changes, and it is nothing else than the progressively developing spirit conscious of its deficiency. Whatever spirit makes its own, does not need force [for its protection]. When conviction, the inner necessity, gives in, no force can sustain it.[74]

The relationship between government and public opinion, as institutionalized in legislatures and in the press, will become in the *Philosophy of Right* a central feature of Hegel's discussion of the sensitive area of policy initiation. Here it serves Hegel only as a way to sum up his historical account of the development of political structures from antiquity to modern times.

This account prefigures in its turn Hegel's later, and much more detailed, historical speculation in his lectures on the philosophy of history. However, the kernel of his basic argument already appears here most clearly. Tyranny, classical polis democracy and the modern monarchy are the three archetypical models which serve Hegel as the various stages through which self-consciousness realizes itself. The route from ancient tyranny to modern constitutional monarchy is, in a sense, the closing of a circle: it is with the rule of one man that it begins, and it is with a structure headed by one man that it culminates. But while ancient tyranny is yet an undifferentiated and crude form of government, modern monarchy represents subjectivity conscious of itself. The discussion of ancient tyranny branches off into a general analysis of the conditions under which new states are created, and here Hegel focuses on the role of great men in history.

Hegel maintains that all states were founded through the extraordinary efforts of great men. Neither a social contract nor sheer force are at the historical roots of the founding of states: rather they were initiated through the spiritual power of a great leader.

[73] *Ibid. II*, 251.   [74] *Ibid. II*, 260.

Government and its forms

The place of the great man in Hegel's early works is similar to that of the legislator in Rousseau's *Contrat Social*; in fact, we have seen Hegel searching for just such a figure in his *The German Constitution*. This leader and founder of a state is the educator of his people: he teaches them how to practice discipline, obedience and societal action, he forces them to obey the common weal. Out of a multitude he creates a people. 'Machiavellianism' is a term used by Hegel in this context to denote the art of founding states, not the way in which they should be run once they have been founded.[75] This constituent dictatorship disappears once its task has been achieved: 'Tyranny is overthrown by the peoples because it is abhorrent, degrading, etc.; but the real cause for this is that it has become superfluous.'[76]

Once constituent tyranny is overthrown after having performed its historical function, it is replaced by a form of government which emerges out of those popular forces which have overthrown it; this is the type of democracy practiced by the classical polis. It is however an undifferentiated form of democracy; far from idealizing the polis, Hegel points to its lack of universality, to the absence of a general norm, to the fact that since everything is decided by the populace, everything is open to the arbitrary will, and nothing stands as a general rule above the accidentality of opinion as expressed in the marketplace:

In this democracy, the will of the individuals is still accidental, since it appears generally as opinion, and the individual has to give in when faced with the majority... Decisions and laws relate only to particular circumstances... The election of public and military leaders is entrusted to the community; but this trust is tested and vindicated only by success, and thus the circumstances are always different.[77]

This lack of a universal law turns the polis into an expression of beautiful liberty – the immediate, unreflective, direct unity of the particular and the universal. The polis knows not distinction between private and public; the individual is subsumed under the totality of the body politic. In a passage strongly reminiscent of the description of the polis in his early theological writings, Hegel says:

[75] *Ibid. II*, 246–7.
[76] *Ibid. II*, 247–8. The resemblance of this paradigm to Marx's *Aufhebung* of the state through the dictatorship of the proletariat is truly remarkable. The dialectics of *Aufhebung* calls forth this necessary abolition of both types of dictatorships once their aim has been achieved.
[77] *Ibid. II*, 249.

This is the beautiful happy liberty of the Greeks, which has been and is admired so much. The people is at the same time split up into citizens as well as constituting the *one* individual, the government. It inter-relates with itself alone. The same will is the individual and the universal. The alienation of the particularity of the will is its immediate preservation . . . There is no protest here: everyone knows himself immediately as universal, i.e. he gives up his particularity without knowing it as such, as a self, an essence.[78]

The polis is thus an entity which despite its apparent beauty enslaves the individual, and the democratic nature of its structure only accentuates the individual's total absorption in the political system. The alternative to this form is, according to Hegel, the modern constitutional monarchy, which is based on the rule of law and the freedom of the individual who identifies with, and at the same time differentiates himself from, the state.[79] In the monarch, the principle of individuality is expressed in a mediated way; the monarch is 'the higher principle of the new age, which remained unknown to the ancients, to Plato'.[80] The monarch, by expressing his will, by saying 'We command', is thus pure subjectivity willing itself.[81]

This is Hegel's vindication of modern monarchy. Expressing subjectivity, it is the highest form of consciousness seeking recognition through self-realization. It is in modern society, where man is torn to pieces by the workings of the market, that he is also returning to himself and develops towards self-recognition. Modern man, who has found himself in his work, is in danger of losing himself again in his products; the political structure, which reflects this knowledge of man as a subject, is aimed at overcoming this tension. In the *Realphilosophie*, Hegel's solution is a society differentiated into estates, headed by a monarch who symbolizes subjectivity – it is the same solution which will be presented later in the *Philosophy of Right*, although there it will be far more elaborate. Any attempt, therefore, to juxtapose an early, radical Hegel of the Jena period against a later, conservative Hegel of the Berlin period flies in the face of the textual evidence.

[78] *Ibid.* II, 249–50. Hegel sees Plato's *Republic* as an expression of this lack of distinction between the individual and the universal. As in his later writings, Hegel sees here Plato's state as a symbol for what would be called today a totalitarian system: 'In ancient times, beautiful public life was the ethos of all, beauty [was] the immediate unity of the universal and the particular, a work of art in which no part separates itself from the whole . . . Plato's republic is, like the Lacaedemonian state, this disappearance of the self-conscious individual' (*Realphilosophie II*, 251).

[79] *Ibid. II*, 250.

[80] *Ibid. II*, 251.   [81] *Ibid. II*, 252.

Yet it is not with the monarch that Hegel concludes his discussion of man's search for self-recognition. Beyond the realm of objective spirit, Hegel perceived man's need to express himself in philosophy, art, religion. The discussion of these subjects brings out again all the inherent tensions in Hegel's political theory. Hegel begins by forcefully expressing a basic duality in man's nature which drives him beyond the realm of objective spirit, i.e. beyond the state:

Man lives in two worlds. In one he has his actuality (*Wirklichkeit*) which disappears, his naturalness, his sacrifice, his passing away; in the other, his absolute preservation that knows itself as absolute being.[82]

This absolute cannot be realized on earth; it can express itself through the spirit of terrestial institutions, but they cannot be coeval with it. It is the cardinal error of religion to seek 'to introduce the eternal, the Kingdom of Heaven, on earth'; the church thus opposes itself to the state and endeavours, in Hegel's picturesque language, 'to keep a fire [burning] in water'.[83] But the eternal cannot be realized in the finite modes of terrestial life, and therefore the church's claim to supremacy is fallacious. In this world, the state is the ultimate being and the recognition man has achieved through it is the highest achievement possible on earth. Any attempt to institutionalize man's absolute, transcendental being in an objective structure leads to an utter alienation of his objective being. In a passage of religious criticism which recalls later themes developed by Feuerbach and Hess, Hegel says:

In religion man elevates himself to the perception of himself as a universal substance. His nature, his station in life, sinks and disappears like a mirage of a dream, like an island appearing as a cloud on the borderline of the horizon. He is equal to his Prince. It is the knowledge of his own as spirit; he has worth for God as for all the others. It is the alienation of all his spheres, of all his existing world; not an alienation which alienates only form, education and its contents against sensuous existence, but a universal alienation of all actuality. This alienation it then presents to itself as perfection.[84]

Something similar appears in art, where the work of art tries to stand for an essence which cannot be represented within the limitations of the objective world:

Absolute art is the identity of content and form ... Art creates the whole as spiritual and for representation only ... Art can therefore give its shapes only

[82] *Ibid. II*, 270.
[83] *Ibid.*
[84] *Ibid. II*, 267. Cf. p. 266: '[God] is a man who has spatial and temporal existence in thoughts ... Divine nature is not different from human nature ...'

to a limited spirit. This medium of finitude, perception, cannot encompass the infinite. It is only thought of as infinite . . .

Beauty is far more the veil that covers truth than its representation . . . Hence the artist demands very often that the relation to art be merely a relation to forms, abstracting from content. But men do not allow themselves to be deprived of this content. They demand essence, not mere form.[85]

Hence, Hegel sums up, while the realms of art, religion and philosophy are beyond the strict limit of the state, man cannot exist in them independently of his political existence in the objective world.

[85] *Ibid.* II, 264–5.

Chapter Six

THE OWL OF MINERVA AND THE CRITICAL MIND

After two years in Heidelberg, Hegel moved to Berlin in 1818, where he stayed as professor of philosophy until his death in 1831. It is this association with Prussia which was to cause so much adverse comment from later critics.

The first to castigate Hegel for accommodation with Prussia was Rudolf Haym, in his *Hegel und seine Zeit* (1857). At the time of the publication of Haym's volume, Prussia appeared as the arch-enemy of German unification, and Haym, a veteran of the abortive Frankfurt National Assembly of 1848, attacked Hegel as both a pro-Prussian reactionary and an enemy of German nationalism. When a decade and a half later Prussia emerged as the champion of German national unification through 'blood and iron', this new role of Prussia reflected on Hegel who suddenly appeared, especially in many English works, as an advocate of German nationalism.[1]

Much of this rests on anachronistic interpretations of historical facts as well as on backward projections of the meaning of 'Prussia' and 'Prussianism'. To Haym, an 1848 nationalist and liberal, Prussia was the bastion of reaction, conservatism and anti-nationalism; hence Hegel, who had been associated with it, was equally guilty. To twentieth-century English writers, 'Prussianism' was, on the contrary, the evil force of German nationalism and militarism; hence Hegel's connection with it made him, in some way, responsible for Nazism. The changing role of Prussia in the context of

[1] See Popper, *The Open Society*, pp. 244–73; also the exchange between T. M. Knox and E. F. Carritt on 'Hegel and Prussianism', originally published in *Philosophy* of 1940, now reprinted in Kaufmann's *Hegel's Political Philosophy*, pp. 13–52. For a careful study of these controversies, see Kaufmann's own 'The Hegel Myth and Its Method', *ibid.*, pp. 137–71; see also the debate between Sidney Hook, Z. A. Pelczynski and myself, originally conducted in *Encounter*, now reprinted in Kaufmann's volume, pp. 55–105. The section on Hegel and Prussia in Rosenkranz's book has been translated into English and published in the *Journal of Speculative Philosophy* VI (1872), 263–79.

German nationalism created, therefore, a new image of Hegel's politics.

The only way in which this argument can be re-stated in terms relevant to its subject – Hegel's political philosophy – is to consider it within its proper historical context. The point is that the Prussia with which Hegel became associated in 1818 was not the Prussia of 1848, let alone 1914. It was a reformed Prussia, as it emerged after the Napoleonic wars from the modernizing and liberalizing efforts of vom Stein and Hardenberg. Amongst the states of post-1815 Europe, Prussia was surely one of the relatively enlightened ones. Even Hegel's harshest critic, Haym, had to admit that 'though Prussia was not yet a constitutional state, it was administered by its bureaucracy honorably and ably. It is true that Prussia did not yet possess a national representative body, but it still acknowledged the principles of the Enlightenment and scientific progress.'[2] Berlin University, founded in the post-1806 reforms, was one of the symbols of this transformation of the old, barren, militaristic Junker Prussia into a modernized, rationally organized, relatively liberal monarchy. The old feudal system of serfdom was abolished, the cities were granted municipal self-government, the army was transformed through universal conscription, an enlightened and forward-looking bureaucracy took the place of the old military caste, and Berlin appeared to be replacing Jena or Heidelberg as the capital of German letters. It was only the romantic, medievalist reaction of Friedrich Wilhelm IV's rule in the 1840s which restored some of the old Prussian elements.

The old, pre-1806 unreformed Prussia was dismissed by Hegel in *The German Constitution* as a sterile, lifeless mechanism. Post-1815 Prussia, like modernized Bavaria and Württemberg, symbolized for Hegel the new and modern German state, as it emerged out of the turmoil of the previous quarter of a century.

The *Philosophy of Right* was Hegel's most comprehensive attempt to delineate the nature of the modern state in a systematic way. To represent it as Hegel's apotheosis of Prussia is nonsense, for philosophical and biographical reasons alike. No state, as Hegel would point out, could ever be adequate to the philosophical idea of the state as expounded in this work. Furthermore, Hegel prepared the *Philosophy of Right* while he was lecturing on the subject at Heidelberg, in Baden, before he moved to Berlin and ever became associated with Prussia. Lastly, the book contains provisions

2 Haym, *Hegel und seine Zeit*, p. 360.

– like the election of representative assemblies – which were absent in Prussia and which cannot, by any stretch of the imagination, be seen as a reflection of Prussian reality. If anything, the section on representation in the *Philosophy of Right* can be viewed as an oblique critique of Prussian conditions.

Nor did Hegel blindly accept the political realities of Prussia when confronted with them personally. Though he was quite powerful at the University, the more conservative elements at the Court, headed by Count von Wittgenstein, chief of the political police, tried several times to harass Hegel in various ways.[3] The Academy of Sciences, under the influence of Schleiermacher, never admitted Hegel, since his philosophical position was not felt to be sound enough by the theologians. When Hegel remarked to officials in Berlin that Bavaria was more liberal than Prussia, he hardly seemed to have endeared himself to the Prussian bureaucracy.[4] In the last year of his life, Hegel ran into trouble with the Prussian censorship over the publication of his essay on the English Reform Bill; we shall later try to unravel the reason for this extraordinary episode in which the Prussian government tried to muzzle its most eminent philosopher and the former Rector of Berlin University. We also have Hegel's earlier stoic remark in a letter to his publisher, commenting on the death of the Prussian censor Granow, where he says that the censor may be dead, but not, alas, censorship.[5] And when Hegel presented a copy of his *Philosophy of Right* to Prince Hardenberg, the Prussian Chancellor, he inserted into his accompanying note a remark that the volume may help the minister to see the relationship between the theory of the state and the Prussian state as it is and *as it may still develop.*[6]

Yet despite all this, Hegel clearly saw the promise of intellectual life and development in the reformed and reconstructed Prussia. Already in his inaugural lecture at Heidelberg, Hegel had evoked the hope which he would later elaborate in greater detail in his Berlin inaugural: that after the many vicissitudes of war and revolution, philosophy may finally come into its own in Germany and that the Germans, like the Jews of antiquity, would now be entrusted with preserving the heritage of the spirit.[7]

It is true that in his Berlin inaugural Hegel also bowed in the

---

[3] See *Briefe von und an Hegel*, III, 461.
[4] Hegel to Niethammer, 9 June 1821 (*ibid.* II, 270).
[5] Hegel to Freiherr Cotta von Cottendorf, 29 May 1831 (*ibid.* III, 342).
[6] Hegel to Hardenberg, October 1820 (*ibid.* II, 242).
[7] Rosenkranz, *Hegels Leben*, p. 328; Haym, *Hegel und seine Zeit*, p. 335.

direction of the current beliefs of the day, for instance when referring to French rule as a 'foreign tyranny'. Though we know what
Hegel's view on the subject was during the anti-French wars, it
was plainly inconceivable for him to praise Napoleon publicly on
such an occasion – even if his remarks on Napoleon in the *Philosophy of Right* itself are laudatory. Yet despite such obvious lip-
service on the occasion of the inaugural lecture, Hegel's main theme
is a faithful *credo* of his philosophical position.

Hegel's main argument in his Berlin inaugural was directed
against the heritage of Kantian philosophy. By maintaining that
ultimately no adequate knowledge of truth, God and the nature
of the universe is possible, Kantianism led to the substitution of
belief, feeling and intuition for knowledge. Hegel calls such a philosophical position, which stops at the temporal and merely phenomenal, a counsel of despair, adding:

What is true and great and divine in life, is so through the idea. The aim of
philosophy is to comprehend it in its true form and universality.
The courage of truth, the belief in the power of the spirit, is the first
condition for philosophical study; man should honour himself and consider
himself worthy of what is highest. He cannot exaggerate the greatness and power
of spirit; the opaque essence of the universe does not contain any power which
can withstand the force of cognition (*Erkennen*). It must open up before man
and present to his eyes its richness and depth.[8]

Philosophy, to Hegel, has to comprehend that which is, and the
present conditions make it possible for it to fulfill its task; unlike
ancient Greece, where philosophy was a private affair, conducted
by private citizens at their own leisure and expense, the modern
state has realized its duty of making philosophy a part of the *res
publica*. The modern university is an expression of this public
institutionalization of philosophy: 'The time has come when within
the state the free realm of thought should flourish next to the govern-
ance of the actual world . . . Here education (*Bildung*) and the
flower of science are the essential moments in the life of the state.'[9]

The *Philosophy of Right* attempts to achieve the same end in its
preface. It reiterates most forcefully Hegel's contention that the
universe is open to human knowledge and that the structure of the
universe is ultimately rational and can be known as such. At the

---

[8] *Berliner Schriften*, p. 8.
[9] *Ibid.* pp. 3–4; cf. Knox, in Kaufmann's volume, p. 19. The public instruction
of philosophy in secondary schools had, as we have seen, already occupied
Hegel while he was involved in the Bavarian reforms. See also his letter to
Raumer, 2 August 1816 (*Briefe von und an Hegel*, II, 96–102).

same time, the preface is an attack on subjectivism in philosophy; it attempts to point out how a subjectivist philosophy may lead to romantic political terrorism and the loss of any rational criterion for the discussion of public and social life.

Hegel's attack centers on the philosophy and actions of Jacob Fries, and it has brought upon Hegel a great deal of criticism because of the highly personal nature of his polemic.[10] The immediate cause of Hegel's wrath was Fries' participation in a student festival in Wartburg. Because the student fraternities, the *Burschenschaften*, which organized the Wartburg festival, were later ruthlessly repressed by the German governments, their actions received a posthumous halo of sanctity in the eyes of latter-day liberals. The truth of the matter is that in their ideology and actions these fraternities pre-figured the most dangerous and hideous aspects of extreme German nationalism. To present their aim as merely agitation for German unification is simple-minded: they were the most chauvinistic element in German society. They excluded foreigners from their ranks, refused to accept Jewish students as members and participated in the anti-semitic outbursts in Frankfurt in 1819; at the Wartburg festival they burned a huge pile of books by authors to whose work they objected. Finally, one of their members, Karl Sand, murdered the poet Kotzebue whom the students suspected of being a Russian agent. The anti-rationalism, xenophobia, anti-semitism, intolerance and terrorism of the *Burschenschaften* present the same syndrome which, under different circumstances, the Nazis were to institutionalize.[11]

Fries went along with the student movement. His address at the Wartburg festival was a typical example of romantic enthusiasm and obscurantism, and it was for this address that Hegel took him to task in the preface to the *Philosophy of Right*. Fries also published a violent anti-semitic pamphlet, 'On the Danger Posed to the Welfare and Character of the German People by the Jews'. In it he accused the Jews of being the bloodsuckers of the people who contaminate the purity of life in Germany. He advocated the suppression of Jewish educational institutions, encouragement of Jewish

---

[10] Even the admiring Rosenkranz felt uncomfortable about this (*Hegels Leben*, p. 337).

[11] See Marcuse, *Reason and Revolution*, pp. 179–81; Eleonore Sterling, 'Anti-Jewish Riots in Germany 1819: A Displacement of Social Protest', *Historia Judaica* xii (1950), 105–42. On the history of the *Burschenschaften*, see H. Haupt, *Quellen und Darstellungen zur Geschichte der Burschenschaft und der deutschen Einheitsbewegung* (Heidelberg, 1911).

emigration from Germany and prohibition of Jewish immigration into Germany. Laws should be enacted, Fries further suggested, to prohibit Jews from marrying Gentiles; no Christian servants, and especially no maids, should be allowed to work for Jews, and Jews should be made to wear a distinctive mark on their clothes.[12]

In attacking Fries, Hegel pointed to the fact that in him the rigour of Kantian philosophy degenerated into an ethic of mere subjective intentions – a danger which Hegel always discerned in Kantianism:

Besides, this self-styled philosophy has expressedly stated that 'truth itself cannot be known', that that only is true which each individual allows to rise out of his heart, emotion and inspiration about ethical institutions, especially about the state, the government, and the constitution. In this connexion, what a lot of flattery has been talked, especially to the young![13]

Hegel does give subjective beliefs their due place in consciousness, but argues that any attempt to base political allegiance on such foundations leads necessarily to dangerous consequences:

This is the quintessence of shallow thinking, to base philosophic science not on the development of thought and the concept but on immediate sense perception and the play of fancy; to take the rich, inward articulation of ethical life, i.e. the state, the architectonic of that life's rationality ... – and confound the completed fabric in the broth of 'heart, friendship and inspiration'. According to a view of this kind, the world of ethics ... should be given over ... to the subjective accident of opinion and caprice. By the simple family remedy of ascribing to feeling the labour, the more than millenary labour, of reason and its intellect, all the trouble of rational insight and knowledge directed by speculative thinking is of course saved.[14]

This subjectivism, Hegel argues in the body of the *Philosophy of Right*, was responsible for the frame of mind of those who condoned the murder of Kotzebue because the assassin Sand had, after all, 'pure intentions', whatever the nature of his deeds. When the

---

12 J. F. Fries, 'Über die Gefährdung des Wohlstandes und Charakters der Deutschen durch die Juden' (*Heidelberger Jahrbücher*, nos. 16–17 (1816)). Fries' latter-day apologist, Sidney Hook, admits (in Kaufmann's volume, p. 104) that Fries, whom he otherwise characterizes as a liberal, did publish a tract against the Jews 'but *not* on religious or racialist grounds'. One may charitably surmise that Hook had never read Fries' pamphlet, otherwise his statement would be quite incredible: Fries' program reads like a draft version of the Nazi Nuremberg laws. On Hegel's relationship to the *Burschenschaften* and his possible influence on the decision of the Heidelberg fraternity to admit Jews (the only one to do so), see my 'A Note on Hegel's Views on Jewish Emancipation', *Jewish Social History* xxv (1963), 145–51.

13 *Philosophy of Right*, p. 5; see also Hegel's letter to Hinrichs, November 1819 (*Briefe von und an Hegel*, ii, 222).

14 *Philosophy of Right*, p. 6; see also Hegel's article on Hinrichs' philosophy of religion (*Berliner Schriften*, p. 60).

theologian de Wette wrote to Sand's mother in such a vein, Hegel attacked him, pointing out that such a moral subjectivism can be used to justify any crime.[15]

The theoretical consequences of this moral subjectivism are, according to Hegel, firstly, an aversion to any objective, codified system of laws and, secondly, moral relativism. The opposition to codified law characterizes for Hegel all those who are ultimately opposed to rational criteria, be it Württemberg advocates of the 'good old law' or student enthusiasts:

But the special mark which [this school] carries on its brow is the hatred of law. Right and ethics, and the actual world of justice and ethical life, are understood through thoughts; through thoughts they are invested with a rational form, i.e. with universality and determinacy. This form is law; and this is it which the feeling that stipulates for its own whim, the conscience that places right in subjective conviction, has reason to regard as its chief foe. The formal character of the right as duty and a law it feels as the letter, cold and dead, as a shackle . . . Hence law . . . is *par excellence* the shibboleth which marks out these false friends and comrades of what they call the 'people'.[16]

Comparing Fries to the sophists, Hegel notes the relativist consequences of his views:

The result . . . is that the concepts of what is true, the laws of ethics, likewise become nothing more than opinions and subjective convictions. The maxims of the worst of criminals, since they too are convictions, are put on the same level of value as those laws; and at the same time any object, however sorry, however accidental, any material however insipid, is put on the same level of value as what constitutes the interest of all thinking men and the bonds of the ethical world.[17]

The nationalist, populist, romantic and anti-rationalist student movement troubled Hegel deeply: 'I wish that those who shout loudest would busy themselves more with concepts,' he remarks to a correspondent.[18] When he reacts to student riots in Berlin, one hears in Hegel's complaint a fear lest the time of upheaval, which he thought had ended by 1815, was not yet over: 'I shall soon be 50 years old, and 30 years out of it I spent in continually

---

[15] *Philosophy of Right*, §§ 126, 140. In a letter to Creuzer of 30 October 1819 (*Briefe von und an Hegel*, II, 218–19), Hegel says that Fries, de Wette and others are responsible for student extremism because of their advocacy of subjectivist ethics.

[16] *Philosophy of Right*, p. 7; cf. p. 6: 'With godliness and the Bible, however, it has arrogated to itself the highest justification for despising the ethical order and the objectivity of the law.'

[17] *Ibid.* p. 9. As early as 1811, Hegel characterized Fries' views as 'petty-foggery' (*Seichtigkeit*); see Hegel to Niethammer, 10 October 1811 (*Briefe von und an Hegel*, I, 388).

[18] Hegel to Rabow, 30 March 1831 (*ibid.* III, 337).

unquiet periods of fear and hope. I had hoped that those fears and hopes would be over.'[19]

The forces unleashed by the student fraternities and their academic mentors were those same forces that ultimately culminated in the victory of Nazism in Germany more than a century later. Though everything which the governments of the Restoration did is naturally anathema to modern liberal opinion, one should be on guard lest the repressive nature of the measures undertaken by the German governments in 1818–19, the Carlsbard decrees, should blind one to the fact that much of the politics of the fraternities was objectionable, expressing the most rabid elements in German political life. Hegel's defence of the measures taken against these forces may not be unexceptionable; but the opinions which were suppressed, and which Hegel detested and feared, were of the most obscurantist, irrational and chauvinistic kind. If Hegel made a mistake in 1819 it was not in opposing Fries and the Wartburg fanatics; his error lay in his ultimately naïve belief that these forces of nationalism and subjective romanticism were merely a carry-over from the past. Unfortunately, they were later to become the wave of the future in Germany, sweeping away, among others, also Hegel's attempt to confront the problems of modern society through rational means.

But this controversy with immediate adversaries is ultimately nothing but a skirmish on the periphery of the main argument of the *Philosophy of Right*. Hegel's main aim is the attempt to establish, in the preface, his views on the relationship between philosophy and actuality and to bring out what he calls the 'scientific' nature of philosophy.[20]

'Science' is a translation, of course, of the German *Wissenschaft*, and when Hegel maintains that his treatment of philosophy is *wissenschaftlich* one should eschew as much as possible the positivistic analogy with the natural sciences. *Wissenschaft* to Hegel relates to what can be known, it is the Greek *episteme*. Actuality can be known in this sense through a system of rigorous 'scientific' concepts needed to comprehend it, not through loose 'notions' and 'feelings'. What characterizes *Wissenschaft* according to Hegel, is the unity of content and form, and it is this unity which distinguishes reason (*Vernunft*) from mere understanding (*Verstand*),

[19] Hegel to Creuzer, 30 October 1819 (*ibid.* II, 219).
[20] *Philosophy* of Right, pp. 2, 6, 7. See also Hegel's programmatic letter of 30 July 1822 to Duboc, where he sets out his aim of making philosophy *wissenschaftlich* (*Briefe von und an Hegel*, II, 329).

which stops at the dichotomy between content and form and cannot overcome it.

Hegel's attempt in the preface to relate historical actuality to reason has led to a number of serious misunderstandings of his position. The key phrase here is, of course, the statement that 'What is rational is actual and what is actual is rational';[21] a phrase which summarizes Hegel's attempt to emancipate philosophy from the heritage of the Kantian dichotomies. As early as 1821, this phrase had come to be understood as being an overall justification of the powers that be, and it is clear that its epigrammatic pungency made it easy for it to be torn out of its context.[22]

Yet the way Hegel approached the problem was far more complex than could be epitomized in an epigram, brilliant (and, for Hegel's reputation, unfortunate) as it may be. The context of Hegel's argument brings out the *critical* nature of his understanding of the task of philosophy. Philosophy has to understand that which is, the true nature of actuality (*Wirklichkeit*). But such knowledge is dialectical: in order to understand that which is, it does not suffice to be content with outward appearances and forms only; this is mere 'understanding'. 'Scientific' knowledge requires penetrating beyond externalities to the inner core of the object to be known, divining the inner rationale and inherent connections holding it together.[23] Such an understanding in depth is sometimes contrary to accepted public opinion and may run into trouble with positive authority. All of what we saw in Hegel's early confrontation with 'positivity' comes out again in his *credo* that philosophy cannot stop at the merely given and positive. Philosophy will always have to pose questions and not view authority as the ultimate proof of truth:

---

[21] *Philosophy of Right*, p. 10.
[22] See Heinrich Paulus' review of the *Philosophy of Right* in the *Heidelberger Jahrbücher* of 1821, pp. 392–5. See also Rosenkranz, *Hegels Leben*, p. 335, Haym, *Hegel und seine Zeit*, p. 367; also Emil L. Fackenheim, 'On the Actuality of the Rational and the Rationality of the Actual', *Review of Metaphysics* XIII (June, 1970), 690–8. Engels added to the difficulty by distorting the sentence when quoting it in his *Ludwig Feuerbach and the End of Classical German Philosophy*: Engels inverted the sequence of the propositions, making Hegel say 'All that is actual is rational and all that is rational is actual' (Marx–Engels, *Selected Works*, II, 361). Most people seem to recall Hegel's dictum in this garbled and distorted form.
[23] Cf. *Philosophy of Right*, § 324: 'Philosophy knows accident for a show and sees in it its essence, necessity.'

Such thinking does not remain stationary at the given, whether the given be upheld by the external positive authority of the state or the *consensus hominum,* or by the authority of inward feeling and emotion and by the 'witness of the spirit' which directly concurs with it.

The unphilosophical heart takes the simple line of adhering with trustful conviction to what is publicly accepted as true and then building on this firm foundation its conduct and its set position in life.[24]

The critical task of philosophy, however, runs into the danger of substituting mere negation for a critical attitude. Though a 'scientific' knowledge of actuality can be achieved only by going beyond appearances, care should be taken lest the spirit which always negates should put itself up as an alternative to actuality itself. While the quest for truth should not refrain from questioning anything just because it is publicly acknowledged, the very existence and nature of public arrangements should not be put in jeopardy. According to Hegel, it is a mistake to gauge the virtue of philosophical enquiry proportionally to the degree of its direct opposition to the state. Subjectivist ethics tend to make every individual into a focus of opposition to the state as a whole. Governments which 'have proved their trust in their scholars who have made philosophy their chosen field by leaving entirely to them the construction and content of philosophy' have been ill-exploited by some of the philosophers – not because they opposed this or other government steps, but because they questioned the very base of political authority.[25] What has happened is that subjectivist philosophy has made it a rule to see freedom only in opposition to the state, overlooking what is to Hegel the immanent truth of the state as the actuality of rational freedom:

At the present time, the idea that freedom of thought, and of mind generally, evinces itself only in divergence from, indeed in hostility to, what is publicly recognized, might seem to be most firmly rooted in connexion with the state, and it is chiefly for this reason that a philosophy of the state might seem essentially to have the task of discovering and promulgating still another theory, and a special and original one at that. In examining this idea . . . we might suppose that no state or constitution had ever existed in the world at all or was ever in being at the present time . . . and we had to start all over again from the beginning.[26]

The danger of philosophers abstracting from actuality and behaving as if it did not exist is that it leads them to build models out of thin air. Such chimeras are then adopted by people as a substitute for actuality, and the consequences cannot but be catastrophic;

[24] *Ibid.* p. 3.   [25] *Ibid.* p. 7.   [26] *Ibid.* p. 4.

the utopian thinking that went with the system-builders of the Enlightenment gave rise to some of the worst excesses of the French Revolution.[27] Philosophy, Hegel reiterates time and again, deals with the world, with actuality; it should not, we have seen, stop at external appearances, nor should it be deterred by conformist accommodation with the powers that be. But it does have actuality as its object, and this means that if something exists, there must ultimately be a reason for its existence, and this reason, hidden and elusive as it may be, must be brought out into the open. It might then turn out to be that the inner rationale of this existence is totally different from what it appears to be to the uncritical mind, and it would then be the task of philosophy to reconcile appearance and content. But because philosophy has reason for its object, it has to look for it in actuality, not in mere thought. By saying that the world is open to our knowledge, we do not imply that it is rational in any *a priori* sense; its rationality is historical, developing, reason unfolding itself in actuality over time. The Kantian heritage is scathingly criticized by Hegel in a passage which, in another context, may also be used to illustrate the philosophical basis of Marx's later critique of utopian thinking:

It is just this placing of philosophy in the actual world which meets with misunderstanding, and so I revert to what I have said before, namely that, since philosophy is the exploration of the rational, it is for that very reason the apprehension of the present and the actual, not the erection of a beyond, supposed to exist, God knows where, or rather which exists, and we can perfectly well say where, namely in the error of a one-sided, empty, ratiocination.[28]

Such subjective wishful thinking, according to Hegel, lacks any criterion for verification; how does one choose between a variety of programs, all of them emerging from laudable motives? Ultimately one ends up in an impasse – or the force of arms is called upon to decide between the various contenders for the road to the millenium. The Hegelian alternative is to look for the seeds of the city of God hidden in actuality:

This book then, containing as it does the science of the state, is to be nothing other than the endeavour to apprehend and portray the state as something

27 Cf. *Phenomenology*, pp. 599–610, where Hegel relates the 'absolute freedom' of the theories of the Enlightenment to Jacobin terror.
28 *Philosophy of Right*, p. 10. When Hegel says that the state is something, 'inherently rational', it does not follow that everything in every state is rational, but that the very phenomenon of the state – men living under a common bond – expresses a rational aspect of human life. Otherwise, there would be no state.

inherently rational. As a work of philosophy, it must be poles apart from an attempt to construct a state as it ought to be. The instruction which it may contain cannot consist in teaching the state what it ought to be; it can only show how the state, the ethical universe, is to be understood.

Hic Rhodus, hic saltus.

To comprehend what is, this is the task of philosophy, because what is, is reason.[29]

The city of God can be thus reached through an adequate understanding in depth of the earthly city:

To recognize reason as the rose in the cross of the present and thereby to enjoy the present, this is the rational insight which reconciles us to the actual, the reconciliation which philosophy affords to those in whom there has once arisen an inner voice bidding them to comprehend.[30]

It is in this context that Hegel introduces his epigram about the rational and the actual:

What is rational is actual and what is actual is rational ... Once that is granted, the great thing is to apprehend in the show of the temporal and transient the substance which is immanent and the eternal which is present. For since rationality (which is synonymous with the Idea) enters upon external existence simultaneously with its actualization, it emerges with an infinite wealth of forms, shapes and appearances.[31]

It was over this epigram, one should recall, that the Hegelian school later split into a 'left' and a 'right' wing, and a careful study of the text is therefore necessary for this reason too. It should first be pointed out that the German term which is rendered here (following Knox's excellent suggestion) as 'actual' is *wirklich*. Its specific connotation derives from its root in the verb 'to act' (*wirken*), which makes it clear that 'actuality' (*Wirklichkeit*) is not a merely passive, natural given. What is 'actual' is always a consequence of a deed, of action; hence a strong activist undertone runs through this couplet.

Secondly, Hegel does not begin the epigram (as Engels' misquotation would have him do) by saying that what is actual is rational, but by maintaining that what is rational is actual: he starts not by postulating the rationality of the actual but rather the actuality of the rational, i.e. with the statement that what is rational has within itself the power to actualize itself, to turn from *potentia* into *actus*. Reason is not an abstraction, or a mere Humean

---

[29] *Ibid.* p. 11.   [30] *Ibid.* p. 12.

[31] *Ibid.* p. 10. One of the first readers of Hegel's book, Nikolaus von Thadden, attacked Hegel precisely on this point in a private letter of 8 August 1821 (*Briefe von und an Hegel*, II, 278).

faculty; it is power, the Greek *Nous* realized in the world. Only after stating that what is rational will ultimately triumph, will actualize itself, does Hegel add the second part of the couplet 'and what is actual is rational' which is a *corollary* of the first part.

Despite this, Hegel became aware quite clearly that by its sheer force, his epigram was apt to lead him into being very clearly misrepresented. Hence in a lengthy footnote in the 1830 edition of his *Encyclopedia of Philosophical Sciences*, he makes it a point to emphasize that actuality (*Wirklichkeit*) is not identical with all that exists. Hegel distinguishes here between *Dasein* (Existence) and *Wirklichkeit*. *Dasein* encompasses everything which exists, whereas *Wirklichkeit* is only that part of *Dasein* in which essence and existence coincide, and it is because of this that one can say that it is rational.[32] Whatever the philosophical difficulties which arise out of this explanation (they seem to make the couplet into something like a tautology), it clearly indicates that Hegel himself did not intend in any way whatsoever to mean it as an overall legitimization of everything which exists. In the *Philosophy of Right* itself, Hegel makes a similar distinction between actuality and existence:

Philosophy . . . shows that the concept alone . . . has actuality, and further that it gives actuality to itself. All else, apart from this actuality established through the working of the concept itself, is ephemeral existence, external contingency, opinion, unsubstantiated appearance, falsity, illusion and so forth.[33]

There is, however, a further aspect or twist to Hegel's argument towards the end of the preface to the *Philosophy of Right*. We have seen how Hegel has stressed the this-worldliness of philosophy, coupled with the caveat to philosophers not to construct a utopia of a state as it ought to be. The note on which Hegel closes this admonition appears to be one of resignation and quietism. He starts by saying 'Hic Rhodus, hic saltus', then proceeds to warn the philosopher:

Whatever happens, every individual is the child of his time; so philosophy too is its own time apprehended in thoughts. It is just as absurd to fancy that a philosophy can transcend its own contemporary world as it is to fancy that an individual can overleap his own age, jump over Rhodes.[34]

This seemingly open admission of the limits of philosophical consciousness is theoretically nothing else than a reflection of Hegel's views on the historicity of reason. Since the philosopher's rational

---

[32] G. W. F. Hegel, *Enzyklopädie der philosophischen Wissenschaften*, ed. F. Nicolin and O. Pöggeler (Hamburg, 1959), § 6.
[33] *Philosophy of Right*, § 1.   [34] *Ibid.* p. 11.

faculty is, like reason itself, not given *a priori*, but evolves over time, so each philosopher is naturally limited in the scope of his perception by the historical context of his own existence, and cannot overcome this limitation. Hence philosophy is also always an adequate testimony to its generation, and each successive generation standing, as it were, on the shoulders of its predecessors, is in a better position to comprehend its own actuality. The distance between Hegel's position and Marx's dictum that 'consciousness is nothing else than conscious being' is much smaller than the orthodox distinctions between 'idealism' and 'materialism' would lead one to believe.

If philosophy is then nothing else than its own time apprehended in thought, then there is a curious corollary to it: if a philosopher can only comprehend that which is, then the very fact that he has comprehended his historical actuality is evidence that a form of life has already grown old, since only the fully developed can be philosophically comprehended. Thus below the surface of the apparent passivity of Hegel's statement, a basically critical theory can be discerned. Hegel closes his preface to the *Philosophy of Right* with one of the most poetic, and now justly famous, passages ever to have been written by a philosopher. It requires very careful reading:

One word more about giving instructions as to what the world ought to be. Philosophy in any case always comes on the scene too late to give it. As the thought of the world, it appears only when actuality is already there cut and dried after its process of formation has been completed. The teaching of the concept, which is also history's inescapable lesson, is that it is only when actuality is mature that the ideal first appears over against the real and that the ideal apprehends this same real world in its substance and builds it up for itself into the shape of an intellectual realm. When philosophy paints its grey in grey, then has a shape of life grown old. By philosophy's grey in grey it cannot be rejuvenated but only understood. The owl of Minerva spreads its wings only with the falling of the dusk.[35]

Philosophy is the wisdom of ripeness, and whenever a period in history finds its great philosopher who translates into the language of ideas the quintessence of its actual life, then a period in history has come to a close. Earlier in the preface, Hegel mentioned Plato, and surely his example would have been before his eyes: by writing the *Republic* as an ideal of the Greek polis, Plato was doing nothing else than raising to an ideal level institutions and arrangements which existed in real, historical Greek life. While no one

[35] *Ibid.* p. 12.

Greek city resembled the *Republic*, and in it all existing city-states are criticized, Plato's ideal city was nonetheless the distillation of the basic ideals of the polis, cleansed of the accidental and arbitrary of historical incidence. But this ideal apotheosis of the polis was also a mark of its decline, because the *Republic* could not have been written before the polis had run its course. This is the meaning of philosophy as *Nach-denken*, after-thought.

Yet this moving passage is not Hegel's appendix to Plato, but his preface to his own political philosophy. And since his own political philosophy is not aimed at 'giving instruction as to what the world ought to be' but is only aimed at comprehending, on a level of ideas, 'what is', the consequence is inescapable: that though Hegel is not announcing the advent of a new world or preaching it, his very ability to comprehend his own world may already point to its possible demise.

The rose in the cross of the present, the tragic irony of Hegel's dialectical apprehension of his world, means that while Hegel saw himself as comprehending the new world of post-1789 (or post-1815) Europe, this by itself meant that this new world, which Hegel heralded in his *Phenomenology*, is already reaching its maturity and is somehow, slowly but surely, on its way out. True, Hegel saw his own time as the apotheosis of history, as the reconciliation of the actual and the rational. Hegel even goes to the length of suggesting that no higher philosophical level of knowledge is possible. In his *History of Philosophy* he says of his present age that 'it would appear as if the World Spirit had at last succeeded in stripping off from itself all alien objective existence', then adding:

The strife of the finite self-consciousness with the absolute self-consciousness . . . now comes to an end . . . This is the whole history of the world in general up to the present time, and the history of philosophy in particular, the sole work of which is to depict this strife. Now, indeed, it seems to have reached its goal, when this absolute self-consciousness, which it had the work of representing, has ceased to be alien, and when spirit accordingly is realized as spirit.[36]

Yet despite this strong tendency to view his own historical epoch and his own philosophy as absolutes, there is nothing in Hegel's closing remarks in the preface to the *Philosophy of Right* to suggest that what he thinks true of all philosophy – namely, that it sums up to its age – is not true of his own philosophy as well. And all philosophy, by summing up its age, in some way announces the demise

[36] G. W. F. Hegel, *Lectures on the History of Philosophy*, trans. E. S. Haldane and F. H. Simson (London, 1895), III, 551–2.

Appendix

of this age. If Hegel postulates his age as the final triumph of freedom and rationality, there are, on the other hand, strong indications to suggest how much Hegel was aware that this conciliation of the actual and the rational cannot solve some quite crucial problems; and in some unguarded moments we shall see Hegel looking over the horizon of his own epoch, though the vision always remained intentionally dim and blurred.

'The owl of Minerva spreads its wings only with the falling of the dusk': in this seemingly quietistic sentence, full of resignation and apparent conservatism, there lies hidden a critical message about the role of philosophy. True, to borrow and invert a phrase from Marx, philosophy cannot change the world, only interpret it; but by its very act of interpretation it changes it, it tells the world that its time is up.

NOTE

Hegel's attack on Fries and de Wette has given rise to the current opinion that Hegel appeared in the context of his time on the side of the police against freedom of expression. One does not, however, have to subscribe to the details of Hegel's attitude towards Fries to point out that, after all, there was very little on libertarian grounds to defend in Fries' own position.

Be this as it may, Hegel's views have been misconstrued to such a point that it is now wholly unknown that during the period of repression which followed Kotzebue's murder, Hegel was very active in intervening on behalf of students, colleagues and friends who ran into difficulties with the police because of their connections, real or imaginary, with the *Burschenschaften*. A careful study of the cases involved shows that Hegel's store of civil courage was quite impressive, and it may be worthwhile to put this on record because so much has been said against Hegel in this connection without the minimal trouble being taken to look at the evidence available.

(a) Hegel intervened with the authorities when his assistant, Leopold Henning, was arrested; see Hegel to Niethammer, 9 June 1821 (*Briefe von und an Hegel*, II, 271) and *Berliner Schriften*, pp. 598–607.

(b) Hegel tried, though unsuccessfully, to secure a position as assistant in Berlin for one of his former Heidelberg students, Carové, who was denied university employment because of his connections with the fraternities. Hegel wrote on his behalf repeatedly to Solger, Dean of the Philosophical Faculty, but to no avail (*Berliner Schriften*, pp. 581–4).

(c) In 1824 one of Hegel's ex-students in Heidelberg, Gustav Asverus, the son of one of Hegel's friends in Jena, was arrested. He had been very active in the student movement, and was also violently anti-Hegelian. From letters preserved in the Marx–Engels Institute in Moscow, we now know that Hegel repeatedly advised Asverus' father how to proceed in his son's defence (*Briefe*

Note

von und an Hegel, IV, 20–7). Hegel also appealed on Asverus' behalf to the Prussian Ministry of Police (*ibid.* II, 216–17), ultimately secured his release and put up 500 thalers as bail (*ibid.* II, 440).

(d) Though Hegel attacked de Wette very strongly for his letter to Sand's mother, he objected to the arbitrary nature of de Wette's dismissal from the university. When colleagues put up a fund to help de Wette financially, Hegel contributed 25 thalers; cf. Varnhagen von Ense's *Blätter aus der preussischen Geschichte*, ed. Ludmilla Assig (Leipzig, 1868), IV, 235.

(e) The French philosopher Victor Cousin, who was one of Hegel's most devoted disciples, was arrested in 1824 by the Prussian police on suspicion of conspiring with the extreme student fraternities. Hegel intervened on his behalf with the Ministry (*Briefe von und an Hegel*, III, 75–6). The Berlin police chief, von Kamptz, denounced Hegel's intervention on several occasions, especially since it had been publicized in the French press. Hegel's contemporaries, and even his enemies, greatly appreciated his civil courage in this case which dragged on for a year; see von Ense, *Blätter aus der preussischen Geschichte*, III, 155–62, 227.

Chapter Seven

THE POLITICAL ECONOMY OF MODERN SOCIETY

THE PREMISSES

In his *Encyclopedia of Philosophical Sciences*, Hegel divides the section dealing with the philosophy of spirit into three parts: subjective spirit, objective spirit and absolute spirit. The part on objective spirit is then dealt with in much greater detail in the *Philosophy of Right*. It is this part which concerns itself with law, morality and ethical life (*Sittlichkeit*) as the objective, institutional expressions of spirit. And though the state stands, as we shall see, at the apex of objective spirit, it is still inferior (as we have already seen in the *Realphilosophie*) to the realm of absolute spirit – i.e. art, religion and philosophy.

Objective spirit is the realm within which human consciousness comes into its own: 'Ethical life is the unity of the will in its concept with the will of the individual.'[1] This unity of content and form when integrated into consciousness is freedom; its political expression has already been formulated in the *System der Sittlichkeit*, where Hegel said that 'the organic principle is freedom, so that those who govern are themselves the governed'.[2]

Yet the attainment of this freedom is not given; it has to be mediated. The history of man is the history of man gaining self-consciousness through his interaction with the objective world surrounding him. This is education, *Bildung*; man *becomes* free. His freedom is not to be found in any legendary state of nature, but evolves precisely out of his effort to dissociate himself from his state of primeval savagery: 'The savage is lazy and is distinguished from the educated man by his brooding stupidity.'[3]

---

[1] *Philosophy of Right*, addition to § 33.
[2] *Schriften zur Politik*, p. 500.
[3] *Philosophy of Right*, addition to § 197. Cf. addition to § 153: 'The educational experiments, advocated by Rousseau in *Émile*, of withdrawing children from the common life of every day and bringing them up in the country.

132

The premisses

That Rousseau's romantic notions about education had much in common with a mere utilitarian and instrumentalist view of it is sharply hinted at by Hegel when he establishes his own view of *Bildung* as the true self-creation of man by himself:

The idea that the state of nature is one of innocence and that there is a simplicity of manners in uncivilized (*ungebildeter*) peoples, implies treating education (*Bildung*) as something purely external, the ally of corruption. Similarly, the feeling that needs [and] their satisfaction ... are absolute ends, implies treating education as a mere means to this end ...

The final purpose of education, therefore, is liberation and the struggle for a higher liberation still; education is the absolute transition from an ethical substantiality which is immediate and natural to one which is intellectual and so both infinitely subjective and lofty enough to have attained universality of form.[4]

This mediation, leading man to the consciousness of freedom, is the central theme of the *Philosophy of Right*. The stages of this mediation of the will are as follows: (a) the will as immediate – absolute or formal right; (b) the will reflected – subjective morality; (c) the unity of both – ethical life. Ethical life (*Sittlichkeit*) is itself divided into three moments:

(a) Family – ethical life 'in its natural or immediate phase';
(b) Civil society – ethical life 'in its division and appearance';
(c) The state – 'freedom universal and objective even in the free self-subsistence of the particular will'.[5]

In most of the traditional discussion of Hegel's social philosophy, the third moment, the state, has usually been central. Hegel's philosophy of the state is, undoubtedly, his major contribution to the realm of social philosophy, but it becomes utterly incomprehensible and even distorted if it is not discussed on the premisses of the two moments (family and civil society) which precede it within his systematic exposition. Our discussion will try to regain the internal balance of Hegel's social theory by dwelling at some length on these two moments of family and civil society.

The three moments of ethical life can also be projected as three alternative modes of inter-human relationship. Hegel's argument would be that men can relate to each other in either one of the

have turned out to be futile, since no success can attend an attempt to estrange people from the laws of the world. Even if the young have to be educated in solitude, it is still useless to hope that the fragrance of the intellectual world will not ultimately permeate this solitude.'

4 *Ibid.* § 187. On *Bildung*, see the excellent discussion in George A. Kelly's *Idealism, Politics and History* (Cambridge, 1969), pp. 341–8.
5 *Philosophy of Right*, § 33; also § 157.

following three modes: particular altruism – the family; universal egoism – civil society; universal altruism – the state. Let us examine these three modes, beginning with the family, the mode of particular altruism. This is the mode in which I relate to other human beings with a view of *their*, rather than my, interests in mind. Within the family, I am ready to make sacrifices for the other – to work so that the children can go to school, to care for the welfare of the old and infirm, and so on. All these activities are other-oriented, 'altruistic' in this analytical (not moralistic) sense; all of them are performed not for the actor's own benefit but for the benefit of someone else with whom the actor is connected through ties which are called 'family ties'. These activities are also limited to a fixed sphere of human beings: I do not provide for all women or all children, only for *my* wife and *my* children. Hence this altruism is limited and particular and does not apply to all and sundry. This is the family.

Secondly, there is civil society. Civil society is the sphere of universal egoism, where I treat everybody as a means to my own ends. Its most acute and typical expression is economic life, where I sell and buy not in order to satisfy the needs of the other, his hunger or his need for shelter, but where I use the felt need of the other as a means to satisfy my own ends. My aims are mediated through the needs of others: the more other people are dependent on a need which I can supply, the better my own position becomes. This is the sphere where everyone acts according to what he perceives as his enlightened self-interest.

Finally, there is the state. Contrary to the traditional liberal theories originating with Hobbes and Locke, Hegel views the state not as an arrangement aimed at safeguarding man's self-interest (this is done in civil society), but as something transcending it. The state to Hegel is universal altruism – a mode of relating to a universe of human beings not out of self-interest but out of solidarity, out of the will to live with other human beings in a community. In this respect, the state is analogous to the family, but its scope is different and the nexus is based on free consciousness, not on a biological determination. If one views the state in terms of safeguarding one's interests, then, Hegel argues, one mistakes it for civil society. Furthermore, the demands put on us by the state in terms of taxation and military service certainly cannot be legitimized in terms of self-interest – a dilemma with which Hobbes was familiar when he ultimately had to admit that if the sovereign demands the

sacrifice of your life in war, there is no way to legitimize this demand. Taxation, after all, is used to ameliorate the lot of *other*
people, and not only to provide services in return, while the duty of
military service necessarily involves the possibility that I may get
killed so that others may live, a prospect which is nonsensical in
terms of enlightened self-interest. Nor can military service be justified through the traditional explanations of defending one's family
or one's property. By putting myself in a position in which I may
get killed, I am not defending my family or my property at all. If
I really wanted to do this, then the best way would be to clear out
of the country altogether once the danger of war becomes imminent,
making sure that my family will be with me and making doubly sure
that my property will be already awaiting us all at the safe haven to
which we flee from our war-threatened country. This would be the
only rational behaviour in terms of my own enlightened self-
interest. That men in fact usually behave otherwise, and even find
fault in such 'rational' behaviour, clearly indicates that they relate
to the state in a way different from that of mere self-interest. The
mode of universal altruism, the readiness to put up sacrifices on
behalf of the other, the consciousness of solidarity and community
– these, for Hegel, are the ties binding a person to what is commonly called his country or his state.[6]

But before these relationships of ethical life can be discussed in
detail, some prior concepts have to be clarified – those of abstract
right and subjective morality. Abstract right to Hegel is vested
in property, and a whole section of the *Philosophy of Right* deals
with property, followed by a section on contract.[7] Hegel views
property within a context far wider than that of mere necessity and
physical need to which natural law theories have relegated it. For
him, the discussion of property is part of his general philosophical
anthropology.

Property is not only instrumental; as we have seen in the *Realphilosophie*, it is a basic requisite for man in his struggle for recognition and realization in the objective world: 'A person must translate

---

[6] That problems of war and poverty seem to create so much stress in American
society today is probably to be attributed to the fact that America has never
been a state (in the Hegelian sense), only a 'civil society', where the common
bond has always been viewed as a mere instrument for preserving individual
life, liberty and the pursuit of happiness. This, incidentally was Hegel's view
of America in the 1820s (*Vernunft in der Geschichte*, p. 207). It is probably
basically true today as well, despite all the changes America has undergone
since then. In the American social ethos, the 'tax payer' always comes before
the 'citizen'. [7] See §§ 41–71 and §§ 71–81.

his freedom into an external sphere in order to exist as an Idea.'[8] Through property man's existence is recognized by others, since the respect others show to his property by not trespassing on it reflects their acceptance of him as a person. Property is thus an objectification of the self which raises it from the realm of pure subjectivity into the sphere of external existence:

The rationale (*Vernüngtigkeit*) of property is to be found not in the satisfaction of needs but in the suppression (*Aufhebung*) of the pure subjectivity of personality. In his property a person exists for the first time as reason.[9]

Property is thus 'the embodiment of personality',[10] and the existence of private property becomes a *conditio sine qua non* in Hegel's social philosophy:

In property my will is the will of a person; but a person is a unit and so property becomes the personality of this unitary will. Since property is the means whereby I give my will an embodiment, property must also have the character of being 'this' or 'mine'. This is the important doctrine of the necessity of private property.[11]

This inherent connection between property and personality leads to extremely important consequences in the further development of Hegel's social philosophy. One of the immediate corollaries is Hegel's defence of the system of private property and his fundamental opposition to any sort of communism; at one point (§ 46) he actually criticizes Plato's *Republic* for emasculating individual personality through the abolition of private property and the introduction of communism. This is obvious enough. But postulating personality on property must make Hegel conscious of the problem of those deprived of property, i.e. the poor. And since property is basic to Hegel's view of the person, poverty becomes for him not merely the plight of people deprived of their physical needs, but of human beings deprived of their personality and humanity as well.

This concern for the property-less appears very clearly in the passages that deal with property. After rejecting Plato's communism, Hegel remarks that equality of property is not a solution to the problem of lack of property, since even if property were to be equally divided, new inequalities would soon arise as a result of

[8] *Ibid.* § 41.
[9] *Ibid.* addition to § 41; cf. also § 46: 'Since my will, as the will of a person, so as a single will, becomes objective to me in property, property acquires the character of private property.'
[10] *Ibid.* § 51.   [11] *Ibid.* addition to § 46.

differences in human skills and the size of families. Yet while equality of property is undesirable and unattainable, each person, according to Hegel, must be guaranteed *some* property:

> Of course men are equal, but only *qua* persons, that is, with respect only to the source from which possession springs; the inference from this is that everyone must have property.[12]

Hegel suggests no mechanism by which such universal possession of property should or could be secured; but although his awareness of the crucial role of property leads him to criticize communistic schemes, it also makes him conscious later, when discussing the working of civil society, of the problem of pauperization, which he will admit to be one of the most vexing problems facing modern society. This attitude toward poverty is totally incomprehensible unless viewed in the context of Hegel's initially basing his definition of personality on property. Hence the definition of personality in terms of property paradoxically becomes a critical device by which modern society may be judged.

Hegel defines the imperative of personality in a form that is consciously modelled on Kant's categorical imperative: 'The imperative of right is: "Be a person and respect others as persons".'[13] Yet it is at this stage, while paying respect to Kant's moral theory, that Hegel introduces a distinction which ultimately transcends Kant's categorical imperative and leads to its *Aufhebung* into the wider Hegelian system.

This is the distinction between *Moralität*, i.e. individual, subjective morality, and *Sittlichkeit*, the wider totality of ethical life. *Moralität* has a legitimate sphere in Hegel's system, but it is a limited one: it regulates the relations among individuals with one another *qua* individuals. But superimposed on this is the broader ethical life of the community, of people relating to each other not as individuals but as members of a wider community. One of Hegel's major arguments against the Kantian heritage is that just as the categorical imperative is inoperative in the family – where it is superseded by love – so its writ does not run in political life. Moreover, the introduction of considerations of individual morality into political problems may create chaos by substituting, as we have already seen Hegel accuse Fries of doing, purely subjective good intentions, whatever their consequences, for an objective code of behaviour governed by universal considerations. Kant's morality,

---

[12] *Ibid.* addition to § 49.   [13] *Ibid.* § 36.

according to Hegel, remains something which 'has to be' (*Sein-sollendes*) and the point is to find an institutional form that would be comprehensive and universal and could thus be actualized.

Hegel's insistent distinction between subjective intent and objective results, which, as we shall see when discussing his philosophy of history, is crucial to his system, is brought out very forcefully in his argument against the purely subjective moralism:

> It is one of the most prominent of the corrupt maxims of our time to enter a plea for the so-called 'moral' intention behind wrong actions and to imagine bad men with well-meaning hearts, i.e. hearts willing their own welfare and perhaps that of others also ... Today this has been resuscitated in a more extravagant form, and the inner enthusiasm and the heart, i.e. the form of particularity as such, have been made the criterion of right, rationality, and excellence. The result is that crime and the thoughts that lead to it, be they fancies however trite and empty, or opinions however wild, are to be regarded as right, rational and excellent, simply because they issue from men's hearts and enthusiasms.[14]

The universality of law, as expressed by the state, supersedes the mere intentions of individuals. Hegel's contention in his Württemberg essay in favour of rational codification appears here in his plea against romantic subjectivism:

> Similarly, in the state as the objectivity of the concept of reason, legal responsibility cannot be tied to what an individual may hold to be or not to be in accordance with his reason, or to his subjective insight into what is right or wrong, good or evil, or to the demands which he makes for the satisfaction of his conviction ... By means of the publicity of law and the universality of manners, the state removes from the right of insight its formal aspect and the contingency which it still retains for the subject at the level of morality.[15]

It is not difficult to see how such a position could be so construed as to mean that Hegel made individual self-determination 'tributary' to the state.[16] The truth of the matter is that in the context of the debate Hegel has been engaged in, the thrust of his argument is aimed at the terroristic implications of the romantic notion which viewed every limitation coming from the state as purely external coercion. Hegel's argument, which here can be seen following that of Rousseau very closely, is that what we call 'the state' is nothing other than a further aspect of our own self-determination. To view

14 *Ibid.* § 126; cf. also §135, where Kant is accused of 'mere formalism'.
15 *Ibid.* § 132; cf. also § 140: 'This final, most abstruse, form of evil, whereby evil is perverted into good and good into evil, and consciousness, in being aware of its power to effect this perversion, is also made aware of itself as absolute, is the high water mark of subjectivity at the level of morality.'
16 See Haym, *Hegel und seine Zeit*, p. 375.

The family

the state as external, as did so much of subjective romanticism, means dooming men to servitude. Human emancipation, according to Hegel, depends upon the ability to raise the brutal relations of natural dependence and domination into conscious relations of mutual inter-dependence.

THE FAMILY

What stands out in Hegel's treatment of the family is his insistence that it is not a contract. Contractual relations, Hegel argues, are an instrument of civil society and are dissolvable at will. The attempt to view the family – or the state – in contractual terms means subsuming everything under civil society, thus making the relational modes of civil society operative in all spheres of human life. Hegel is aware that this tendency of civil society concepts to arrogate to themselves all other spheres of life is very strong; but he speaks against it when civil society encroaches on the realm of the family as well as when it encroaches on that of the state:

> The object about which a contract is made is a single external thing, since it is only things of that kind which the parties' purely arbitrary will has in its power to alienate.
> To subsume marriage under the concept of contract is thus quite impossible; this subsumption – though shameful is the only word for it – is propounded in Kant's *Philosophy of Law* [§§ 24–7]. It is equally far from the truth to ground the nature of the state on the contractual relation, whether the state is supposed to be a contract of all with all, or of all with the monarch and the government.[17]

If marriage were a contract, Hegel argues, it would degrade marital relations to 'a level of a contract for reciprocal use'.[18] Marriage cannot be a contract because it has a *telos* in ethical life – the achievement of one's consciousness in the other. Though there appears to be an element of contract in the act of entering into the married state, the goal is in fact to transcend it: 'On the contrary, though marriage begins in contract, it is precisely a contract to transcend the standpoint of contract, the standpoint from which persons are regarded in their individuality as self-subsisting units.'[19] Rights are the focus of contractual relations, and in the marriage there are duties, not rights: the rights emanating from marriage appear only at its dissolution – either by death (inheritance) or by

[17] *Philosophy of Right*, § 75. Cf. Hegel's similar argument in *Realphilosophie I*, 222.
[18] *Philosophy of Right*, addition to § 161.   [19] *Ibid.* § 163.

divorce (alimony, maintenance, etc.).[20] A marriage in which each partner claims in court his or her rights is one which is already in the process of breaking up.

The nexus linking members of the family to each other is love. Though Hegel has little patience for the *Schwärmerei* typical of the romantics in their discussion of this subject, he incorporates something of the awareness that characterized their attitude, though in a controlled way, and elevates it to a dialectical realization of the basic contradiction in love. In a family, Hegel maintains, 'one's frame of mind is to have self-consciousness of one's individuality within this unity as the absolute essence of oneself, with the result that one is in it not as an independent person but as a member'.[21] In this unity persons transcend their own egoism and 'renounce their natural and individual personality ... From this point of view, their union is a self-restriction, but in fact it is their liberation, because in it they attain their substantive self-consciousness.'[22] The internal contradiction, however, is always present:

> The first moment of love is that I do not wish to be a self-subsistent and independent person and that, if I were, then I would feel defective and incomplete. The second moment is that I find myself in another person, that I count for something in the other, while the other in turn comes to count for something in me. Love, therefore, is the most tremendous contradiction.[23]

Yet along with the subjective side of love in marriage there is an objective side as well. Though Hegel regards the subjective side, love, as the sublimation of the sexual drive into a will to identify with the other, he also warns against leaving it at that, i.e. at the level of romanticism. Schlegel, for example, would have suggested that if there is love, there is no need for any ceremony or any other 'objective' aspect. Hegel insists here, as elsewhere, on institutionalization, and sees in the family capital (*Vermögen*) this objective side. He even goes to some length to show that family property is

---

[20] *Ibid.* § 159: 'The right which the individual enjoys on the strength of the family unity ... takes on the *form* of right (as the abstract moment of determinate individuality) only when the family begins to dissolve.' Hegel allows divorce, but maintains that it should not be made too easy, so that marriage should not turn into mere caprice (addition to § 163).

[21] *Ibid.* § 158.

[22] *Ibid.* § 162. Cf. Hegel's earlier fragment on 'Love' (*Early Theological Writings*, pp. 302–8). In *Realphilosophie II*, 228, Hegel sees marriage as the unity of personality and impersonality, of the natural and the spiritual. All this is interestingly similar to Marx's extraordinary excursus on sexual relations in *Early Writings*, p. 154.

[23] *Philosophy of Right*, addition to § 158.

not vested in the individual but in the family unit, since otherwise inheritance by relatives would have no justification whatsoever.[24]

The family's own objectification appears in the children. Following a theme developed in the *Realphilosophie*, Hegel argues that 'it is only in the children that the unity [of marriage] exists externally, objectively, and explicitly as a unit, because the parents love the children as their love, as the embodiment of their substance'.[25]

But the family, by its own definition, is a transitory stage; its natural unity is integrated 'into a plurality of families, each of which conducts itself as in principle a self-subsistent concrete person'.[26] We have thus arrived at civil society.

CIVIL SOCIETY: UNIVERSAL INTERDEPENDENCE

Civil society is the tremendous power which draws men into itself and claims from them that they work for it, owe everything to it, and do everything by its means.[27]

This realization of the power of civil society in the world of man is central to Hegel's discussion of it in the *Philosophy of Right*. We have already seen how in his *Realphilosophie* Hegel came to attribute a crucial position to labour within his system of a philosophical anthropology; but the discussion about the division of labour and commodity-producing society was still, despite its astonishing foresight, rather rudimentary on the conceptual level. Only at a later stage did the term 'civil society' (*bürgerliche Gesellschaft*) differentiate itself in his thought, though the internal subdivisions of the relevant chapters in the *Realphilosophie* already correspond to those of the *Philosophy of Right*. It is true that the *Philosophy of Right* seems to lack some of the forceful critical thrust of the *Realphilosophie* in its discussion of the working of civil society; yet it would be a mistake to see it merely as quietistic. Though the criticism in the later work may be more guarded in its language, its theoretical significance is unmistakable and, as we shall see, the critical arguments are sometimes worked out in even more detail in their implications when compared with the parallel statements of the *Realphilosophie*.[28]

---

[24] *Ibid.* §§ 170–1, 178.
[25] *Ibid.* § 173: cf. also additions to §§ 123 and 125. See *Realphilosophie I*, 221, 223.   [26] *Philosophy of Right*, § 181.   [27] *Ibid.* addition to § 238.
[28] There is also evidence that during his years in Berlin Hegel had been re-reading Adam Ferguson's *Essay on the History of Civil Society*: see *Berliner Schriften*, p. 690.

The political economy of modern society

What stands out in Hegel's account of civil society as the sphere of self-regarding aims is its relation to historical developments. As a differentiated and institutionalized sphere, civil society is the child of the modern world:

The creation of civil society is the achievement of the modern world which has for the first time given all determinations of the Idea their due.[29]

A distinction has to be made here between the principle of civil society as a sphere of universal egoism, which exists in every society, and its fully developed institutionalization into a distinct and differentiated social sphere. It is the latter which is typical of modern societies, where individual self-interest receives legitimization and is emancipated from the religious and ethico-political considerations which until then had hampered the free play of individual interests to their full extent.

Hegel's definition of civil society follows the classical economists' model of the free market, and Hegel's early acquaintance with Steuart and Smith is evident in this definition:

Civil society – an association of members as self-subsistent individuals in a universality which, because of their self-subsistence, is only abstract. Their association is brought about by their needs, by the legal system – the means to security of person and property – and by an external organization for attaining their particular and common interests.[30]

Hegel is aware that the similarity between this model and the natural law heritage could lead to a confusion of civil society with the state (and the English term of 'civil society' certainly echoes some of this confusion). Hence he issues a warning against it:

This system [of universal interdependence] may be *prima facie* regarded as the external state, the state based on need, the state as the understanding envisages it (*Not- und Verstandesstaat*).[31]

This confusion, Hegel adds, is very common in political thought: 'If the state is represented as a unity of different persons, as a unity which is only a partnership, then what is really meant is only civil society. Many modern constitutional lawyers have been able to bring within their purview no theory of state but this. In civil

---

[29] *Philosophy of Right*, addition to § 182.
[30] *Ibid.* § 157.
[31] *Ibid.* § 183. The specific difference of the state is stressed also in § 258: 'If the state is confused with civil society, and if its specific end is laid down as the security and protection of property and personal freedom, then the interest of the individuals as such becomes the ultimate end of their association, and it follows that membership of the state is something optional.'

society, each member is his own end, everything else is nothing to him.'[32] What social contract theories call a state is, to Hegel, but civil society, based, as it were, on needs and a lower kind of knowledge – 'understanding'. This lower kind of knowledge, *Verstand*, is juxtaposed against the higher level of reason, *Vernunft*, which is to be found in the state. 'Understanding' implies in this context cognitive ability grasping only the external necessity binding people together, not realizing the inherent reason for it. This expresses itself, for example, in the fact that civil society, though it precedes the state in the logical order, is ultimately dependent upon the state for its very existence and preservation.[33]

This epistemological distinction also leads Hegel to regard political economy, the theory of civil society, within its proper context. Hegel's discussion brings out the dialectical nature of political economy; while paying tribute to its theoretical achievements, Hegel points to its limitations, which he then attributes to its belonging to the level of 'understanding':

Political economy is the science which starts from the view of needs and labour but then has the task of explaining mass-relationships and mass-movements in their complexity and their qualitative and quantitative character. This is one of the sciences which have arisen out of the conditions of the modern world. Its development affords the interesting spectacle (as in Smith, Say and Ricardo) of thought working upon the mass of details which confront it at the outset and extracting therefrom the simple principles of the thing, the understanding effective in the thing and directing it ... But if we look at it from the opposite point of view, this is the field in which the understanding with its subjective aims and moral fancies vents its discontent and moral frustration.[34]

It is for this reason that the universality of civil society is merely instrumental, not – as in the state – an end in itself:

Individuals in their capacity as burghers in this state are private persons whose end is their own interest. This end is mediated through the universal which thus appears as a means to its realization.[35]

The basis of civil society is the system of needs; yet human needs are not raw, natural needs, rather they are mediated through man's labour:

[32] *Ibid.* addition to § 182.
[33] *Ibid.*: 'Civil society is the [stage of] difference which intervenes between the family and the state, even if its formation follows later in time than that of the state, because as [the stage of] difference, it presupposes the state: to subsist itself, it must have the state before its eyes as something self-subsistent.' See also § 256.
[34] *Ibid.* § 189.   [35] *Ibid.* §187; see also § 182 and addition to § 184.

The means of acquiring and preparing the particular means appropriate to our similarly particularized needs is work. Through work the raw material directly supplied by nature is specifically adapted to these numerous ends by all sorts of different processes. Now this formative change confers value on means and gives them their utility, and hence man in what he consumes is mainly concerned with the products of men. It is the product of human effort which man consumes . . .

There is hardly any raw material which does not need to be worked on before use.[36]

Labour is thus the mediator between man and nature and therefore in labour there always exists an intrinsic moment of liberation, since labour enables man to transcend the physical limits set upon him by nature. Not only is the satisfaction of human needs dependent upon human labour and consciousness but human needs themselves are not purely material, physical needs. Their articulation implies the mediation of consciousness and hence human needs are of a different order from animal needs which are purely physical. Because human needs are 'a conjunction of immediate or natural needs with mental needs arising from ideas', there is a liberating aspect in the very process of defining and satisfying these needs:

Since . . . [needs arising from ideas] because of their universality make themselves preponderant, this social moment has in it the aspect of liberation, i.e. the strict natural necessity of need is obscured and man is concerned with his own opinion, indeed with an opinion which is universal, and with a necessity of his own making alone, instead of with an external necessity, an inner contingency, and mere caprice.[37]

This mediation and generation of human needs through consciousness implies that, unlike animal needs, human needs have no fixed and determinable limits:

An animal's needs and its ways and means of satisfying them are both alike restricted in scope. Though man is subject to this restriction too, yet at the same time he evinces his transcendence of it and his universality, first by the multiplication of needs and means of satisfying them, and secondly by the differentiation and division of concrete need into single parts and aspects which in turn become different needs . . .

An animal is restricted by particularity. It has its instincts and means of

---

[36] *Ibid.* § 196 and addition.
[37] *Ibid.* § 194. The similarity between this and Marx's view of man as *homo faber* is again striking. While the parallel passages in the *Realphilosophie* were unknown to Marx, he was, of course, acquainted with the *Philosophy of Right*, though his detailed commentary on it, written in 1843, limits itself to §§ 261–313; see Marx's *Critique of Hegel's 'Philosophy of Right'*, ed. J. O'Malley (Cambridge, 1970).

144

satisfying them, means which are limited and which it cannot overstep . . . Intelligence, with its grasp of distinction, multiplies these human needs, and since taste and utility become criteria of judgement, even the needs themselves are affected thereby.[38]

Such a view is, of course, diametrically opposed to the proto-romantic idealization of the 'state of nature' as a model of an equilibrium between man and his needs and between human consciousness and nature. Hegel takes up here an argument with Rousseau which goes to the roots of their opposing views about human civilization:

The idea has been advanced that in respect of his needs man lived in freedom in the so-called 'state of nature' when his needs were supposed to be confined to what are known as the simple necessities of nature . . . This view takes no account of the moment of liberation intrinsic to work . . . Apart from this, it is false, because to be confined to mere physical needs as such and their direct satisfaction would simply be the condition in which the mental is plunged in the natural and so would be one of savagery and unfreedom, while freedom itself is to be found only in the reflection of mind into itself, in mind's distinction from nature, and in the reflex of mind in nature.[39]

Yet it is precisely this liberating aspect of man as not being limited in his needs by his natural determination which also drives human society to the endless pursuit of commodities. This is the inner restlessness of civil society to which Hegel had already alluded in his *Realphilosophie*. Man imagines that he expands his consciousness by acquiring new commodities, while in actual fact he only satisfies the desire for more profit by the producer. Civil society is the mechanism through which not only felt needs are satisfied but through which a new demand is also created consciously by the producers: 'Hence the need for greater comfort does not exactly arise within you directly; it is suggested to you by those who hope to make a profit from its creation.'[40] In a passage strongly reminiscent of Tocqueville, Hegel maintains that the tendency toward equality which is typical of modern society pushes civil society ever more into the direction of expanding production since equality means pressure for more consumption:

[The social moment in needs] directly involves the demand for equality of satisfaction with others. The need for this equality and for emulation, which is the equalizing of oneself with others, as well as the other need also present here, the

[38] *Philosophy of Right*, § 190 and addition. Cf. addition to § 185: 'By means of his ideas and reflections man expands his desires, which are not a closed circle like animal instinct, and carries them on to the false infinite.'
[39] *Ibid.* § 194.   [40] *Ibid.* addition to § 191.

need of the particular to assert itself in some distinctive way, become themselves a fruitful source of the multiplication of needs and their expression.[41]

This craving after unlimited desires creates, however, its necessary opposite – poverty. Society creates not only 'new desires without end'; 'want and destitution are measureless too', and the pursuit of unlimited wealth breeds poverty: 'In these contrasts and their complexity, civil society affords a spectacle of extravagance and want as well as of the physical and ethical degeneration common to them both.'[42]

Poverty is then not an accidental by-product of civil society; it is inherent in it. Hegel's position on this is as critical in the *Philosophy of Right* as it had been almost twenty years earlier in the *Realphilosophie*.

The dialectics of civil society create a universal dependence of man on man. No man is an island any more, and each finds himself irretrievably interwoven into the texture of production, exchange and consumption: 'In the course of the actual attainment of selfish ends – an attainment conditioned in this way by universality – there is formed a system of complete interdependence, wherein the livelihood, happiness, and legal status of one man is interwoven with the livelihood, happiness and rights of all.'[43]

This universal interdependence is further enhanced through the division of labour, which in its turn tends towards the maximization of production and profit through the introduction of machinery:

[The division of labour] makes necessary everywhere the dependence of men on one another and their reciprocal relation in the satisfaction of their other needs. Further, the abstraction of one man's production from another's makes work more and more mechanical, until finally man is able to step aside and install machines in his place.[44]

Mechanization and industrialization are therefore the necessary consequences of civil society. Thus civil society reaches its apex – and it is here that Hegel integrates the Smithian model of a free market into his philosophical system, by transforming Smith's 'hidden hand' into dialectical reason working in civil society, un-

[41] *Ibid.* § 193.   [42] *Ibid.* § 185.
[43] *Ibid.* § 183; cf. addition to § 192: 'The fact that I must direct my conduct by reference to others introduces here the form of universality. It is from others that I acquire the means of satisfaction and I must accordingly accept their views. At the same time, however, I am compelled to produce means for the satisfaction of others. We play into each other's hands and so hang together. To this extent everything private becomes something social.'
[44] *Ibid.* § 198.

beknownst to its own members. Self-interest and self-assertion are
the motives of activity in civil society; but these can be realized
by the individual only through inter-action with others and recognition by them.[45] The mutual dependence of all on all is inherent
in every individual's self-oriented action:

> When men are thus dependent on one another and reciprocally related to one
> another in their work and the satisfaction of their needs, subjective self-seeking
> turns into a contribution to the satisfaction of the needs of everyone else.
> That is to say, by a dialectical advance, subjective self-seeking turns into the
> mediation of the particular through the universal, with the result that each man
> in earning, producing, and enjoying on his own account is *eo ipso* producing
> and earning for the enjoyment of everyone else.[46]

This is the role political economy plays in Hegel's system. The
political economists are mistaken when they represent their limited
reasoning as an ultimate explanation of human behaviour. Yet there
is more to political economy than meets the eye or than political
economists themselves are aware of. Economics is the handmaid of
reason acting in the world; behind the self-seeking, accidentality
and arbitrariness of civil society there looms inherent reason:

> It is to find reconciliation here to discover in the sphere of needs this show of
> rationality lying in the thing and effective there . . .
> To discover this necessary element here is the object of political economy, a
> science which is a credit to thought because it finds laws for a mass of accidents.
> It is an interesting spectacle here to see all chains of activity leading back to the
> same point; particular spheres of action fall into groups, influence others, and
> are helped or hindered by others. The most remarkable thing is this mutual
> interlocking of particulars.[47]

Civil society thus becomes integrated into Hegel's system as a
necessary moment in man's progress towards his realization of the
consciousness of freedom. But it is subordinated to the higher
universality of the state. Adam Smith is thus *aufgehoben* – both
preserved and transcended – into the Hegelian system.

POVERTY AND THE LIMITS OF CIVIL SOCIETY

We have previously seen how in his *Realphilosophie* Hegel
realized that the mechanism of the market creates social polarization, poverty and alienation; in the *Philosophy of Right* the same
radical critique of civil society emerges from Hegel's discussion of
the consequences of allowing it free reign. In both works Hegel
suggests state intervention in order to mitigate some of the harsher

[45] This is a recurring theme: see §§ 48, 57, 133, 153, 207, 214–15, 218–19, 355.
[46] *Ibid.* § 199.   [47] *Ibid.* § 189 and addition.

aspects of poverty; yet ultimately he is unable to provide a radical solution.

Hegel's acceptance of Smith's 'hidden hand' does not entail following the optimistic and harmonistic implications of the model. Smith contended that if everyone were to follow his enlightened self-interest rationally, the general good of all would evolve out this clash of interests. Hegel accepts Smith's view that behind the senseless and conflicting clash of egoistic interests in civil society a higher purpose can be discerned; but he does not agree with the hidden assumption which implies that everyone in society is thus being well taken care of. Poverty, which for Smith is always marginal to his model, assumes another dimension in Hegel. For the latter, pauperization and the subsequent alienation from society are not incidental to the system but endemic to it. Moreover, Hegel goes to some length to show that every suggested remedial policy put forward to overcome poverty in modern society seems to be useless, and some of these policies may even boomerang. The extraordinary thing about Hegel's discussion of these social problems in the *Philosophy of Right* is that in an analysis which attempts to depict how modern society in its differentiated structure is able to overcome its problems through mediation, the only problem which remains open and unresolved according to Hegel's own admission is the problem of poverty.

Poverty, according to Hegel, grows in proportionate ratio to the growth of wealth; they are the two aspects of a zero-sum equation, and poverty in one quarter is the price society pays for wealth in another. Far from being a relic of the old, undeveloped society, poverty in modern society is a phenomenon as modern as the structure of commodity-producing society itself:

When social conditions tend to multiply and subdivide needs, means and enjoyments indefinitely – a process which, like the distinction between natural and refined needs, has no qualitative limits – this is luxury. In this same process, however, dependence and want increase *ad infinitum*, and the material to meet this is permanently barred to the needy man because it consists of external objects with the special character of being property, the embodiment of the free will of others, and hence from his point of view its recalcitrance is absolute.[48]

It is the economic expansion of civil society which brings about social polarization and intensifies it. Modern poverty is accompanied by industrial overproduction which cannot find enough

[48] *Ibid.* § 195.

Poverty and the limits of civil society

consumers who have sufficient purchasing power to buy the products offered on the market. Not the malfunction of civil society causes poverty, but precisely its opposite, the smooth functioning of the powers of the market:

When civil society is in a state of unimpeded activity, it is engaged in expanding internally in population and industry. The amassing of wealth is intensified by generalizing (a) the linkage of men by their needs, and (b) the methods of preparing and distributing the means to satisfy these needs, because it is from this double process of generalization that the largest profits are derived. That is one side of the picture. The other is the subdivision and restriction of particular jobs. This results in the dependence and distress of the class tied to the work of that sort, and these again entail inability to feel and enjoy the broader freedoms and especially the intellectual benefits of society.[49]

One of Hegel's most fascinating insights into the dialectical working of civil society is his awareness of the fact that poverty is not to be understood in objective terms only. When discussing previously the system of needs, Hegel had clearly indicated that needs have both an objective and a subjective aspect; he had also pointed out that there is no minimum standard of living which can be fixed and determined beforehand. The historicity of needs and the development of civil society turn the minimum standard of living into a measure always relative to prevailing conditions.[50] The main problem of the poor is that while they cannot attain that which is considered as the minimum in their particular society, they nevertheless have the felt need to achieve this level. Civil society thus succeeds in internalizing its norms about consumption into the consciousness of its members even while it is unable to satisfy these norms. This is exacerbated because civil society continuously overproduces goods which the masses cannot buy because of their lack of purchasing power. Thus poverty becomes a dialectical concept; it is the expression of the tension between the needs created by civil society and its inability to satisfy them:

Not only caprice, however, but also contingencies, physical conditions, and factors grounded in external circumstances may reduce men to poverty. The poor still have the needs common to civil society, and yet since society has withdrawn from them the natural means of acquisition and broken the bond of the family ... their poverty leaves them more or less deprived of all the advantages of society, of the opportunity of acquiring skill or education of any

49 *Ibid.* § 243. It should be noted that just as in the *Realphilosophie* Hegel is using here the modern term *Klasse* to denote the workers, rather than *Stand* which he always uses otherwise.
50 Addition to § 244: 'The lowest subsistence level, that of a rabble of paupers, is fixed automatically, but the minimum varies considerably in different countries. In England, even the very poorest believe that they have rights.'

kind, as well as of the administration of justice, the public health services, and often even of the consolations of religion, and so forth.[51]

This is a strikingly modern and sophisticated description of the culture of poverty and it parallels many much more recent attempts by social scientists to drive home the point that poverty cannot be described merely in quantitative terms. To Hegel, the culture of poverty entails the deprivation of educational and vocational skills, exclusion from the normal working of the system of justice and the public welfare services and exclusion even from the institutional organs of society – organized religion – which aim at alleviating man's suffering on a spiritual level. Since Hegel in his social philosophy was searching for a system through which man could be integrated into his world, he must have been more aware than many of his contemporaries what an exclusion from these integrative organs would entail.

It is only when poverty reaches this qualitative dimension of exclusion that a rabble (*Pöbel*) is created – a heap of human beings utterly atomized and alienated from society, feeling no allegiance to it and no longer even wishing to be integrated into it. The element of consciousness is once again central to Hegel's description of the emergence of this group within civil society which finds itself totally outside it:

When the standard of living of a large mass of people falls below a certain subsistence level – a level regulated automatically as the one necessary for a member of the society – and when there is a consequent loss of the sense of right and wrong, of honesty and the self-respect which makes a man insist on maintaining himself by his own work and effort, the result is the creation of a rabble of paupers.[52]

Hegel stresses again and again the dialectical nature of the emergence of poverty, the fact that pauperization is accompanied by enormous enrichment: 'At the same time this brings with it, at the other end of the social scale, conditions which greatly facilitate the concentration of disproportionate wealth in a few hands.'[53]

[51] *Ibid.* § 241; cf. addition to § 244: 'Poverty in itself does not make men into a rabble; a rabble is created only when there is joined to poverty a disposition of mind, an inner indignation (*Empörung*) against the rich, against society, against the government, etc. A further consequence of this attitude is that through their dependence on chance men become frivolous and idle, like the Neapolitan *lazzaroni* for example. In this way there is born in the rabble the evil of lacking self-respect enough to secure subsistence by its own labour and yet at the same time of claiming to receive subsistence as its right.'
[52] *Ibid.* § 244.   [53] *Ibid.*

Poverty and the limits of civil society

This analysis leads Hegel to call for the intervention of the state. The situation, he believes, can be brought into harmony only by means of the state which has power over it.[54] Yet, just as in the *Realphilosophie*, Hegel's program of state intervention is fraught with internal difficulties for it is clear that Hegel sees it necessary, from the theoretical premises of his system, to preserve the autonomy of civil society. Therefore he limits his advocacy of state interference to external control only, and avoids the conclusion that the state should simply take over economic activity. And when he calls for more direct initiative, he himself quickly realizes that it will be no more than a palliative so long as the whole system is not overhauled. Hegel's dilemma is acute: if he leaves the state out of economic activity, an entire group of civil society members is going to be left outside it; but if he brings in the state in a way that would solve the problem, his distinction between civil society and the state would disappear, and the whole system of mediation and dialectical progress towards integration through differentiation would collapse.

Hegel's call for curbs on industry, mainly through price controls, is grounded in his insistence that after all civil society exists in a public context. The clash of interests can be overcome not through an automatic 'hidden hand' but only through conscious direction and supervision:

The differing interests of producers and consumers may come into collision with each other; and although a fair balance between them on the whole may be brought about automatically, still their adjustment also requires a control which stands above both and is consciously undertaken. The right to the exercise of such control in a single case (e.g. in the fixing of prices of the commonest necessities of life) depends on the fact that, by being publicly exposed for sale, goods in absolutely universal daily demand are offered not so much to an individual as such but rather to a universal purchaser, the public; and thus both the defence of the public's right not to be defrauded, and also the management of goods inspection, may lie, as a common concern, with a public authority.[55]

Hegel is further conscious of the fact that it is the large industrial concerns which also require public control:

But public care and direction are most of all necessary in the case of larger branches of industry, because these are dependent on conditions abroad and on combinations of distant circumstances which cannot be grasped as a whole by the individuals tied to these industries for their living.[56]

[54] *Ibid.* § 185.   [55] *Ibid.* § 236.
[56] *Ibid.* See also what follows in the same paragraph: 'Control is also necessary to diminish the danger of upheavals arising from clashing interests and to

151

The political economy of modern society

Yet in the same paragraph Hegel mentions ancient Oriental societies, such as Pharaonic Egypt, in which the state had taken over the function of civil society and had itself become the economic entrepreneur. Hegel objects to such a system as injurious to freedom and emphatically warns against the tendency of the state to encroach upon economic activity and step directly into it in its zeal to protect its weaker citizens. Whatever the ills of civil society, it should not be crushed by the state.

Hegel does, however, proceed to discuss various mechanisms through which the lot of the industrial poor could be alleviated. This discussion brings out both his rare and astonishing grasp of the nature of civil society as well as his ultimate inability to cope with the problem of poverty. While he commends individual charity, he clearly sees that it is not enough: 'A false view is implied . . . when charity insists on having this poor relief reserved solely to private sympathy and the accidental occurrence of knowledge and a charitable disposition.'[57] Alongside private charity, public authority must step in.

Hegel sees three alternative ways in which the alleviation of poverty can be approached: (a) through voluntary institutions; (b) by redistribution of wealth through direct taxation; (c) through public works. The point, however, is that none of these methods solves the problem, which is one of overproduction and underconsumption, and it is in these terms that Hegel understands the intrinsic problem of modern society. Solutions (a) and (b) do not restore to the recipient of welfare, whether voluntary or public, his own dignity and self-consciousness as a self-subsistent member of civil society, since civil society is based, according to Hegel, on individuals who view themselves as capable of maintaining themselves. Solution (c), on the other hand, only adds more goods to a market that is already glutted with unsaleable goods. Though Keynsian welfare economics was later able to find a way out of this latter predicament by resorting to public works which did not produce immediate consumer goods, Hegel's dissatisfaction with the third solution derives from his familiarity with the economic theory of his day and bears witness to his basic insight that the crisis of modern society differs from the traditional problem of poverty in ages past. Society can now produce an unlimited

abbreviate the period in which their tension should be eased through the working of a necessity of which they themselves know nothing.'
[57] *Ibid.* § 242.

152

quantity of goods; the problem is one of distribution and of consumption, not of production. The relevant passage should be quoted here in its entirety:

> When the masses begin to decline into poverty, (a) the burden of maintaining them at their ordinary standard of living might be directly laid on the wealthier classes, or they might receive the means of livelihood directly from other public sources of wealth (e.g. from the endowments of rich hospitals, monasteries, and other foundations). In either case, however, the needy would receive subsistence directly, not by means of their work, and this would violate the principle of civil society and the feeling of individual independence and self-respect in its individual members. (b) As an alternative, they might be given subsistence directly through being given work, i.e. the opportunity to work. In this event the volume of production would be increased, *but the evil consists precisely in an excess of production and in the lack of a proportionate number of consumers who are themselves also producers,* and thus it is simply intensified by both of the methods (a) and (b) by which it is sought to alleviate it. *It hence becomes apparent that despite an excess of wealth civil society is not rich enough, i.e. its own resources are insufficient to check excessive poverty and the creation of a penurious rabble.*[58]

After thus discarding the various possible alternatives for the elimination of poverty, Hegel gloomily remarks that it remains inherent and endemic to modern society. The very text attests to the depth of his pessimism: 'Against nature man can claim no right, but once society is established, poverty immediately takes the form of a wrong done to one class by another. The important question of how poverty is to be abolished is one of the most disturbing problems which agitate modern society.'[59] Yet no solution is offered by Hegel himself.

To these observations Hegel adds the remark that any given civil society may attempt to find a solution to its particular problem of industrial overproduction and poverty by seeking markets as well as raw materials abroad. Again, it is fascinating to reflect that the following was written around 1820:

[58] *Ibid.* § 245 (my italics). Hegel then proceeds to cite Britain as an example for these conditions.

[59] *Ibid.* addition to § 244. In a surprising aside on the Cynic school, Hegel sees its emergence as a protest against the extremes of luxury and poverty in late Athenian society: 'The entire Cynical mode of life adopted by Diogenes was nothing more or less than a product of Athenian social life, and what determined it was the way of thinking against which his whole manner protested. Hence it was not independent of social conditions but simply their result; it was itself a rude product of luxury. When luxury is at its height, distress and depravity are equally extreme, and in such circumstances Cynicism is the outcome of opposition to refinement' (addition to § 195).

This inner dialectic of civil society thus drives it – or at any rate drives a specific civil society – to push beyond its own limits and seek markets, and so its necessary means of subsistence, in other lands which are either deficient in the goods it has overproduced, or else generally backward in industry, etc.[60]

A further aspect of these drives by civil society to seek solutions to its problems outside itself is colonization, i.e. the export and emigration of superfluous members of society to overseas territories. There they are able to find not only economic security but also the ethical sustenance and social integration which the brutalizing conditions of their life in the metropolis have denied them:

This far-flung connecting link [i.e. the sea] affords the means for the colonizing activity – sporadic or systematic – to which the mature civil society is driven and by which it supplies to a part of its population a return to life on the family basis in a new land and so also supplies itself with a new demand and field for its industry . . .

Civil society is thus driven to found colonies. Increase of population alone has this effect, but it is due in particular to the appearance of a number of people who cannot secure the satisfaction of their needs by their own labour once production rises above the requirements of consumers.[61]

We have thus seen Hegel analyse the functioning of civil society and come up with a theory of pauperization, social polarization, economic imperialism and colonization. Few people around 1820 grasped in such depth the predicament of modern industrial society and the future course of nineteenth-century European history. What is conspicuous in Hegel's analysis, however, is not only his far-sightedness but also a basic intellectual honesty which makes him admit time and again – completely against the grain of the integrative and mediating nature of the whole of his social philosophy – that he has no solution to the problems posed by civil society in its modern context. This is the only time in his system where Hegel raises a problem – and leaves it open. Though his theory of the state is aimed at integrating the contending interests of civil society under a common bond, on the problem of poverty he ultimately has nothing more to say than that it is one of 'the most disturbing problems which agitate modern society'. On no other occasion does Hegel leave a problem at that.

[60] *Ibid.* § 246. This process has, however, an obvious geographical limitation since it cannot go on forever and hence cannot be a solution to the intrinsic problem of civil society.

[61] *Ibid.* § 248 and addition. In the addition Hegel further remarks that ultimately the European colonies will gain independence, as in the case of the English and Spanish colonies in America, but adds that 'colonial independence proves to be of the greatest advantage to the mother country, just as the emancipation of slaves turns out to the greatest advantage of the owners'.

Chapter Eight

SOCIAL CLASSES, REPRESENTATION
AND PLURALISM

BUREAUCRACY — THE UNIVERSAL CLASS

Hegel's theory of social classes in the *Philosophy of Right* follows his general outline in the *Realphilosophie*; hence only a number of salient points need to be repeated here. However, the *Philosophy of Right* does contain a more detailed discussion of the universal class, the bureaucracy.

The origins of social differentiation are traced by Hegel to the social division of labour which is the consequence of social production:

The infinitely complex, criss-cross, movements of reciprocal production and exchange, and the equally infinite multiplicity of means therein employed, become crystallized, owing to the universality inherent in their content, and distinguished into general groups. As a result, the entire complex is built up into particular systems of needs, means, and the types of work relative to these needs, modes of satisfaction and of theoretical and practical education, i.e. into systems, to one or other of which individuals are assigned — in other words, into class-divisions.[1]

There is however another aspect of class division, and this is the moment of integration. Belonging to a class links a person to a universal and hence classes are a mediator between man's purely individual existence and the wider context of his life: 'When we say that a man must be a "somebody", we mean that he should belong to some specific social class, since to be a somebody means to have a substantive being. A man with no class is a mere private person and his universality is not actualized.'[2]

This seems to be a throwback to the old system of estates and guilds, in which a person's *Stand* really did determine his overall status in society and thus the nature of his personality. Yet Hegel quite specifically points out that class distinctions should not be

---

[1] *Philosophy of Right*, § 201. [2] *Ibid.* addition to § 207.

hereditary; the picture of society he presents is that of an open, mobile society, of a *carrière ouverte aux talents*, in which distinctions represent ability and not inherited privilege. This may be naïve but it is not the closed system of the old society; it is modern, free bourgeois society which Hegel describes here and to its divisions he attempts to add the dimension of integration:

It is in accordance with the concept that class-organization, as particularity became objective to itself, is split in this way into its general divisions. But the question of the particular class to which an individual is to belong is one on which natural capacity, birth, and other circumstances have their influence, though the essential and final determining factors are subjective opinion and the individual's arbitrary will, which win in this sphere their right, their merit, and their dignity. Hence what happens here by inner necessity occurs at the same time by the mediation of the arbitrary will, and to the conscious subject it has the shape of being the work of his own will ...

The recognition and the right that what is brought about by reason of necessity in civil society and the state at the same time be effected by the mediation of the arbitrary will is the more precise definition of what is primarily meant by freedom in common parlance.[3]

Class divisions determine not only a person's purely economic mode of life but are a totality which impinges on the whole of his life. A person's consciousness is moulded in accordance with his membership of a particular class. The three classes – the agricultural class, the business class and the bureaucracy – thus reflect three modes of consciousness: conservatism, individualism and universality.

Hegel's account of the agricultural class in the *Philosophy of Right* differs from his earlier discussion of the subject as now this class includes not only the peasantry but the landed aristocracy as well. The agricultural class is thus a curiously bicephalous entity, encompassing the two extreme poles of the social spectrum. In the *Realphilosophie*, there was no aristocracy at all, probably as a result of the immediate impact on Hegel of the French revolutionary experience; its introduction into the system in the early 1820s is clearly a bow in the direction of the Restoration. Hegel attempts, however, to minimize this by incorporating the aristocracy, in a somewhat mechanical way, into the top of the agricultural class. In this way he could avoid having to change his overall system of three classes. It must be admitted, however, that this manoeuvre has the effect of turning Hegel's account into a far less adequate theory of social classes than it might otherwise have been.

[3] *Ibid.* § 206.

Bureaucracy – the universal class

Yet despite this flaw, Hegel's description of the agricultural class expresses in a most succinct way his contention that social existence determines the modes of consciousness:

The substantial [or agricultural] class has its capital in the natural products of the soil which it cultivates – soil which is capable of exclusively private ownership and which demands formation in an objective way and not mere haphazard exploitation ... But owing to the conditions here, the agricultural mode of subsistence remains one which owes comparatively little to reflection and independence of will, and this mode of life is in general such that this class has the substantial disposition of an ethical life which is immediate, resting on family relationship and trust ...

The agricultural class will always retain a mode of life which is patriarchal and the substantial frame of mind proper to such a life. The member of this class accepts unreflectively what is given him and takes what he gets, thanking God for it and living in faith and confidence that this goodness will continue. What comes to him suffices him; once it is consumed, more comes again. This is the simple attitude of mind not concentrated on the struggle for riches. It may be described as the attitude of the old nobility which just ate what there was ...

The agricultural class ... has little occasion to think of itself; what it obtains is the gift of a stranger, of nature. Its feeling of dependence is fundamental to it, and with this feeling there is readily associated a willingness to submit to whatever may befall it at other men's hands. The agricultural class is thus more inclined to subservience, the business class to freedom.[4]

Because the landed aristocracy's property is in the form of primogeniture and entailed estates relatively free from the fluctuations of the market and the direct interference of the state, members of this class are *prima facie* more suited than members of less independent classes for public office. The pragmatic version of the 'gentleman of independent means' as an optimal political actor receives here speculative justification.[5]

The business class represents for Hegel both man's creative power and the ethos of individualism, law and order. The business class 'has for its task the adaptation of raw materials, and for its means of livelihood it is thrown back on its work, on reflection and intelligence, and essentially on the mediation of one man's needs and work with those of the other.'[6] Craftsmanship, mass production and exchange are the three main modes through which this class establishes itself.

Although Hegel places the aristocracy on a higher level in terms of possible public service, it is the business class which represents

---

[4] *Ibid.* § 203 and addition, and addition to § 204.
[5] *Ibid.* § 306.   [6] *Ibid.* § 204.

a higher order of consciousness. The consciousness of the agricultural class, aristocratic and peasant alike, is, after all, still enclosed in natural relations – the family, the soil. In the business class a higher consciousness is at work:

> In the business class, however, it is intelligence which is the essential thing, and natural products can be treated only as raw materials . . .
>
> In the business class, the individual is thrown back on himself, and this feeling of selfhood is most intimately connected with the demand for law and order. The sense of freedom and order has therefore arisen above all in towns.[7]

On another occasion Hegel says that the middle class is the 'pillar of the state'. Though the term 'middle classes' in this particular context includes also the civil servants and is not exactly identical with the business class, Hegel's statement that 'a state without a middle class must therefore remain at a low level' is a clear indication of the kind of social structure – and political consciousness and organization – Hegel was aiming at. In the same paragraph Hegel adds that it should be 'the prime concern of the state that a middle class should be developed', since without the countervailing powers of a middle class the state may develop into ruthless authoritarianism. It is the lack of a middle class in Russia, Hegel maintains, that is responsible for the authoritarianism of the czarist system: 'Russia, for instance, has a mass of serfs on the one hand and a mass of rulers on the other.'[8]

It is on the class of civil servants, however, that Hegel's discussion of social classes in the *Philosophy of Right* concentrates. This class is the crucial link between the particularism of civil society and the universality of the state. On the one hand, it is one class among the classes of civil society; on the other, it does not have its own interests as the aim of its activities but is motivated by the interests of society as a whole. Hegel's attempt to find a sphere which transcends private interests is similar to the Platonic endeavour, but while Plato tried to neutralize his Guardians totally from 'civil society' by depriving them of family and private property, Hegel's solution is less radical; it is also, after all, the very method commonly used by modern states in their attempt to ensure the relative independence of their civil service from the pressures of civil society. Hegel defines the universal class as follows:

> The universal class [the class of civil servants] has for its task the universal interests of the community. It must therefore be relieved from direct labour to supply its needs, either by having private means or by receiving an allowance

[7] *Ibid.* additions to §§ 203 and 204.   [8] *Ibid.* addition to § 297.

from the state which claims its industry, with the result that private interest finds its satisfaction in the work for the universal. [9]

Today this sounds, of course, quite commonplace. One has to recall, however, that at the time when Hegel wrote this, many public offices were still venal, as for example, in England where no real civil service as yet existed. Prussia, with its relatively enlightened bureaucracy, was surely far more modern in this respect in 1820 when compared with the corrupt practices prevailing in England at that period.

The civil service has a specific mode of behaviour which, according to Hegel, is characterized by its being 'dispassionate, upright and polite'.[10] Though civil servants constitute 'the greater part of the middle class',[11] appointment to civil service positions should be by merit alone. The Napoleonic idea of a meritocracy is strongly echoed in Hegel's insistence that:

Individuals are not appointed to office on account of their birth or native personal gifts. The *objective* factor in their appointment is knowledge and proof of ability. Such proof guarantees that the state will get what it requires; and since it is the sole condition of appointment, it also guarantees to every citizen the chance of joining the class of civil servants.[12]

Universalistic, achievement-oriented criteria imbue the whole structure of the civil service, and a place in the civil service, according to Hegel, should never be construed as constituting a claim to something resembling private property. According to Hegel, the property-oriented criteria of civil society are totally out of place in the public realm of the civil service and he sees the institution of a modern, rationally organized bureaucracy as one of the characteristics of the new state:

The individual functionaries and agents are attached to their office not on the strength of their immediate personality, but only on the strength of their universal and objective qualities ... The functions and the powers of the state cannot be private property.

The business of the state is in the hands of individuals. But their authority to conduct its affairs is based not on their birth but on their objective qualities. Ability, skill, character, all belong to a man in his particular capacity. He must be educated and be trained to a particular task. Hence an office may not be saleable or hereditary. In France, seats in parliament were formerly saleable, and in England army commissions up to a certain rank are saleable to this day.

⁹ *Ibid.* § 205; cf. § 303: 'The universal class, or, more precisely, the class of civil servants, must purely in virtue of its character as universal, have the universal as the end of its activity.' See also Hegel's discussion of the role of an independent civil service in his essay on Württemberg, *Political Writings*, pp. 257–8.

¹⁰ *Philosophy of Right*, § 296.   ¹¹ *Ibid.* § 297.   ¹² *Ibid.* § 291.

The saleability of office, however, was or is still connected with the medieval constitution of certain states, and such constitutions are nowadays gradually disappearing.[13]

Civil servants should also have tenure and be thus independent of immediate political pressure:

Once an individual has been appointed to his official position by the sovereign's act, the tenure of his post is conditional on his fulfilling his duties. Such fulfillment is the very essence of his appointment, and it is only consequential that he finds in his office his livelihood and the assured satisfaction of his particular interests, and further that his external circumstances and his official work are freed from other kinds of subjective dependence and influence . . .

What the service of the state really requires is that men shall forgo the selfish and capricious satisfaction of their subjective ends; by this very sacrifice, they acquire the right to find their satisfaction in, but only in, the dutiful discharge of their public functions.[14]

What we have here is a model of a bureaucracy almost identical with the Weberian ideal type. According to Hegel the modern state needs a tenured bureaucracy with an ethos of service to the commonwealth, recruited according to merit and compensated according to its performance. In its autonomy and independence from the economic powers of civil society, this bureaucracy acts as a brake on civil society itself and ensures that public policy should not be an immediate reflection of the interests of civil society. Hegel is aware of the danger that members of such a bureaucracy may tend to view themselves as 'owning' the state;[15] but he posits the multiplicity of corporations and other voluntary organizations as effective checks and balances on the power of the civil service.[16] Because Hegel was aware of the immense power of civil society, he saw as the utmost necessity the development within the social structure of foci of power that would be relatively independent of it. In his Jena writings the 'universal' or 'absolute' class is mainly occupied with defending the state; only over time does Hegel shift the emphasis from mere defence to administration, and this occurs parallel to his own growing awareness of the power of civil society. Hegel's theory of bureaucracy is thus not only a reflection of the

[13] *Ibid.* § 277 and addition.
[14] *Ibid.* § 294.
[15] *Ibid.*: 'The opposite extreme . . . would be an official who clung to his office purely and simply to make a living without any real sense of duty and so without any real right to go on holding it.' It was on this issue of the bureaucracy ultimately imagining that it 'owns' the state that Marx attacked Hegel's notion of the bureaucracy as a universal class; see his *Critique of Hegel's 'Philosophy of Right'*, pp. 46–8, which refer to these paragraphs.
[16] *Philosophy of Right*, addition to § 297.

functional needs of a complex and differentiated society, but also represents a critique of the claims of civil society to absolute and paramount power.

REPRESENTATION AND CORPORATIONS

In his essay on Württemberg, Hegel had discussed representation at some length; his views on this subject in the *Philosophy of Right* generally follow his observations on the constitutional debate in his native Württemberg. The fact that what he advocates in the *Philosophy of Right* concerning representative organs is quite different from the existing practices then prevailing in Prussia, should again make clear that for all his sympathy for Prussia, Hegel never saw its political arrangements as a model for his political theory.

Representation for Hegel is a system of mediation between the population and the government, between the interests of civil society and the universalism of the state. As such, it is a necessary element in the political structure. The absence of mediation is despotism. In a despotism, 'where there are only rulers and people, the people is effective, if at all, only as a mass destructive of the organization of the state'.[17] Hence mediation and representation are crucial if an attempt is to be made to integrate the contending particularisms into a political whole:

The Estates have the function of bringing public affairs into existence not only implicitly, but also actually, i.e. of bringing into existence the moment of subjective formal freedom, the public consciousness as an empirical universal, of which the thoughts and opinions of the Many are particulars . . .

Hence the specific function which the concept assigns to the Estates is to be sought in the fact that in them the subjective moment in universal freedom — the private judgement and private will of the sphere called 'civil society' in this book — comes into existence integrally related to the state . . .

The real significance of the Estates lies in the fact that it is through them that the state enters the subjective consciousness of the people and that the people begins to participate in the state.[18]

The assembly of estates is thus the aggregation and articulation of the interests of civil society and hence its composition should reflect the divisions of civil society. According to Hegel, it should be bi-cameral, with an Upper House composed of members of the nobility, and a Lower House which should be elected.[19]

[17] *Ibid.* addition to § 302.
[18] *Ibid.* § 301 and addition.   [19] *Ibid.* §§ 306–7.

Social classes, representation and pluralism

But the electoral basis for the Lower House should not be founded on merely direct, universal suffrage. As in the Württemberg essay, Hegel holds that undifferentiated suffrage causes atomization and political alienation: we have seen how much his theory is akin to current views of group representation prevalent in contemporary Western political theory. If people vote according to their corporate affiliation, Hegel argues, the gap between civil society and the state, which remains wide open in the case of direct elections, can be overcome:

The circles of association in civil society are already communities. To picture these communities as once more breaking up into a mere conglomeration of individuals as soon as they enter the field of politics, i.e. the field of the highest concrete universality, is *eo ipso* to hold civil and political life apart from one another and as it were to hang the latter in the air, because its basis could then only be the abstract individuality of caprice and opinion.[20]

Hegel thus adds the integrative function to the representative function ascribed to Assemblies in traditional theories of representation. While he stresses that individual representatives are not to be bound by any *mandat impératif*,[21] he sees in their very relation to an identifiable and articulate interest a guarantee against atomization:

Regarded as a mediating organ, the Estates stand between the government in general on the one hand and the nation broken up into particulars (people and associations) on the other . . .

[They prevent] individuals from having the appearance of a mass or an aggregate and so from acquiring an unorganized opinion and volition and from crystallizing into a powerful *bloc* in opposition to the organized state.[22]

Hegel is also very much aware of the dimension of scale as a variable when working out a system of representation; the ancient theories of democracy cannot be applicable to the modern state, with its wide territory and complex social organization, and, if introduced, would constitute a travesty of representation:

As for popular suffrage, it may be further remarked that especially in large states it leads inevitably to electoral indifference, since the casting of a single vote is of no significance where there is a multitude of electors.
. . . Thus the result of an institution of this kind is more likely to be the opposite of what was intended; election actually falls into the power of a few,

[20] *Ibid.* § 303. Cf. § 308, where Hegel says that if elections are based on groups, 'society is not dispersed into atomic units, collected to perform only a single and temporary act, and kept together for a moment and no longer. On the contrary, it makes the appointment as a society, articulated into associations, communities, and corporations, which although constituted already for other purposes, acquire in this way a connexion with politics.'
[21] *Ibid.* § 309.   [22] *Ibid.* § 302.

of a caucus, and so of the particular and contingent interest which is precisely what was to have been neutralized.[23]

Hegel is thus among the first political theorists to recognize that direct suffrage in a modern society would create a system very different from that envisaged by the advocates of such a system of direct representation. The emergence of the modern party fulfilled the mediating role Hegel assigned to corporations. As to the general function of the assembly of estates, Hegel sees in it an organ of control as well as the expression of the subjective aspect of freedom – public opinion:

> The Estates are a guarantee of the general welfare and public freedom ...
> The guarantee lies ... in the fact that the anticipation of criticism from the Many, particularly of public criticism, has the effect of inducing officials to devote their best attention beforehand to their duties and the schemes under consideration.[24]

The sphere of activities of the Assembly should include deliberations about problems of war and peace. Referring to the British parliamentary example, Hegel maintains that no war should be waged without the express approval of the Assembly.[25] Again basing himself on the British model as against continental examples, Hegel opposes the exclusion of crown ministers from the Assembly:

> The proposal to exclude members of the executive from legislative bodies, as for instance the Constituent Assembly did, is a consequence of false views of the state. In England, ministers must be members of parliament, and this is right, because executive officers should be linked with and not opposed to the legislature.[26]

Deliberations in the Assembly have a further function: truth comes out in a dialectical fashion and is never an *a priori* given. Debates in the Assembly, with their quality of give and take, are thus a device through which truth, and what is best for the body politic, can emerge. In a passage reminiscent of some of John Stuart Mill's later arguments, Hegel maintains that 'the idea usually dominant is that everyone knows from the start what is best for the state and that the Assembly debate is a mere discussion of this knowledge. In fact, however, the precise contrary is the truth. It is here that there first begin to develop the virtues, abilities, dexterities, which have to serve as an example to the public.'[27]

---

[23] *Ibid.* § 311. Cf. Dante Germino, 'Hegel as a Political Theorist', *The Journal of Politics* xxxi (1969), esp. pp. 900–5.
[24] *Philosophy of Right*, § 301.   [25] *Ibid.* addition to § 329.
[26] *Ibid.* addition to § 300.   [27] *Ibid.* addition to § 315.

Social classes, representation and pluralism

This is also Hegel's argument against keeping Assembly debates closed to the public; all debates should be open, for the public nature of Assembly debates is by itself an act of political education.[28] The public nature of the debate is also an excellent method of control over ministers, though 'of course such debates are irksome to ministers, who have to equip themselves with wit and eloquence to meet the criticisms there directed against them'.[29]

If the picture which thus emerges from this exposition is quite different from the one usually to be found in many accounts of Hegel's political philosophy, this is so because on this matter of representation, as on many others, commentators have preferred to limit themselves to a number of Hegel's aphorisms, sometimes quoted from secondary sources, instead of carefully making their way through the bulk of the text of the *Philosophy of Right*. It should also be borne in mind that Hegel uttered these views when there was no system of representation in Prussia and when freedom of expression was very severely limited. If one were to draw practical political conclusions from Hegel's discussion of representation, one would have to view it as a direct critique of Prussian, and generally German, conditions, with the British model as a possible desideratum. That Hegel has very little sympathy for the French experiences with representative government should not divert one's attention from the implied criticism of conditions in Prussia. And, after all, the French example does not get more than it deserves from Hegel's hands; despite all ideological pronouncements, the French model has not been particularly successful in evolving a system of representation and Hegel's criticism of it indicates some of the structural weaknesses which have bedevilled it even up to our own times.

A similar picture emerges out of Hegel's discussion of the role of corporations. Again, as in the Württemberg essay, these are not the traditional, restrictive old guilds, but voluntary organizations into which persons organize themselves according to their professions, trades and interests. The poverty of traditional democratic and liberal theory has been specifically accentuated by its hostility

[28] *Ibid.*: 'Estate Assemblies, open to the public, are a great spectacle and an excellent education for the citizens, and it is from them that the people learn best how to recognize the true character of its interests ... Publicity here is the chief means of educating the public in national affairs. A nation which has such public sittings is far more vitally related to the state than one which has no Estates Assembly or one which meets in private.'

[29] *Ibid.*

164

to any intermediate groupings standing between the individual and the state. Like Tocqueville a decade or two later, Hegel wants to redress the balance.

Hegel's point of departure is again his concern for the individual who may become atomized and alienated if left completely to himself. Once more Hegel's awareness of the nature of modern society helps him to articulate what would only later become evident, and even commonplace, to others:

Unless he is a member of an authorized corporation . . . an individual is without rank or dignity, his isolation reduces his business to mere self-seeking and his livelihood and satisfaction become insecure. Consequently, he has to try to gain recognition for himself by giving external proofs of success in his business, and to these proofs no limit can be set. He cannot live in the manner of his class, for no class really exists for him . . .

The sanctity of marriage and the dignity of corporation membership are the two fixed points round which the unorganized atoms of civil society revolve.[30]

Hegel opposes the abolition of corporations in the name of individualistic theories, and his argument is an expression of a critical realization of the perils of modern conditions:

The consideration behind the abolition of corporations in recent times is that the individual should fend for himself. But we may grant this and still hold that corporation membership does not alter a man's obligation to earn his living. Under modern political conditions, the citizens have only a restricted share in the public business of the state, yet it is essential to provide men – ethical entities – with work of a public character, over and above their private business. This work of a public character, which the modern state does not always provide, is found in the corporation.[31]

These voluntary organizations also help to channel the egoistic ends of members of civil society into a universal structure, so that even a member of the business class, who is totally immersed in his particularistic pursuits, will have to relate in some reciprocal way to other members of his trade. While he would normally view them as competitors, in the fraternity of the corporation a sense of solidarity with them (against everybody else, of course) should lay the foundations for a relation of mutuality. Because of the strength of the disruptive forces of civil society, Hegel realized that the kind of solidarity he envisaged in the state cannot be created in an unmediated way: antagonistic *bourgeois* cannot become co-operative *citoyens* without a lengthy process of mediation and *Bildung*, and the corporation is one of the prime vehicles for this political education of modern man. Without it 'fraternity' would disappear under 'liberty' and 'equality'.

[30] *Ibid.* §§ 253, 255.   [31] *Ibid.* addition to § 255.

Social classes, representation and pluralism

By educating man towards the state, corporations also institution-alized the legitimate functions of aggregated interests which should not be subsumed under the state, though they should not, on the other hand, rule it. Corporations are thus the institutionalized guarantee against state encroachment upon economic activity:

Particular interests which are common to everyone fall within civil society and lie outside the absolutely universal interest of the state proper. The administration of these is in the hands of the corporations, commercial and professional as well as municipal, and their officials, directors, managers, and the like. It is the business of these officials to manage the private property and interests of these particular spheres and, from that point of view, their authority rests on the confidence of their commonalties and professional equals.[32]

Corporations should defend the aggregate interests of their members, provide for their education and 'in short . . . to come to the scene like a second family for [their] members'.[33] One of their chief aims is to cushion their members against the contingencies and vicissitudes of civil society: 'Within the corporation the help which poverty receives loses its accidental character and the humiliation wrongfully associated with it. The wealthy perform their duties to their fellow associates and thus riches cease to in-spire either pride or envy, pride in their owners, envy in others.'[34]

Hegel takes special care to point out that corporations should not neglect to represent the interests of the poorer classes in society and observes that the poor can attain their share of power through organization. While more affluent groups in society have been well-organized, Hegel maintains that:

For some time past . . . the lower classes, the mass of the population, have been left more or less unorganized. And yet it is of the utmost importance that the masses should be organized, because only so do they become mighty and powerful. Otherwise they are nothing but a heap, an aggregate of atomic units. Only when the particular associations are organized members of the state are they possessed of legitimate power.[35]

On the other hand, the dialectical position of corporations be-tween civil society and the state calls for some sort of state super-vision of their activities and structures, 'otherwise they would ossify, build themselves in, and decline into a miserable system of castes. In and by itself, however, a corporation is not a closed caste.'[36] Like so much else in the structure of Hegel's political

[32] *Ibid.* § 288.
[33] *Ibid.* § 252.   [34] *Ibid.* § 253.
[35] *Ibid.* addition to § 290.   [36] *Ibid.* addition to § 255.

system, an interdependence of the various members of the organism is a necessary prerequisite for its proper functioning. The integrated state Hegel has in mind is a pluralistic structure in which corporations, assemblies of estates and other bodies jointly regulate each other, so that out of the warring interests of civil society, integration, leading to the state, may emerge.

IN DEFENCE OF PLURALISM

Hegel's insistence that the state embodies a higher, universal orientation in inter-human relations is premised upon the preservation of the lower, less comprehensive spheres. A wide sphere of activities should be left to individual subjective decision and personal choice. This sphere should be institutionalized, and the institutions thus safeguarding the individual's choice 'are the pillars of public freedom since in them particular freedom is realized'.[37] Though subjective freedom is not, to Hegel, the *ultima ratio* of political organization, he cannot conceive of a state that will not incorporate it and allot to it its due place. A state which will be all-encompassing, which will leave nothing to the individual, will be an empty structure:

What is of the utmost importance is that the law of reason should be shot through and through by the law of particular freedom, and that my particular freedom should become identified with the universal end, or otherwise the state is left in the air. The state is actual only when its members have a feeling of their own self-hood and it is stable only when public and private ends are identical.[38]

The effective guarantee of individual freedom lies in the distribution of social powers; though we shall later see how the classical theory of the separation of powers has little appeal for Hegel, he goes beyond a formal distribution of power to the sphere of social organization and calls for a proliferation of voluntary organizations which can counterbalance the authority of government:

The security of the state and its subjects against the misuse of power by ministers and their officials lies directly in their hierarchial organization and their answerability; but it lies too in the authority given to societies and corporations, because in itself this is a barrier against the intrusion of subjective caprice

[37] *Ibid.* § 265. See also addition to § 289, where Hegel insists on a realm of privacy to be reserved exclusively to the individual's own decision. In the addition to § 46 Hegel maintains that only in extreme cases of emergency may the state infringe upon the individual's right to private property.
[38] *Ibid.* addition to § 265.

into the power entrusted to a civil servant, and it completes from below the state control which does not reach down as far as the conduct of individuals.[39]

Even the existence of a strong middle class – which we have already seen as constituting for Hegel a guarantee for a well-ordered state – is made dependent upon social pluralism:

> It is a prime concern of the state that a middle class should be developed, but this can be done only if the state is an organic unity like the one described here, i.e. it can be done only by giving authority to spheres of particular interests, which are relatively independent, and by appointing an army of officials whose personal arbitrariness is broken against such authorized bodies. Action in accordance with everyone's rights, and the habit of such action is a consequence of the counterpoise to officialdom which independent and self-subsistent bodies create.[40]

Thus while he undoubtedly gives the bureaucracy a dominant position in his state, Hegel is much concerned to limit and balance its power. Moreover, what he understands by an 'organic' structure of a state is not the unitary image usually associated with organistic theories of political organization, but precisely its opposite – a differentiated social structure in which relatively autonomous bodies counterbalance the center.

As an example of how things should not be organized, Hegel cites the case of France. As in *The German Constitution*, the bureaucratic centralism of France, which allows no leeway for voluntary organizations and pluralism, transforms the state into a lifeless machine:

> But the result of this is that once more everything may have its source in the Minister's power, and the business of the state is, as we say, centralized. This entails the maximum of simplification, speed and efficiency in meeting state requirements. A system of this kind was introduced by the French Revolutionaries, elaborated by Napoleon, and still exists in France today. On the other hand, France lacks corporations and local government, i.e. associations wherein particular and universal interests meet. It is true that these associations won too great a measure of self-subsistence in the Middle Ages, when they were states within states and obstinately persisted in behaving like independent corporate bodies. But while this should not be allowed to happen, *we may none the less affirm that the proper strength of the state lies in these associations.* In them the executive meets with legitimate interests which it must respect.[41]

[39] *Ibid.* § 295. On another occasion, in § 289, Hegel contends that the constitutional principle of hereditary monarchy goes hand in hand with the preservation of public freedom through well-defined institutions.
[40] *Ibid.* addition to § 297.
[41] *Ibid.* addition to § 290 (my italics). In his lecture on the *Philosophy of History*, Hegel similarly remarks that 'Nowhere can people less tolerate free action on the parts of others than in France' (Sibree's translation, p. 454).

In defence of pluralism

This plea for pluralism manifests itself also in Hegel's attitude to the complex relationship between state and religion. Opposition to Catholicism as well as his own experience in the Bavarian school controversy made Hegel sensitive to church interference in public affairs, especially in matters of education. In his *Positivity of the Christian Religion* Hegel had already established his theoretical argument against vesting education in the hands of the church.[42] But his position has further consequences. Though the institutional corollary of Hegel's view on state and church leads to the separation of the two, his argument follows a unique line and does not derive from the traditional libertarian theory which finds its justification in the individual's right of choice alone.

Hegel sets out his view in a long excursus in § 270 of the *Philosophy of Right*. To Hegel, both the state and religion are two necessary moments of self-consciousness. Yet while in religion the Idea appears as mere representation, is grounded on feeling, in the state it is founded on reason. Hence the realm of the state is superior to that of the church, though the absolute truth of religion is, on the other hand, beyond the finite limits of the state as an objective, terrestrial institution. Thus the state should on no account be subservient to the church, and the unity of church and state is therefore something which characterizes an oriental despotism rather than a modern state.[43] Furthermore, it was religious disunity which brought out the true nature of the state. Only after the church had been subjected to outward division did the state as such attain 'universality of thought' against the particular sects: 'It is only as a result of that disunion that the state has been able to reach its appointed end as a self-consciously rational and ethical organization.'[44]

Hence the stronger and more mature and developed a state is, the more liberal it can be in matters of religion. Only a state sure of itself can allow people to find their own form of worship. A truly strong state may even 'tolerate a sect (though, of course, all depends on its numbers) which on religious grounds declines to recognize even its direct duties to the state'.[45]

Hegel's views on religious tolerance are quite outspoken, and it should be borne in mind that they are based neither on prudential

[42] *Early Theological Writings*, p. 107.
[43] *Philosophy of Right*, § 270: 'This often desired unity of church and state is found under oriental despotism, but an oriental despotism is not a state, or at any rate not the self-conscious form of state which is alone worthy of mind.'
[44] *Ibid.*   [45] *Ibid.*

169

grounds nor on an individualistic ethic, but on his conviction that the state as an institution bringing out the universalistic aspects of inter-human relations has to overlook the differences emanating from man's particular associations:

> It is part of education (*Bildung*), of thinking as the consciousness of the single in the form of universality, that the ego comes to be apprehended as a universal person in which all are identical. A man counts as a man in virtue of his manhood alone, not because he is a Jew, Catholic, Protestant, German, Italian, etc.[46]

The political consequences are clear for Hegel. He calls for tolerance for Quakers and Anabaptists and maintains that the state should find a way which will enable members of these sects not to serve in the army while fulfilling all other duties of citizenship.[47] In a long footnote dealing with dissenters and religious minorities, he defends at some length the Jewish claim for political and social emancipation as against both traditional Christian fundamentalists and the newly emerging secular German nationalists. Arguing against the view that the Jews should first of all shed their peculiar customs and usages before being admitted into citizenship, Hegel even makes Jewish emancipation into a criterion of whether a state is conscious of its own universal nature:

> Thus technically it may have been right to refuse a grant of even civil rights to the Jews on the ground that they should be regarded as belonging not only to a religious sect but to a foreign people (*Volk*). But the fierce outcry raised against the Jews, from that point of view and others, ignores the fact that they are, above all, *men*; and manhood, so far from being a mere superficial, abstract quality, is on the contrary itself the basis of the fact that what civil rights arouse in their possessors is the feeling of oneself as counting in civil society as a person with rights, and this feeling of self-hood, infinite and free from all restrictions, is the root from which the desired similarity in disposition and ways of thinking comes into being. To exclude the Jews from civil rights, on the other hand, would rather be to confirm the isolation with which they have been reproached – a result for which the state refusing them rights would be blamable and reproachable, because by so refusing it would have misunderstood its own basic principle, its nature as an objective and powerful institution.[48]

Few observers in Hegel's time, Jewish or Gentile, exhibited a similar awareness of the complexities surrounding the arguments about Jewish emancipation. It should again be noted that it was not until 1848 that Jews in Prussia were granted civil emancipa-

---

[46] *Ibid.*, § 209. [47] *Ibid.* § 270.
[48] *Ibid.*: In one of the rare lapses in his otherwise remarkable translation, Knox translates here *Volk* as 'race' rather than 'people'. But this reflects both later racist views about the Jews as well as a completely innocent nineteenth-century English usage, which is however wholly out of context vis-à-vis the problem Hegel is here trying to confront.

tion and that despite a general atmosphere of benevolent tolerance, Jews were not admitted into public service in Germany – and this included the teaching profession – until 1918.

This call for pluralism was a direct corollary to Hegel's theory about the various spheres of social relations and it led to numerous comments by Hegel criticizing Plato's attempt to make the state – at least as far as the Guardians were concerned – into the only legitimate social nexus. Though there obviously are a number of Platonic overtones in some aspects of Hegel's political philosophy – notably in his theory of the connection between social classes and modes of consciousness – on the basic issue of monism versus pluralism Hegel emerges very strongly as an opponent of Plato.

What is utterly lacking in Plato's *Republic*, according to Hegel, is the moment of subjective freedom. Trying to relate Plato to the intellectual and social milieu of his time, Hegel shows a rare insight into the dilemma faced by Plato which ultimately vitiated his whole attempt at constructing an ideal society:

> In his *Republic*, Plato displays the substance of ethical life in its ideal beauty and truth; but he could only cope with the principle of self-subsistent particularity, which in his day had forced its way into Greek ethical life, by setting up in opposition to it his purely substantial state. He absolutely excluded it from his state, even in its very beginnings in private property and the family, as well as in its more mature form as the subjective will, the choice of a social position, and so forth . . .
> Plato wished to exclude particularity from his state, but this is no help.[49]

Since property is to Hegel the prime condition for personality, implied in the element of recognition which appears in property as an external object, the abolition of private property by Plato spells for Hegel the disappearance and emasculation of personality: 'The general principle that underlies Plato's ideal state violates the right of personality by forbidding the holding of private property.'[50]

Plato's insistence that people should have their roles determined for them by the state implies that ultimately there is no civil society in his system: 'In Plato's state, subjective freedom does not count, because people have their occupations assigned to them by the Guardians. In many oriental states, this assignment is determined by birth. But subjective freedom, which must be respected, demands that individuals should have free choice in this matter.'[51]

[49] *Ibid.* § 185 and addition.   [50] *Ibid.* § 46.
[51] *Ibid.* addition to § 262. Cf. also § 299, where Plato's commonwealth is compared to an oriental despotism.

This lack of social mobility is common to Plato and the Indian caste system, in both of which 'the principle of subjective particularity was . . . denied its rights'. Hegel's own theory of social classes, on the other hand, stresses the principle of mobility and the idea of an open society:

> The question of the particular class to which an individual is to belong is one on which natural capacity, birth and other circumstances have their influence, though the essential final determining factors are subjective opinion and the individual's arbitrary will, which win in this sphere their right, their merit, and their dignity.[52]

Hegel's critique of Plato's *Republic* is thus identical with the views of those contemporary observers who see Plato as one of the forerunners of totalitarianism. Without using the term, Hegel expressly accuses Plato of wishing to subsume all particularisms under the totality of the universal – whereas his own solution attempts to integrate particularism into a legitimate, though clearly delineated, autonomous sphere:

> It might seem that universal ends would be more readily attainable if the universal absorbed the strength of the particulars in the way described, for instance, in Plato's *Republic*. But this, too, is only an illusion, since both universal and particular turn into one another and exist only for and by means of one another.[53]

A further aspect of Hegel's theory about the need for a differentiated and pluralistic structure has to do with public opinion. Here there is an obvious ambiguity in Hegel's views which has to be traced not only to the dialectical structure of his thought, but also to the extreme delicacy with which such a subject had to be approached in the wake of the Carlsbad Decrees and the prevalence of quite strict censorship. Even so, Hegel's attitude represents such a sophisticated view of public opinion that it strikes one today as even more remarkable than it must have sounded to Hegel's own contemporaries. Compared to it, so much of the conventional wisdom of orthodox liberal thought appears trite, jejune and even banal.

What Hegel says about the legal aspects of public opinion seems nowadays commonplace, though one has again to recall that it

[52] *Ibid.* § 206.
[53] *Ibid.* addition to § 184. This critique of Plato can be found in Hegel's early writings as well. After criticizing the ancient polis for its subsumption of the individual under the beautiful totality of public *virtus*, Hegel says (*Realphilosophie II*, p. 251): 'Plato's republic is, like the Lacaedemonian state, this disappearance of the self-conscious individual.'

required some courage to advocate in his circumstances 'the freedom of public communication – of the press and the spoken word'.[54]

There are, however, qualifications and Hegel enumerates the following as being beyond the pale of the freedom of expression: 'slander, libel, abuse, the contemptuous caricature of government, its ministers, officials, and in particular the monarch, defiance of the laws, incitement to rebellion'. Though this leaves open too much that is questionable, all liberal Western legal systems have clauses even today that fit quite well into the limits imposed by Hegel on freedom of speech and communication.

However, what is remarkable in Hegel's discussion of public opinion is his awareness of the specific modernity of it and its central position in modern society. Furthermore, since the modern state is based on the principle of subjectivity come to consciousness, and public opinion is the expression of subjectivity, the two are interrelated. Public opinion and the modern state belong to each other:

At all times public opinion has been a great power and it is particularly so in our day when the principle of subjective freedom has such importance and significance. What is to be authoritative nowadays derives its authority, not at all from force, only to a small extent from habit and custom, really from insight and argument.[55]

Yet, according to Hegel, there is an inherent tension in public opinion: as an aggregate of the bulk of various individual opinions, it is unwieldy and unstructured and hence, though it represents subjective freedom, it may be contradictory, disoriented and incoherent:

The formal subjective freedom of individuals consists of their having and expressing their own private judgements, opinions, and recommendations on affairs of state. This freedom is collectively manifested as what is called 'public opinion', in which what is absolutely universal, the substantive and the true, is linked with its opposite, the purely particular and private opinions of the Many. Public opinion as it exists is thus a standing self-contradiction, knowledge as appearance, the essential just as directly present as the inessential.[56]

[54] *Philosophy of Right*, § 319.
[55] *Ibid.* addition to § 316. Cf. addition to § 317: 'The principle of the modern world requires that what anyone is to recognize shall reveal itself as something entitled to recognition.' Hegel further adds that enforced silence causes people to 'bottle up their objections, whereas argument gives them an outlet and a measure of satisfaction'. Hence in France 'freedom of speech has turned out far less dangerous than enforced silence'. Hegel is here quite openly criticizing conditions in Prussia and advocating, though on purely prudential grounds in this instance, the relatively more liberal approach of post-1815 France.   [56] *Ibid.* § 316.

Social classes, representation and pluralism

In his discussion of parliamentary debates, Hegel has already made the point that truth emerges dialectically from the harsh clash of contending opinions. But this means that the conglomerate of public opinion is not, in any way, sacrosanct and it includes the false and the trivial just as much as the truthful and the sublime. Because a view is held by some members of the public, or, put otherwise, because it is part of public opinion, is not in itself a warranty for its intrinsic worth. Though Hegel believes that all opinions should be heard, and none should be suppressed, the immediate result may be a rather confusing cacophony, where every view, silly, dishonest and venal as it may be, appears to rank equally with the most profound and responsible opinion:

> Public opinion, therefore, is a repository not only of genuine needs and correct tendencies of common life, but also, in the form of common sense ... of the eternal, substantive principles of justice, the true content and result of legislation, the whole constitution ... At the same time ... it becomes infected by all the accidents of opinion, by its ignorance and perversity, by its mistakes and falsity of judgement.[57]

This leads Hegel to his ambivalent conclusion that 'public opinion therefore deserves to be as much respected as despised – despised for its concrete expression and for the concrete consciousness it expresses, respected for its essential basis, a basis which only glimmers more or less dimly in that concrete expression'.[58] Though this may leave one quite perplexed, it is meant to bring out Hegel's feeling that public opinion cannot be summed up under the harmonistic and simple-minded rubric of *vox populi, vox dei*. Few nineteenth-century thinkers were aware of this ambiguity inherent in the media of modern communication – something of which we today are much more conscious. Yet Hegel does indicate that there is a way out of the cacophonous confusion of public opinion. For him it is the test of political leadership to be able to discern between the false and the true in public opinion. Political leadership has, to Hegel, an ambivalent relation to public opinion: on the one hand, it has to express it, on the other, it should lead it; on the one hand, a political leader should bow to the wishes of the led, while on the other, he should be discriminating enough to disregard immediate public opinion, and be strong enough to claim that the latest editorial in a daily paper may not be the ultimate expression of the consummate wisdom of the community. Hegel offers no criteria to the political leader by which he should decide what is passing and

[57] *Ibid.* § 317.   [58] *Ibid.* § 318.

174

In defence of pluralism

what is eternal in the opinions of the day. But the scenario is fascinating, representing as it were Hegel's own attempt to reach a position which could be justified by a dialectical synthesis of will and reason. The whole complexity of what constitutes rational freedom in public choice seems to be encapsulated in Hegel's seemingly contradictory statement about the relationship of political leadership and public opinion:

Thus to be independent of public opinion is the first formal condition of achieving anything great or rational whether in life or in science. Great achievement is assured, however, of subsequent recognition and grateful acceptance by public opinion, which in due course will make it one of its own prejudices.

Public opinion contains all kinds of falsity and truth, but it takes a great man to find the truth in it. The great man of the age is the one who can put into words the will of his age, tell his age what its will is, and accomplish it. What he does is the heart and the essence of his age, he actualizes it. The man who lacks sense enough to despise public opinion expressed in gossip will never do anything great.[59]

Napoleon must have been in Hegel's mind when writing these words, and though a bit of hero-worship is obviously apparent here, this emerges after all in the context of a discussion about public opinion, amid Hegel's insistence that it should be guaranteed 'by laws and by-laws'.[60] Again, Hegel seemed to be nearer to an understanding of the *Zeitgeist* of the modern age than most of his contemporaries, few of whom sensed the intensely ambiguous and dialectical relationship about to evolve in modern society between political leadership and public opinion.

[59] *Ibid.* and addition.   [60] *Ibid.* § 319.

175

Chapter Nine

THE STATE – THE CONSCIOUSNESS OF FREEDOM

THE HIEROGLYPH OF REASON

Any discussion of Hegel's theory of state proper has to contend with a prevalent built-in preconception holding that Hegel advocated an authoritarian, if not outright totalitarian, form of government. The preceding chapters have attempted to show how far from the truth such a simple-minded explication of Hegel's political theory is. Now that we arrive at the core of Hegel's theory of the state proper, as expounded in the *Philosophy of Right*, a further caveat should be registered about the construction of Hegel's statements regarding the role of the state.

Of Hegel's statements the one which perhaps more than any other has been responsible for creating the above-mentioned pre-conception appears in the addition to § 258. In the original German it reads as follows: 'Es ist der Gang Gottes in der Welt, dass der Staat ist.' This has been variously rendered into English as 'The State is the march of God through the world',[1] 'The existence of the State is the presence of God upon earth',[2] or 'The march of God in the world, that is what the state is'.[3]

The implications are clear, yet none of these translations is adequate. Hegel's German syntax is undoubtedly slightly curious in this sentence and this may be attributed to the fact that the sentence comes from an 'addition', i.e. from a text not included in Hegel's own edition of the *Rechtsphilosophie*, but added by his posthumous editor, Eduard Gans, from notebooks of students who attended Hegel's lectures. As Kaufmann has recently shown, a

---

[1] Hegel, *Selections*, ed. J. Loewenberg (New York, 1929), p. 443.
[2] In E. F. Carritt's article on 'Hegel and Prussianism', reprinted in Kaufmann's *Hegel's Political Philosophy*, p. 36.
[3] Knox's translation, p. 279. A further variant is: 'It is the course of God through the world that constitutes the state'; in *The Philosophy of Hegel*, ed. C. J. Friedrich (New York, 1953), p. 283.

correct translation of this sentence would have to read 'It is the way of God in the world, that there should be [literally: is] the state.'[4] What Hegel meant to say was not that the state is the 'March of God' on earth or anything of this nature, but that the very existence of the state is part of a divine strategy, not a merely human arbitrary artefact. One may, of course, argue with such a view but it has none of the odious overtones attributed to Hegel by all those other translators who have read into him a message that most clearly, whatever the failings of the syntax, was not there. Were this just a matter of a mistranslation, it would be pointless to waste time on it; but this misconstrued rendering of Hegel's phrase became in the critical literature an irrefutable proof of the authoritarianism inherent in Hegel's theory of the state.

Furthermore, it has to be pointed out that on no account can Hegel's theory be so construed as to refer to any existing state; it is the *idea* of the state with which Hegel is dealing and any existing state cannot be anything but a mere approximation to the idea.[5] On the level of historical evidence we have already seen that Hegel's attitude to Prussia was far from that of quietistic acceptance; what has to be stressed is that on theoretical grounds also, the idea of the state could not be identified with any given state, just as the model of civil society could not be identical with the working of any actual market mechanism. In the same paragraph as that from which the preceding much mistranslated sentence has been taken, Hegel is very explicit about this:

In considering the idea of the state, we must not have our eyes on particular states or on particular institutions ... On some principle or other, any state may be shown to be bad, this or that defect may be found in it ... The state is no ideal work of art; it stands on earth and so in the sphere of caprice, chance and error, and bad behaviour may disfigure it in many respects. But the ugliest of men, or a criminal, or an invalid, or a cripple, is still a living man. The affirmative, life, subsists despite his defects, and it is this affirmative which is our theme here.[6]

It is this which Hegel means when he refers to the state as a 'hieroglyph of reason'[7] which has to be deciphered through a discarding of the accidental and arbitrary, beneath which the rational and the essential is then to be found.

[4] Kaufmann, *Hegel's Political Philosophy*, p. 279.
[5] J. N. Findlay, *The Philosophy of Hegel*, 2nd printing (New York, 1966), p. 326; cf. Rosenkranz, *Hegels Leben*, p. 332.
[6] *Philosophy of Right*, addition to § 258.
[7] *Ibid.* addition to § 279.

The state – the consciousness of freedom

The rationality which permeates the world of man becomes apparent for the first time in the state, Hegel argues. In the family, it is still hidden behind feeling and sentiment; in civil society it appears as an instrumentality of individual self-interest. Only in the sphere of the state does reason become conscious of itself; in other words, only in the state are the actions of man one with his intentions – man knows what he wants and acts according to it:

The state is the actuality of the ethical idea. It is ethical mind *qua* the substantial will manifest and revealed to itself, knowing and thinking itself, accomplishing what it knows and in so far as it knows it . . . Self-consciousness . . . finds in the state, as its essence and the end and product of its activity, its substantive freedom.[8]

This is the ethical moment in the state, the unity of subjective consciousness and the objective order: 'The substantial order, in the self-consciousness which it has thus actually attained in individuals, knows itself and so is an object of knowledge.'[9] Human activity in the state is thus motivated by the recognition that what is being ordered has its ultimate source in the subjective will: law is not an external imposition, which has subsequently to be legitimized in one way or another, but an expression of the individual's will:

On the other hand [the laws] are not something alien to the subject. On the contrary, his spirit bears witness to them as to its own essence, the essence in which he has a feeling of his own self-hood, and in which he lives on in his own element which is not distinguished from himself. The subject is thus directly linked to the ethical order by a relation which is more like an identity than even the relation of faith or trust.[10]

The political consequences of such a view are made abundantly clear by Hegel: 'Now to say that men allow themselves to be ruled counter to their own interests, ends and intentions is preposterous.'[11] And elsewhere he remarks:

When we walk the streets at night in safety, it does not strike us that this might be otherwise. This habit of feeling safe has become second nature, and we do not reflect on just how this is due solely to the working of special institutions. Commonplace thinking often has the impression that force holds the state together, but in fact its only bond is the fundamental sense of order which everybody possesses.[12]

This conscious identity of the subject and the state is a condition for the adequate functioning of the commonwealth. When this

[8] *Ibid.* § 257.
[9] *Ibid.* § 146; cf. also § 144. [10] *Ibid.* § 147.
[11] *Ibid.* addition to § 281. [12] *Ibid.* addition to § 268.

consciousness of identity does not work, the state is in danger of falling apart:

> The state is actual only when its members have a feeling of their own self-hood and it is stable only when the public and private ends are identical. It has often been said that the end of the state is the happiness of its citizens. This is perfectly true. If all is not well with them, if their subjective aims are not satisfied, if they do not find that the state as such is the means to their satisfaction, then the footing of the state itself is insecure.[13]

Patriotism, Hegel remarks, is not only a readiness for exceptional sacrifices in times of emergency; it is rather my knowledge that I am fulfilled through my living in communion with other human beings, in 'the consciousness that my interests, both substantive and particular, are contained and preserved in another's (i.e. in the state's) interests and ends, i.e. in the other's relations to me as an individual'.[14] The secret of patriotism, according to Hegel, lies in the citizens' realization 'that they know the state as their substance, because it is the state that maintains their particular spheres of interest together with the title, authority and welfare of these'.[15]

In a statement strongly reminiscent of Rousseau, Hegel remarks that 'in the state, as something ethical, as the inter-penetration of the substantive and the particular, my obligation to what is substantive is at the same time the embodiment of my particular freedom'.[16] In this identity of the universal and the particular will, Hegel adds, 'right and duty coalesce', since a man 'has rights insofar as he has duties, and duties insofar as he has rights'.[17]

The state, then, is based on rational freedom, organized in such a way as to enable each to realize his freedom in conjunction with others, while in civil society one can realize one's ends only by disregarding everyone else's aims. Hence the purely individualistic concept of freedom, which maintains no limits on one's arbitrary choice, has to be superseded by the ethical order which makes my freedom dependent on that of the other. The state is 'freedom universal and objective'.[18] Yet the idea of the state is not given, but is the consequence of historical development; hence it is only in the modern era that the element of subjectivity, of freedom, appears in the state; this element was absent from the ancient polis: 'In the states of antiquity, ethical life had not grown into this free system of an objective order self-subsistently developed, and

---

[13] *Ibid.* addition to § 265.
[14] *Ibid.* § 268.
[15] *Ibid.* § 289.
[16] *Ibid.* § 261.
[17] *Ibid.* § 155.
[18] *Ibid.* § 33.

consequently it was by the personal genius of individuals that this defect had to be made good.'[19]

Thus we arrive at the modern state which is based on the principle of subjectivity. In his lectures on the *Philosophy of History* Hegel suggests how the emergence of the principle of subjectivity gradually developed through the successive stages of Christianity and then through the Reformation and the French Revolution.[20] While in the ancient polis subjectivity was subsumed under the unmediated universality of the political, in feudalism the particular will managed to subsume the universal, the state; only the modern state succeeds in synthesizing these two moments within its differentiated structure:

The principle of modern states has prodigious strength and depth because it allows the principle of subjectivity to progress to its culmination in the extreme of self-subsistent personal particularity, and yet at the same time brings it back to the substantive unity and maintains this unity in the principle of subjectivity itself . . .

The essence of the modern state is that the universal be bound up with the complete freedom of its particular members and with private well-being . . . The universal must be furthered, but subjectivity on the other hand must attain its full and living development. It is only when both these moments subsist in their strength that the state can be regarded as articulated and genuinely organized.[21]

Seen from another angle, this implies that in modern society the political relationship of man becomes the dominant relationship, 'the principle of the modern state requires that the whole of an individual's activity shall be mediated through his will'.[22] This autonomy of the will, expressed in political institutions, means the politicization of life. Not that the non-political spheres cease to exist; on the contrary, we have seen how Hegel insists on the necessity of the existence of autonomous, voluntary bodies and how the non-political spheres of human life – the family, civil society and, in this context, the church as well – should lead a life that is separate from and independent of the state. Yet it is a political decision that it be so and hence the pluralism advocated by Hegel

[19] *Ibid.* § 150. Cf. addition to § 261: 'In the states of antiquity the subjective end simply coincided with the state's will. In modern times, however, we make claims for private judgement, private willing, and private conscience.'
[20] *Philosophy of History*, pp. 413–37, 438–57.
[21] *Philosophy of Right*, § 260, and addition. The addition then continues: 'Immature states are those in which the idea of the state is still veiled and where its particular determinations have not yet attained free self-subsistence.'
[22] *Ibid.* addition to § 299.

should not divert attention from the fact that it coexists with a pronounced primacy of the political. It is this primacy which many commentators have mistakenly taken to reveal the authoritarian moment in Hegel. Though such an interpretation is erroneous, it does not, of course, mean that Hegel's position is that of classical liberalism. While the latter was always, to various degrees, suspicious of the state and saw its structures at best as guarantees for individual liberty, the existence of which was anchored outside the state, Hegel's vision of the state invests it with the positive role of being itself the embodiment of man's self-consciousness.

This, however, also reflects the potentially critical attitude Hegel develops against the state. The state embodies man's highest relationship to other human beings yet this function of the state is conditional, not absolute. In order to qualify for such a role, the state has to reflect the individual's self-consciousness. Hence not every state qualifies for those attributes with which Hegel invests the idea of the state. Furthermore, it is the way the institutions of the state are organized which determines whether individual self-consciousness does or does not find its adequate expression in any individual state:

The state is absolutely rational inasmuch as it is the actuality of the substantial will which it possesses in the particular self-consciousness once that consciousness has been raised to consciousness of its universality. This substantial unity is an absolute unmoved end in itself, in which freedom comes into its supreme right. On the other hand, this final end has a supreme right against the individual, whose supreme duty is to be a member of the state.[23]

External conformity with the law, however, is by itself an empty ritual, since it lacks the moment of consciousness.[24] When Hegel says in the preface to the *Philosophy of Right* that the state is 'reason as it actualized itself in the element of self-consciousness',[25] this implies that institutions are not conceived as external coercive organs but become extensions of man's own self-consciousness:

The state is the actuality of concrete freedom. But concrete freedom consists in this, that personal individuality and its particular interests not only achieve their complete development and gain explicit recognition for their gift (as they do in the sphere of the family and civil society) but, for one thing, they also pass over of their own accord into the interest of the universal, and, for another thing, they know and will the universal ... The result is that the universal does not prevail or achieve completion except along with particular interests and through co-operation of particular knowing and willing; and individuals likewise do not live as private persons for their own ends alone, but in the very act of

[22] *Ibid.* § 258.   [24] *Ibid.* addition to § 150.   [25] *Ibid.* p. 4.

willing these they will be universal in light of the universal, and their activity is consciously aimed at none but the universal.[26]

Despite this, Hegel is aware that from the point of view of the individual's purely private interests the state may sometimes appear as an external necessity,[27] and, in fact, we have encountered a similar notion in the *Realphilosophie*. But beyond this external appearance, the state is immanent in the individual's self-consciousness to the extent that a person needs the other for the recognition of his own personality. The same applies to the concept of duty, which Hegel sees as a restriction only in a purely external sense. Echoing a Kantian theme – though in a different institutional context – Hegel maintains that man's freedom can express itself only through overcoming abstraction and becoming concreticized in a relationship:

The bond of duty can appear as a restriction only on indeterminate subjective or abstract freedom, and on the impulses either of the natural will or of the moral will which determines its indeterminate good arbitrarily. The truth is, however, that in duty the individual finds his liberation; first, liberation from dependence on mere natural impulse and from the depression which as a particular subject he cannot escape in his moral reflections on what ought to be and what might be; secondly, liberation from the indeterminate subjectivity which, never reaching reality or the objective determinacy of action, remains self-enclosed and devoid of actuality. In duty the individual acquires his substantive freedom.[28]

A critical element appears again in this context when Hegel uses his distinction between *Wirklichkeit* and *Dasein* to suggest that a state in which the unity of the particular and the universal is lacking, i.e. a 'bad' state, belongs merely to the realm of *Dasein* and hence lacks the characteristic of rationality:

The state is actual, and its actuality consists in this, that the interest of the whole is realized in and through particular ends. Actuality is always the unity of universal and particular . . . Where this unity is not present, a thing is not actual even though it may have acquired existence. A bad state is one which merely exists; a sick body exists too, but it has no genuine reality . . .[29]

This also explains the ground for Hegel's attack on the three theoretical pillars of the Restoration – Savigny, Müller and Haller. In all three Hegel discerns a political philosophy which ultimately bases the state on prescription and power and on an uncritical

[26] *Ibid.* § 260.
[27] *Ibid.* § 261.
[28] *Ibid.* § 149. Cf. addition to § 155: 'A slave can have no duties; only a free man has them.'
[29] *Ibid.* addition to § 270.

acceptance of 'positive' existence as it is. In a long footnote attacking von Haller's *Restauration der Staatswissenschaften* Hegel characterizes Haller's traditionalism as 'dispensing with thought' and imbued with a 'hatred of all laws and legislation'. He goes on to say that: 'The hatred of law, of right made determinate in law, is the shibboleth whereby fanaticism, flabby-mindedness, and the hypocrisy of good intentions are clearly and infallibly recognized for what they are, disguise themselves as they may.'[30]

Haller's rejection of the rationality of codification basically implies that might is right and that the animal kingdom is the paradigm for political society. According to Haller, 'this, therefore, is the eternal, unalterable, ordinance of God, that the mightier rule, must rule and will always rule . . . [To Haller] it is not that might of justice and ethics, but only the irrational power of brute force.'[31] Hegel does concede that it is possible that historical states did arise as a consequence of force, but 'the question of the form in which they arose or were introduced is entirely irrelevant to a consideration of their rational basis'.[32] For Hegel, Haller's ultimate mistake is that he takes everything that ever happened in an undifferentiated way as an overall legitimization for the future; there is no developmental criterion and nothing can be overcome, changed or elevated to a higher plane. The most primitive stage of human history appears as legitimizing present-day conduct.

It is in the context of his argument with Haller that Hegel makes an interesting comment about Rousseau. Since he himself acknowledges that the modern state is based on will, he cannot but give Rousseau his due credit:

The merit of Rousseau's contribution to the search for this [philosophical concept of the state] is that, by adducing the will as the principle of the state, he is adducing a principle which has thought for both its form and its content, a principle indeed which is thinking itself, not a principle, like gregarious instinct, for instance, or divine authority, which has thought as its form only.[33]

[30] *Ibid.* § 258. Cf. § 219: 'To regard the introduction of a legal system no more than an optional act of grace or favour on the part of monarchs and governments (as Herr von Haller does) is a piece of mere thoughtlessness. The point is that legal and political institutions are rational in principle and therefore absolutely necessary.'
[31] *Ibid.* § 258. Cf. Wilhelm Metzger, *Gesellschaft, Recht und Staat in der Ethik des deutschen Idealismus*, new ed. (Aalen, 1966), esp. pp. 251–78; Carl Schmitt, *Politische Romantik* (München and Berlin, 1925). For further remarks by Hegel on Haller, see *Berliner Schriften*, pp. 678–84.
[32] *Philosophy of Right*, § 219.
[33] *Ibid.* § 258.

The state – the consciousness of freedom

This, however, is accompanied by a reservation which points to what Hegel saw as Rousseau's main limitation, viz. that he put no rein on the purely individualistic will. It seems that here Hegel misses the significance of Rousseau's distinction between *la volonté générale* and *la volonté des tous*. Hegel apparently sees Rousseau's 'general will' as a pure aggregate of individual wills and overlooks the fact that it represents a higher, community-oriented level of consciousness, transcending the 'lower' will which is oriented towards merely individual goals. Be that as it may, Hegel's critique of Rousseau provides at least an indication of the dialectical way in which Hegel conceived the place of the individual will in the state. For him, it is the basis of the state, yet it has to be *aufgehoben* – transcended and preserved – on the level at which individuals will each others' goals, i.e. the common weal, and not only their own, particular good.[34]

It is to this purely individualistically oriented will that Hegel attributes the basic fallacy which expressed itself in the extremist tendencies of the French Revolution. The idea that it was possible to abstract from historical reality and construct a political order according to the mere will of an aggregate of human beings led to the chaos and terror in which such utopian dreams had ultimately to end:

For this reason, when these abstract conclusions came into power they afforded for the first time in human history the prodigious spectacle of the overthrow of the constitution of a great actual state and its complete reconstruction *ab initio* on the basis of pure thought alone, after the destruction of all existing and given material. The will of its refounders was to give it what they alleged was a purely rational basis, but it was only abstractions that were being used; the Idea was lacking; and the experiment ended in the maximum of frightfulness and terror.[35]

On a parallel level, one has to note Hegel's warning not to view the state as a contract, terminable at will: 'We are already citizens of the state by birth, the rational end of man is life in the state.'[36] Man is a *zoön politikon* and severing him from his political relationships diminishes his humanity.

It is in this sense that Hegel views his own idea of the state, especially as expressed in § 258, as transcending the political philosophies of both revolution and restoration.

[34] *Ibid.* [35] *Ibid.* [36] *Ibid.* addition to § 75.

The state – the consciousness of freedom

THE CONSTITUTION AND THE MONARCHY

Hegel's discussion of the constitutional structure of the state centers round the idea of the monarchy and his conception of the monarchy has a number of peculiarities which it is worthwhile to discuss in some detail.

The kind of monarchy Hegel has in mind is one that is moving away from the absolutist and authoritarian tradition towards that of a limited form of constitutional monarchy: 'The development of the state to constitutional monarchy is the achievement of the modern world.'[37] This system cannot, however, be imposed *a priori* on any given society; rather, it is an outgrowth of a whole sub-structure of institutions and mores and any attempt to impose the form of a constitutional monarchy on a society as yet unripe for it is doomed to failure. Hegel relates how Napoleon gave the Spaniards a constitution that was far more rational than the one they had possessed earlier, but 'they recoiled from it as from something alien, because they were not yet educated up to its level'.[38] In the same paragraph Hegel states that 'the constitution of any given nation depends in general on the character and development of its self-consciousness . . . A nation's constitution must embody its feeling for its rights and its position, otherwise, there may be a constitution there in an external way, but it is meaningless and valueless.'

This view, with its heavy indebtedness to Montesquieu, implies the possibility and necessity of over-all social change as a pre-requisite for political development; and Hegel draws examples to this effect from English and German constitutional history. In holding this view, Hegel brings out his dialectical understanding of the nature of historical change; but his statement is also a reflection of his opposition to violent change, which in his view lacks this dialectical dimension: 'Hence the advance from one state of affairs to another is tranquil in appearance and unnoticed. In this way a constitution changes over a period of time into something quite different from what it was originally.'[39]

Hegel's espousal of the constitutional monarchy as his model of the modern state raises the problem of the separation of powers. Here Hegel's view diverges, as one might expect, from any orthodox interpretation of the theory of the separation of powers. Though

[37] *Ibid.* § 273.
[38] *Ibid.* addition to § 274. Also: 'Every nation has the constitution appropriate to it and suitable for it.'   [39] *Ibid.* addition to § 298.

he praises the principle of the division of powers as 'the guarantee of public freedom',[40] he opposes any system which would like to achieve a separation of powers by investing each political *institution* with a separate and exclusive *function*. This Hegel dismisses as an abstraction worthy of 'understanding', not of reason. What Hegel is looking for is a system wherein each power would, in a fashion, include within itself all the others as well. Such an organic interdependence would ensure that the function of mutual limitation would not obliterate the function of integration:

The powers of the state, then, must certainly be distinguished, but each of them must build itself inwardly into a whole and contain in itself the other moments. When we speak of the distinct activities of these powers, we must not slip into the monstrous error of so interpreting their distinction as to suppose that each power should subsist independently in abstraction from the others.[41]

In a way this may not be all that different from what ultimately became constitutional practice in the United States, where the President came to have a share in legislation, while the Senate, through its power to confirm or block appointments and through its powerful committees, achieved a voice in administration. Hegel expressly wants to distinguish between the legislative and the judiciary functions – his opposition to customary, unwritten law even rests on this principle, since under a system of customary law the judge is, for all practical purposes, the legislator, and this Hegel believes to be pernicious and unacceptable.[42]

Yet the classification of the various powers is slightly different from that of the customary three powers as envisaged by Montesquieu and it is here that the special role Hegel assigns to the monarch becomes apparent. The powers are:

(a) the power to determine and establish the universal – the Legislature;
(b) the power to subsume single cases and the spheres of particularity under the universal – the Executive;
(c) the power of subjectivity, as the will with the power of ultimate decision – the Crown. In the Crown, the different powers are bound into an individual unity which is thus at once the apex and basis of the whole, i.e. of the constitutional monarchy.[43]

The monarchy is thus basic to Hegel's political structure but the way he conceives of it is unique and rather different from the views

---

[40] *Ibid.* § 272.
[41] *Ibid.* addition to § 272. Hegel advocated the identical view in his 'System der Sittlichkeit', *Schriften zur Politik*, pp. 489–90.
[42] *Philosophy of Right*, § 211.
[43] *Ibid.* § 273. Similarly the legislature deals not only with legislation proper but also concerns itself (§ 298) 'with the content of home affairs'.

prevalent among the political theorists of the Restoration, who saw the monarchy as rooted in the principle of legitimacy and divine right. In his critique of Haller, Hegel makes short shrift of the claim for divine right; Montesquieu's views on the monarchy, on the other hand, he sees as steeped in the feudal tradition, 'in which relationships recognized in the constitutional law are crystallized into the rights of private property'.[44] To Hegel, the monarchy integrates the various moments of the constitution and brings out the element of self-determination upon which the modern state is founded:

> The power of the Crown contains in itself the three moments of the whole, viz. (α) the *universality* of the constitution and the laws; (β) counsel, which refers the *particular* to the universal; and (γ) the moment of ultimate decision, as the *self-determination* to which everything else reverts and from which everything else derives the beginning of its actuality.[45]

This is an unusual and highly original way of looking at the monarchy. Since the modern state is, according to Hegel, based on subjectivity, on self-determination, there has to be an expression of this subjectivity in the objective institutions of the state:

> The truth of subjectivity . . . is attained only in a subject, and the truth of personality only in a person; . . . Hence this absolutely decisive moment of the whole is not individuality in general, but a single individual, the monarch . . .
>
> This last re-absorbs all particularity into its single self, cuts short the weighing of pros and cons between which it lets itself oscillate perpetually now this way and now that, and by saying 'I will' makes its decision and so inaugurates all activity and actuality.[46]

Herein lies the paradox of Hegel's theory of the monarchy. While keeping the traditional form of the monarchy, Hegel divests the monarch himself of any real power by making the Crown into the symbol of self-determination. Hegel, it seems, thought that the only effective way of combating the old absolutist idea of the monarchy and the legitimist theories of the Restoration would be to keep the form of the monarchy as a symbol for the modern political idea of subjectivity and self-determination. Undoubtedly this is in tune with Hegel's own views, quoted earlier, about political change which, he maintains, occurs 'unnoticed'.

Here Hegel formulates what was to become a famous simile – comparing the monarch's function to that of dotting the 'i's:

---

[44] *Ibid.* § 273. For Hegel's argument against the divine right theorists, see addition to § 281.
[45] *Ibid.* § 275.   [46] *Ibid.* § 279.

The state – the consciousness of freedom

In a completely organized state, it is only a question of the culminating point of formal decision. [The monarch] has only to say 'yes' and dot the 'i', because the throne should be such that the significant in its holder is not his particular make-up ... In a well-organized monarchy, the objective aspect belongs to the law alone, and the monarch's part is merely to set to the law the subjective 'I will'.[47]

The king can thus be both essential – without him the 'i's go undotted – but also ultimately trivial. Hence the system of primogeniture is as good as any other in securing royal succession. If some rational faculties were to be required of the monarch, primogeniture would be a haphazard system; but anyone can say 'I will', provided there is agreement about who this individual should be and the hereditary principle guarantees continuity and acceptance. One has the impression that Hegel must have had his tongue in his cheek when writing, for example, the following:

What is more difficult is to apprehend this 'I will' as a person. To do so is not to say that the monarch may act capriciously. *As a matter of fact, he is bound by the concrete decisions of his counsellors, and if the constitution is stable, he has often no more to do than sign his name.* But this name is important. It is the last word beyond which it is impossible to go ...

This 'I will' constitutes the great difference between the ancient world and the modern, and in the great edifice of the state it must therefore have its appropriate objective existence.[48]

The king is thus a mere symbol of the unity of the state. While ministers and officials are answerable for their actions, he is not.[49] Ministers and officials are appointed on the basis of their capabilities; but everyone can be king, and that is how it should be. The king should be above the strife of the various contending forces in society. This is a theory of the monarchy which, at the time Hegel formulated it, was far from being actualized anywhere in Europe. It is surely not a paradigm of the Prussian monarchy and only later, in the nineteenth century, was it to slowly evolve:

In this unity lies the actual unity of the state, and it is only through this ... that the unity of the state is saved from the risk of being drawn into the sphere of particularity and its caprices, ends, opinions, and saved too from the war of factions round the throne and from the enfeeblement and overthrow of the powers of the state.[50]

[47] *Ibid.* addition to § 280.
[48] *Ibid.* addition to § 279 (my italics). In earlier times, Hegel says, the oracle fulfilled the same function of absolute subjectivity. The irony of this statement could not have been lost on his contemporaries when they compared it with the lofty claims of Adam Müller and Ludwig von Haller for the monarchical principle. [49] *Ibid.* § 284.
[50] *Ibid.* § 281. Hegel adds that 'monarchs are not exactly distinguished for their bodily prowess or intellectual gifts'.

The constitution and the monarchy

This elevated and neutralized nature of the monarchy would also resolve, according to Hegel, the traditional dichotomy between classical democracy and classical monarchism. 'The principle of the modern world', Hegel maintains, 'is freedom of subjectivity'; classical democracy was as one-sided as classical monarchy. Hence, he goes on, 'Which is the better form of government, monarchy or democracy? We may only say that all constitutional forms are one-sided unless they can sustain in themselves the principle of free subjectivity and know how to correspond with a matured rationality.'[51]

The parallel controversy about popular versus royal sovereignty is similarly overcome according to Hegel by positing the state as such, and not one of its institutions or parts, as the bearer of sovereignty.[52]

Of all Hegel's political writings, it is in the *Philosophy of Right* that the role of the monarchy is most minimal. During the rule of Napoleon, Hegel attributed to the great Emperor a much more central role than he did to the Prussian monarch. While paying tribute to its symbolic role, Hegel opposes any attempt to invest the monarchy with the reality of power or to ground its position on legitimist arguments: a powerful monarch becomes himself a party in the political struggle. The Prussian age of reform under vom Stein and Hardenberg might have given rise to a hope that the monarchy was moving in such a direction; but the resurgence of a legitimist, Christian and romanticist view of the monarchy in Prussia in the 1830s, under the aegis of Friedrich Wilhelm IV, also led to a repudiation of Hegel's theory of the monarchy. It was at that time, immediately after Hegel's death, that numerous tracts and pamphlets were published in Germany attacking Hegel's theory of the state and the monarchy as incompatible with the principles of the Prussian state and the Hohenzollern dynasty.[53] As in so many other cases, Hegel's contemporaries understood only too well the critical message of Hegel's theory of politics.

[51] *Ibid.* addition to § 273.
[52] *Ibid.* §§ 278–9.
[53] The most influential among them was K. E. Schubart's *Über die Unvereinbarkeit der Hegelschen Staatslehre mit dem obersten Lebens- und Entwicklungsprinzip des preussischen Staats* (Breslau, 1839). On this whole legitimist anti-Hegelian literature, see my 'Hegel Revisited', *Journal of Contemporary History* III (1968), 133–47.

THE RULE OF LAW

Though the title of Hegel's *Rechtsphilosophie* comprehends the whole realm of objective spirit and not only the legal sphere in its narrower sense, it is, of course, natural that the law proper should be central to Hegel's theory of institutional and public life. Ever since *The German Constitution*, Hegel had been most outspoken about the need to distinguish between the sphere of private and public law. His arguments against the jurists of the Old Reich, the Württemberg traditionalists, as well as against Haller, had always been that they did not make this necessary distinction and hence the state sank, under them, to the level of private interests and, with it, the *res publica* disappeared.

Very early in the *Philosophy of Right* Hegel argues that law is the realm of freedom.[54] The growing rationalization of legal structures is one of the criteria for historical progress.[55] Codification, which attempts to systematize and rationalize the legal heritage of past ages in any given society, is welcome and rulers which have initiated such comprehensive codifications 'have been the greatest benefactors of peoples'.[56]

Furthermore, what distinguishes, according to Hegel, between despotism and a well-ordered state is the existence of fixed and known rules, binding upon the government. Hegel's objection both to monarchical absolutism as well as to majoritarian democracy has this in common, that in both cases the law, as an objective institution regulating behaviour, disappears; a majority can be as tyrannical as an individual despot:

Despotism means any state of affairs where law has disappeared and where the particular will as such, whether of a monarch or a mob (ochlocracy) counts as law or rather takes the place of law; while it is precisely in legal, constitutional, government that sovereignty is to be found as the moment of ideality – the ideality of the particular spheres and functions.[57]

The general principles of the rule of law are elaborated in §§ 221–228 of the *Philosophy of Right*, and the courts of law are here made the repository of the individual's rights. These rights the individual possesses as a member of civil society and the administration of justice is invested with the duty of protecting them. Every individual

[54] *Philosophy of Right*, § 4.
[55] *Ibid.* § 216.
[56] *Ibid.* § 215. Justinian, Frederick the Great and Napoleon are variously cited by Hegel as examples for this kind of ruler.
[57] *Ibid.* § 278; also § 286.

The rule of law

has the right *in judicio stare*, and 'in court the specific character which rightness acquires is that it must be demonstrable'.[58]

Laws must be promulgated and made public; hence case-law, as distinct from formal codification, may vitiate this public nature of the law:

If laws are to have a binding force, it follows that, in view of the right of self-consciousness, they must be universally known.

To hang the laws so high that no citizen could read them (as Dionysius the tyrant did) is injustice of one and the same kind as to bury them in row upon row of learned tomes, collections of dissenting judgements and opinions, records of customs, etc., and in a dead language too, so that knowledge of the law of the land is accessible only to those who have made it their professional study.[59]

Making legal proceedings public is a corollary of the universality of the law. At a time when most continental governments were sliding back into *in camera* legal proceedings, Hegel's warning carried with it not only a theoretical argument for publicity but also a strong political message:

Amongst the right of the subjective consciousness [is] . . . the publicity of judicial proceedings. The reason for this is that a trial is implicitly an event of universal validity, and although the particular content of the action affects the interests of the parties alone, its universal content, i.e. the right at issue and the judgement thereon, affects the interests of everybody.

It is straightforward common sense to hold that the publicity of legal proceedings is right and just . . . An integral part of justice is the confidence which citizens have in it, and it is this which requires that proceedings shall be public.[60]

On another issue Hegel admits that it is difficult to postulate general rules on the exact scope of affairs about which it is permissible for the state to legislate. In times of war, government may have to legislate on matters that would be outside its proper scope in normal circumstances. Hegel is also aware that such a necessity usually causes the government to 'acquire a measure of odium' in the eyes of the public.[61] But outside these contingencies, Hegel maintains, legislation should not interfere with matters of subjective belief and preference; privacy and individual morals should not be subject to legislation:

Morality and moral commands concern the will in its most private, subjective, and particular side, and so cannot be a matter for positive legislation . . .

The legislation of the ancients in earlier times was full of precepts about

---

[58] *Ibid.* § 222. [59] *Ibid.* § 215.
[60] *Ibid.* § 224 and addition. [61] *Ibid.* addition to § 234.

191

uprightness and integrity which are unsuited by nature to legal enactment because they fall wholly within the field of inner life.[62]

Through a complex and sometimes abstruse argument Hegel arrives at the conclusion that the nature of law as the expression of self-consciousness should lead to trial by jury – again, something which was far from the prevalent practice in Prussia or on the continent generally. Hegel argues that in adjudication there are always two aspects – the question of fact and the question of law. The latter requires a judge's decision, but as far as the question of fact is concerned 'no grounds can be adduced for supposing that the judge, i.e. the legal expert, should be the only person to establish how the facts lie, for ability to do so depends on general, not on purely legal, education'.[63] Hence, as in English law, this question of fact should be decided upon by a jury.

To this common sense justification of trial by jury Hegel adds the more speculative one of self-consciousness: the verdict of one's peers is the criminal's own verdict upon himself, mediated through the self-consciousness of people who represent the same level of consciousness as the accused himself.[64]

Hegel's persistent distrust of lawyers also provides him with an argument about trial by jury. Jury trials help to prevent the monopolization of the legal process by professional lawyers who have an obvious interest in keeping the proceedings as arcane and obscurantist as possible. If law is monopolized by the legal profession, 'members of civil society . . . are kept strangers to the law', and the citizen is prevented from participation in the legal process through which the legal norms are internalized by the public.[65]

To the progressive rationalization of the law over time Hegel finds a corollary in the decreasing severity of the penal code: 'The fact that society has become strong and sure of itself diminishes the external importance of the injury and so leads to a mitigation of its punishment.'[66] A Draconian penal code is a mark of a society's inner

---

[62] *Ibid.* § 213 and addition. Hegel also says that in affairs like 'marriage, love and religion' the state should regulate only those aspects that are 'in principle external'.

[63] *Ibid.* addition to § 227.

[64] *Ibid.* § 228.

[65] *Ibid.*; also addition to § 215: 'The legal profession, possessed of a special knowledge of the law, often claims this knowledge as its monopoly and refuses to allow any layman to discuss the subject . . . But we do not need to be shoemakers to know if our shoes fit, and just as little have we any need to be professionals to acquire knowledge of matters of universal interest.'

[66] *Ibid.* § 218.

The rule of law

uncertainty. Like every other institution, Hegel suggests, a penal code is 'the child of its age and the state of civil society at the time'. This progressive minimalization of the necessity to use penal measures ultimately reflects what is the basis of Hegel's theory of the state – that the modern state, based on self-consciousness and the citizens' readiness to cooperate with each other, calls for increasingly less and less coercion. Coercion is the mark of undeveloped, undifferentiated structures. Where self-consciousness comes into its own, coercion becomes superfluous.

Chapter Ten

WAR

Hegel's theory of war led various commentators to find a connection between Hegelian political theory and the fascist, totalitarian ideas about war and the state.[1] There is no doubt that what Hegel has to say on the subject of war is rather unusual and sometimes quite startling, and it is easy to see how his unorthodox views, when taken out of the context of his general political philosophy, could have been so misconstrued.

Nothing could be more unsettling than the way in which Hegel criticizes the conventional wisdom about war, derived from the heritage of Natural Law theories. This heritage, both in its ecclesiastical and its secular version, tended to look upon war as something deviating from the norm of peace and harmony unless war was waged for what could be declared to be a 'just' cause. Since the avowed aim of Natural Law theories was to achieve a system of harmonious cooperation among individuals as well as among states, a strong undercurrent of negative value judgement accompanied anything deemed to be injurious to this effort. War, or strife generally, always meant, therefore, that something went wrong.

This left Natural Law theories with somewhat Manichean explanations about the origins and causes of war. A theological Natural Law theory could always refer either to God's inscrutability, or to man's fall, or to both; secular theories had no such convenient refuge, and thus had no choice but to acknowledge the chasm between the 'is' and the 'ought'. The legacy of this dichotomy is, of course, strongly felt in Kant as well.

The comprehensiveness of Hegel's theoretical attempt to give an adequate explanation to the world of man in terms of Spirit's actualization in the phenomenal world led him to seek an explanation

[1] See Popper, *The Open Society*, p. 259; Hermann Heller, *Hegel und der nationale Machtstaatsgedanke in Deutschland* (Leipzig and Berlin, 1921), p. 118; W. M. McGovern, *From Luther to Hitler* (New York, 1940); D. A. Routh, 'The Philosophy of International Relations', *Politica* (September, 1938), pp. 223–35.

of the historical phenomenon of war which would transcend the mere moralism of condemnation. If war has been until now a permanent feature of human history, its instrumentality in man's development could not be denied; since so much of what happened in history is the outcome of war and discord rather than of harmony and co-operation, a theory which would just dismiss the means as utterly unworthy while welcoming the results, would be both a very poor theory on theoretical grounds, and hypocritical, if not outright immoral, on ethical ones. Such a theory would fail to provide man with adequate ethical criteria by which to judge war itself.

Hegel's way of confronting this dilemma begins by questioning some of the conventional theories about the legitimacy of war and military service. Conventional theory condemns war on general moral principles but ultimately finds justification for legitimizing some kind of military service. The problem which is consequently conveniently obscured is, how can a political authority issue a command to a citizen to serve in the army in times of war and thus expose himself to the peril of being killed or wounded, while at the same time founding the legitimacy of its authority on the postulate of preserving the individual's safety and on condemning violence. As we briefly observed when dealing with Hegel's distinction between civil society and the state, conventional wisdom tries to overcome the dilemma by stating that by thus exposing himself the individual is defending his family and his property. But this, to Hegel, is pure nonsense; it views the state – and military service – in terms of individual self-interest, i.e. of civil society, while a true 'civil society' view of the matter would urge the individual to eschew military service and betake himself, with his family and property, to a safe shelter. Hegel is scathing in his rejection of this version of the conventional wisdom:

An entirely distorted account of the demand for this sacrifice [of property and life] results from regarding the state as a mere civil society and from regarding its final end as only the security of individual life and property. This security cannot possibly be obtained by the sacrifice of what is to be secured – on the contrary.[2]

Hegel also mentions that historically the decline of the ancient polis got under way when people began to feel that they were fighting for their property only, not for the commonwealth, and hence they felt very little inclination to risk their life for it; if it is only

2 *Philosophy of Right*, § 32.

property that is to be defended, then there are less costly ways of doing so than to die for it.[3]

If the aim – and legitimacy – of war is not to defend life and property, what, then, is it?

War, to Hegel, is precisely the transcendence of material values – the ability of the individual to go beyond his own, narrow, civil society interests and coalesce with his fellow citizens for a common endeavour:

> War is the state of affairs which deals in earnest with the vanity of temporal goods and concerns – a vanity at other times a common theme of edifying sermonizing. This is what makes it the moment in which the ideality of the particular attains its right and is actualized. War has the higher significance that by its agency, as I have remarked elsewhere 'the ethical health of peoples is preserved in their indifference to the stabilization of finite institutions; just as the blowing of the winds preserves the sea from the foulness which would be the result of prolonged calm, so also corruption in nations would be the product of prolonged, let alone "perpetual", peace'. This, however, is said to be only a philosophical idea, or, to use another common expression, a 'justification of providence', and it is maintained that actual wars require some other justification.[4]

This has to be read very carefully: just as a situation of stress – like a plague – brings out the solidarity of a family, so a situation of warfare brings out the ability of men to transcend their self-centered interests. From this there follows no glorification of the plague – or of war. According to Hegel, the insecurity of property, brought about by war, is, after all, 'necessary' in the sense that it resides in the nature of property as an external object, only tenuously connected with the subject. As such, this insecurity is ultimately accepted by everyone; the problem is that when this transient nature of worldly goods is proven 'in the form of hussars with shining sabres and [when] they actualize in real earnest what the preachers have said, then the moving and edifying discourses which foretold all these events turn into curses against the invader'.[5]

War is thus the ultimate proof that the values of civil society are only relative. This leads Hegel to his radical conclusion that one

[3] *Early Theological Writings*, pp. 164–5: 'The preservation of the city could only have been important to them as a means to the preservation of their property and its enjoyment. Therefore, to have exposed themselves to the danger of death would have been to do something ridiculous, since the means, death, would have forthwith annulled the end, property and enjoyment.'

[4] *Philosophy of Right*, § 324; Hegel's reference is to his treatise on Natural Law (*Gesammelte Werke*, IV, 450).

[5] *Philosophy of Right*, addition to § 324.

of the dangers of continuous peace would be to give rise to the illusion that the power of civil society is absolute and supreme. In a situation of peace there is very strong pressure on the individuals to consider their own self-interest as the *ultima ratio* of social organization and to absolutize it. We have already noted Hegel's repeated insistence that civil society, though an essential moment in the development of inter-human relations, should not be considered as the final end of human life. A situation in which people do not hold anything beyond civil society as binding upon them, is a situation of social disintegration – and of hubris. Hence Hegel is led to see in war the *momento mori* which shakes human beings out of their complacent preoccupation with their narrow and limited self-interests:

In peace civil life continually expands; all its departments wall themselves in, and in the long run men stagnate. Their idiosyncracies become continually more fixed and ossified. But for health the unity of the body is required, and if its parts harden themselves into exclusiveness, that is death.[6]

Hence there always is in war a hidden meaning beyond the immediate causes which have precipitated one or another particular war. The phenomenology of war has to be understood in its wider context, and here, as elsewhere, philosophy has to 'recognize reason as the rose in the cross of the present', even at the cost of taking up a position which could be so easily misunderstood:

War is not to be regarded as an absolute evil and as a purely external accident, which itself therefore has some accidental cause, be it injustices, the passions of nations or the holders of power, etc., or in short, something or other which ought not to be. It is to what is by nature accidental that accidents happen, and the fate whereby they happen is thus a necessity. Here as elsewhere, the point of view from which things seem pure accidents vanishes if we look at them in the light of the concept and philosophy, because philosophy knows accident for a show and sees in it its essence, necessity. It is necessity that the finite – property and life – should be definitely established as accidental, because accidentality is the concept of the finite.[7]

This is the general background to Hegel's view of war, and it appears in various formulations and nuances throughout his writings. War is the attempt to overcome the individual's 'rootedness

[6] *Ibid.* Despite what he says in his *Perpetual Peace*, Kant has a similar insight into war: 'War itself, if it is carried on with order and with a sacred respect for the rights of citizens, has something sublime in it ... On the other hand, a long peace generally brings about a predominant commercial spirit and, along with it, low selfishness, cowardice and effeminacy, and debases the disposition of the people' (Immanuel Kant, *Critique of Judgment*, trans. J. H. Bernard (New York, 1959), § 28).

[7] *Philosophy of Right*, § 324.

in his own existence [*Dasein*], this disintegration of the whole into atoms'.[8] In the *Phenomenology*, Hegel even makes the extreme suggestion that 'in order not to let [the particular ends] get rooted and settled in their isolation and thus break up the whole into fragments and let the common spirit evaporate, governments have from time to time to shake them to the very core by war'.[9] Although Hegel never comes back to this radical counsel, its true nature is revealed in the same passage when Hegel argues that by thus confronting its citizens with the spectre of war, government lets them 'feel the power of their lord and master, death'. War is the power of negativity, and this is significant, since even if one rejects Hegel's reasoning altogether, one should bear in mind that the ends of this initiated war are not political, that its aim is not the aggrandizement of states or princes, but rather the bringing out of the relativity of human existence. Furthermore, there is no glory in such a war. Since Hegel's above-quoted statement has often been used to emphasize the similarity between his and the fascist theories of war, this distinction should be recalled, as it shows that whatever reservations one may have about Hegel's theory of war, it remains basically different from anything even vaguely resembling modern totalitarian justifications – and glorifications – of war.[10]

War thus draws the citizens together, brings down the walls created by ossified self-interests:

> In times of peace, the particular spheres and functions pursue their paths of satisfying their particular aims and minding their own business, and it is in part only by way of the unconscious necessity of the thing that their self-seeking is turned into a contribution to the reciprocal support and to the support of the whole . . .
>
> In a situation of exigency, however, whether in home or foreign affairs, the organism of which these particular spheres are members fuses into the concept of sovereignty. The sovereignty is entrusted with the salvation of the state at the sacrifice of these particular authorities whose powers are valid at other times, and it is then that that ideality comes into its proper actuality.[11]

Because of this, it is in war that the strength of a state is tested. In *The German Constitution* Hegel remarks that the wars against revolutionary France have finally proved that the Old Reich is not

---

8 *Realphilosophie II*, 262.

9 *Phenomenology*, p. 474. The irony of this statement is that during the Battle of Jena Hegel's house was severely damaged and in the chaos he almost lost the only manuscript of the *Phenomenology*.

10 The element of inherent negativity is also referred to in the 'System der Sittlichkeit' (*Schriften zur Politik*, p. 471) and *Realphilosophie II*, 261.

11 *Philosophy of Right*, § 278.

a state any more, since 'the health of a state is generally revealed
not so much in the calm of peace as in the stir of war. Peace is the
state of enjoyment and activity in seclusion . . . But in war the
power of association of all with the whole is in evidence.'[12] Again,
it is Hegel's argument that war as such is no more than what a
disease is to a body: only when attacked by disease can one form a
judgement of whether a particular body is healthy or not. War is
not *the* health of a state – *in* it a state's health is put to the test.

The sacrifice demanded of the citizen in a state of war is by its
nature a test of his solidarity with his fellow citizens. Hence Hegel's
view of courage in war is far from the romantic notions of subjective valour. To Hegel, courage is not a subjective psychological
trait, but a moment of identification with the commonalty:

Courage to be sure is multiform. The mettle of an animal or a brigand, courage
for the sake of honour, the courage of a knight, these are not true forms of
courage. The true courage of civilized nations is readiness to sacrifice in the
service of the state, so that the individual counts as only one amongst many.
The important thing here is not personal mettle but aligning oneself with the
universal. In India five hundred men [under Clive] conquered twenty thousand
who were not cowards, but who only lacked this disposition to work in close co-
operation with others.[13]

That Hegel has no illusions about the conditions of actual warfare can be seen from an interesting passage in the *System der
Sittlichkeit*, where he notes the extreme ambivalence of the human
attributes brought out by war. There he says that war gives rise
both to the best and worst passions in men.[14]

Yet there is another level on which Hegel discusses the immanence
of war and it is here that his speculative views are translated into a
language which tries to explain how actual wars get started; it is
here too that Hegel enlarges upon his view of the state as an
individual. The individual attains to his personality through his
relation to other individuals. Similarly, according to Hegel, the
essence of the state's existence as a unity, as an individuality, lies in
its relationship with other states: 'A state is as little an actual individual without relations to other states as an individual is

---

[12] *Political Writings*, pp. 143–4. Uncomfortable as one may feel about the
implications of this statement, one could be hard pressed to deny its validity
as a statement of fact. Marx similarly refers to war as 'this great common
task, this great communal labour'; see K. Marx, *Grundrisse zur Kritik der
politischen Ökonomie* (Berlin, 1953), p. 378.

[13] *Philosophy of Right*, addition to § 327. For a similar non-romantic view of
military courage, see *Schriften zur Politik*, p. 470.

[14] *Ibid.* pp. 470–1.

actually a person without *rapport* with other persons.'[15] This personality of the state must be distinguished and differentiated from other personalities in order to find its own identity:

> The nation as state is mind in its substantive rationality and immediate actuality and is therefore the absolute power on earth. It follows that every state is sovereign and autonomous against its neighbours. It is entitled in the first place and without qualification to be sovereign from their point of view, i.e. to be recognized by them as sovereign.[16]

The paradox inherent in Hegel's position is that just as in the case of the individual person, the main problem is that of recognition: even while postulating the state's 'absolute power on earth' Hegel has to premiss it on recognition by others. The 'absolute power on earth' is further reminiscent of Hegel's reference (in § 186) to the individual's 'inherently infinite personality'; in the specific context of the paragraph just quoted, Hegel is obviously referring to Spinoza's contention (to which he expressly alludes in the addition to § 339) that the notion of sovereignty is a corollary of the situation in which the nations have no Praetor to preside over them and settle their disputes. This view is at the root of Hegel's view of international relations, and it is on this issue that he differs so radically from the Kantian approach to international affairs.

Hegel is adamant about the basic distinction between the nature of internal and international law. While internal law is binding, under penalty of sanctions, and in case of infringement there exist both an objective criterion for judgement as well as an objective judge to administer it, international law is binding only insofar as the parties concerned are willing to abide by it. It is of the nature of a voluntary act, expressing the subjective wills of the parties involved, not of a binding, objective law. Hence international law remains always an 'ought':

> The fundamental proposition of international law . . . is that treaties, as the ground of obligation between states, ought to be kept. But since the sovereignty of a state is the principle of its relations to others, states are to that extent in a state of nature to each other. Their rights are actualized only in their particular wills and not in a universal will with constitutional powers over them. This universal proviso of international law therefore does not go beyond an ought-

---

[15] *Philosophy of Right*, § 331. See also the essay on Natural Law (*Gesammelte Schriften*, IV, 449–50), and *Schriften zur Politik*, p. 489: 'A nation which is not being recognized must produce this recognition through war or colonies.'

[16] *Philosophy of Right*, § 331. Hegel writes: 'Das Volk als Staat . . .'; since Knox's translation of this is 'the nation-state', which may lead to misunderstandings, I have suggested a more neutral translation of Hegel's phrase. Cf. also § 323.

to-be, and what really happens is that international relations in accordance with treaty alternate with the severance of these relations.

There is no Praetor to judge between states; at best there may be an arbitrator or a mediator, and even he exercises his functions contingently only, i.e. in dependence on the particular will of the disputants.[17]

Because of this, international treaties do not have 'the actuality (*Wirklichkeit*) of actual contracts . . . Hence they should not be viewed according to the way of civil contracts'.[18]

What is important to grasp here is that Hegel is not preaching a gospel of international behaviour as it should be, but is attempting to understand that which *is*, and he wishes to disentangle this understanding from the erroneous notions that have crept into it because of mistaken analogies with internal law. He even goes a bit further, when he maintains that whatever wishful thinking and pious hope would like to imagine, there is *on principle* no way of ever achieving the possibility of perpetual peace. The idea of a league of nations, according to Hegel, would never solve the real problem, since in order to be effective such a league would itself have to be ready to wage war. Such a league may avert this or that war (and there are after all numerous other modes of averting individual wars), but the immanence of war itself will not be exorcized just by having it waged under the auspices of a league of nations rather than under the flag of individual states. As Hegel himself points out (and this has sometimes been overlooked by some observers), he is criticizing here not only the Kantian idea of perpetual peace, but also the theoretical premises of the Holy Alliance of post-1815 Restoration Europe. According to Hegel, Kant and Metternich share the same fallacy and illusion:

Perpetual peace is often advocated as an ideal towards which humanity should strive. With that end in view, Kant proposed a league of monarchs to adjust differences between states, and the Holy Alliance was meant to be a league of much the same kind. But the state is an individual, and individuality implies negation. Hence even if a number of states make themselves into a family, this group as an individual must engender an opposite and create an enemy.[19]

---

[17] *Ibid.* § 333; also addition to § 330: 'Since there is no power in existence which decides in face of the state what is right in principle and actualizes this decision, it follows that so far as international relations are concerned we can never get beyond an "ought". The relation between states is a relation between autonomous entities which make mutual stipulations but which at the same time are superior to these stipulations.'

[18] *Realphilosophie II*, 261.

[19] *Philosophy of Right*, addition to § 324. The Korean and Congolese experiences might perhaps be cited as illustrations for Hegel's contention that the existence of an international organization might enmesh this very body in what is to

War

Such a league, Hegel would argue, would be effective only if it would behave like a state, like a person – distinguish itself from others, and thus attain its self-identification through recognition. One may paradoxically say that if *states*, in the plural, were to cease to exist, there could not, by definition, remain *a state* in the singular.[20]

It is from this conditional and incomplete nature of international law that Hegel deduces his explanation about the causes of actual wars. What is extremely interesting to note is the almost identical language which Hegel uses on the two occasions on which he discusses this problem – in *The German Constitution* and the *Philosophy of Right*. While the first was written at the time of the French revolutionary victories over the German states and the second at the height of the Restoration, Hegel's views in both cases follow the same pattern: whenever war breaks out it is because two sets of rights, each legitimate in its own way, clash. And since there is no accepted way to adjudicate such disputes, the sword comes in as the arbiter. Wars to Hegel are always such clashes *between two rights* – not between right and wrong, as the partisans and contenders themselves see the conflict. Hence the outcome of a war never proves one side right and the other wrong. It only regulates which right will yield to the other. The outcome of any given war is by itself neutral to the problem of justice or justification, and there is no way of reading into Hegel anything resembling the maxim of 'might is right'.

Hegel's formulation of the above view in the *Philosophy of Right* is as follows:

It follows that if states disagree and their particular wills cannot be harmonized, the matter can only be settled by war. A state through its subjects has widespread connections and many-sided interests, and these may be readily and considerably injured; but it remains inherently indeterminable which of these injuries is to be regarded as a specific breach of the treaty or an injury to the honour and autonomy of the state. The reason for this is that a state may regard its infinity and honour as at stake in each of its concerns, however minute, and it is all the more inclined to susceptibility to injury the more its strong

all practical purposes an act of war. Assertions that such experiences tend to strengthen the authority of the UN only corroborate Hegel's insight, since the same might be said of an individual state confronted with the challenge of war.

20 Hegel similarly remarks that a 'general league of nations for perpetual peace would be the domination of one nation, or would merely be one people; its universality would be obliterated' (*Realphilosophie II*, 261).

individuality is impelled as a result of long domestic peace to seek and create a sphere of activity abroad.[21]

In the more rambling language of *The German Constitution*, written almost twenty years earlier, Hegel goes into greater detail:

The relation of states to one another is so many-sided, and every single matter settled in a peace treaty has in turn so many facets, that despite all their precise determination there still remain innumerable facets of the matter about which dispute is possible . . .

Wars, be they called wars of aggression or defense – a matter on which the parties never agree – would be called unjust only if the peace treaty had stipulated an unconditional peace on both sides . . . No state can bind itself to let itself be attacked or treated as an enemy and yet not to arm itself but to keep the peace.

But the potential modes of enmity are so infinite that there is no determining them by the human intelligence, and the more determinations there are, i.e. the more the rights that are established, the more readily does a contradiction between such rights arise . . .

Each party grounds its behaviour on rights and accuses the other of an infringement of a right. The right of one state *A* is infringed by state *B* in a right *a* which accrues to *A*, but state *B* avers that it has upheld its right *b* and that this is not to be taken as an infringement of the right of *A*. The public takes sides; each party claims to have right on its side; *and both parties are right. It is just the rights themselves which come into contradiction with one another* . . .

Right is the advantage of one state, acknowledged and settled by treaties. Since in treaties generally the varying interests of the states are settled, though as rights these interests are so infinitely many-sided, they must come into contradiction, and so must the rights themselves. It depends entirely on circumstances, on the combinations of power, i.e. on the judgement of politics, whether the interest and right which is coming into jeopardy is to be defended by the power with its whole strength, since it too has just the opposite interest which collides with the first, and therefore a right too. *Thus war, or the like, has now to decide, not which of the rights alleged by the two parties is the genuine right – since both parties have a genuine right – but which of the two rights is to give way.* War, or whatever it may be, has to decide this, precisely because both contradictory rights were equally genuine; thus a third thing, i.e. war, must make them unequal so that they can be unified, and this happens when one gives way to the other.[22]

---

[21] *Philosophy of Right*, § 334. In § 335 Hegel points out the manifold ways in which a state may think itself as being threatened: 'The state is in essence a mind and therefore cannot be prepared to stop at just taking notice of an injury *after* it has actually occurred. On the contrary, there arises in addition as · a cause of strife the *idea* of such an injury as the idea of a danger *threatening* from another state, together with calculations of degrees of probability on this side and that, guessing at intentions, etc., etc.' This sounds ominously contemporary.

[22] *Political Writings*, pp. 208–10 (my italics).

This passage has been quoted at length since it clearly shows that Hegel's view is obviously at odds with any ideological interpretation of war. It certainly cannot fit into any nationalistic, or totalitarian, ideology which naturally would tend to glorify and romanticize both the conduct of the war itself and its results. Hegel leaves the results of war in a neutral, indeterminable zone, completely free from any value judgement concerning the significance of its outcome. Though in the long march of history Hegel quotes Schiller's dictum that 'the history of the world is the world's court of judgement', this refers to the overall outcome of historical development and does not apply to the outcome of any particular war.[23]

There is thus a curious dichotomy in Hegel's view on war between the significance he attaches to the readiness of the citizen to go to war and the ultimate meaninglessness of the act of war itself and its results. This is also borne out by Hegel himself when in his *System der Sittlichkeit* he refers to war as 'aimless labour'.[24] Ultimately, war is the power of negativity. On the subject of war, therefore, Hegel comes nearer perhaps than anywhere else in his political philosophy to the borders of what would be called today existentialist thought.

What is surprising to a certain extent, however, is that despite Hegel's insistence that international law always remains on the level of an 'ought', his very theory of sovereignty as based on reciprocal recognition brings forth a system of a limited, yet effective, *comitas gentium*. There is nothing more dialectical than Hegel's assertion that it is precisely in the moment of sovereignty, which appears as power unlimited by any other factor, that the ultimate limitation of the state's actions is inherent.

In *The German Constitution* Hegel says: 'It happens of course that a state against which war is actually being waged is not recognized; but in reality it *is* recognized by the very fact that war is being waged against it, and it gains full recognition when peace is made with it.'[25]

Though sovereignty is absolute, a state's sovereignty needs recognition by other states in order to be recognized as such, just as a person's recognition as an individual and an independent being

---

[23] *Philosophy of Right*, § 340 (my italics). Even this should be understood in light of what Hegel says in § 342, that 'world history is not the verdict of mere might'.
[24] *Schriften zur Politik*, p. 471.
[25] *Political Writings*, p. 201.

ultimately rests upon recognition by another.[26] Hence even in war there are a number of norms which should be preserved, the foremost among them being that ultimately war is to be seen as something transient. Another such norm is that war should not be waged against families and individual members of civil society:

The fact that states reciprocally recognize each other as states remains, even in war – the state of affairs when rights disappear and force and chance hold sway – a bond wherein each counts to the rest as something absolute. Hence in war, war itself is characterized as something which ought to pass away. It implies therefore the proviso of the *jus gentium* that the possibility of peace be retained (and so, for example, that envoys must be respected), and, in general, that war be not waged against domestic institutions, against the peace of family and private life, or against persons in their private capacity.[27]

Hegel also adds that foreign nationals should be protected in situations of war.[28] He thus arrives at a picture of war which is limited in its scope, a far cry from modern total wars. Hegel further insists that wars should be carried on by professional armies, and only in extreme cases, if 'the state as such, if its autonomy, is in jeopardy', should the whole citizenry be called up in arms.[29] Politically, the army should be wholly under civilian control and its functions should be limited to external affairs. Hegel cites the Praetorian guard as a lamentable example of the army taking part in politics.[30]

Despite Hegel's strictures against an *a priori* concept of international law, his views lead to a pragmatic system of customary international behaviour, 'custom being the inner universality of behaviour maintained in all circumstances'.[31] The irony of the matter is that what must finally be said about the way Hegel saw the conduct of war evolving in the modern age is that it seriously misjudged future developments.

When Hegel envisaged wars as waged on a limited basis, he made the same misjudgement which had led him to underestimate the enormous force of modern nationalism: he totally failed to see the prevalence of modern, total war. The Napoleonic example seems to have passed him by without leaving any trace in this quarter. This naïveté, and ultimately Hegel's wishful thinking, appear several times in his describing modern warfare as being more humane and less barbaric than the wars of yesteryear:

[26] *Philosophy of Right*, § 331.
[27] *Ibid.* § 338. Cf. 'System der Sittlichkeit' (*Schriften zur Politik*, p. 471), where Hegel says that since war is not fought between families, 'hatred itself is undifferentiated, free from all personal aspects'.
[28] *Philosophy of Right*, § 339.   [29] *Ibid.* § 326.
[30] *Ibid.* addition to § 271.   [31] *Ibid.* § 339.

War

Modern wars are therefore humanely waged, and person is not set over against person in hatred. At most, personal enmities appear in the vanguard, but in the main body of the army hostility is something vague and gives place to each side's respect for the duty of the other.[32]

On several occasions Hegel appears to associate this more humane, impersonal nature of modern warfare with the introduction of the gun:

The principle of the modern world – thought and the universal – has given courage a higher form, because its display now seems to be more mechanical, the act not of this particular person, but of a number of a whole ... It is for this reason that thought had invented the gun, and the invention of this weapon, which has changed the purely personal form of bravery into a more abstract one, is no accident.[33]

If this may seem today to have been totally negated by later developments, the vision inherent in Hegel's theory should not be overlooked. For him the contemporary world presented a picture of ever-narrowing differences between states whose cautious, pragmatic coexistence was now finally becoming a possibility due to the ever-growing rationalization of life:

The European peoples form a family in accordance with the universal principle underlying their legal code, their customs, and their civilization. This principle has modified their international conduct accordingly in a state of affairs [i.e. war] otherwise dominated by the mutual infliction of evil.[34]

Thus even war itself, with all its negativity, does finally receive a meaning within the wider scheme of things. Out of the vortex of clashes characterizing international relations, an inner order emerges and reason appears in history not as something given *a priori* – as an axiomatic system of norms – but as an end product of a long, arduous and sometimes seemingly meaningless process. The various principles underlying the different states, the *Volksgeister*, in contending blindly with each other, are nothing else than tools in the hands of reason. Thus reason establishes itself cunningly in the world of man:

It is as particular entities that states enter into relations with one another. Hence their relations are on the largest scale a maelstrom of external contingency and the inner particularity of passions, private interests and selfish ends, abilities and virtues, vices, force, and wrong. All these whirl together ... Their deeds and destinies in their reciprocal relations to one another are the dialectic of the finitude of these minds, and out of it arises the universal mind, the mind of the world, free from all restriction, producing itself as that which exercises its right

---

32 *Ibid.* addition to § 338.
33 *Ibid.* § 328. See also *Schriften zur Politik*, pp. 471–2.
34 *Philosophy of Right*, addition to § 339.

– and its right is the highest right of all – over these finite minds in the 'history of the world which is the world's court of judgement'.[35]

The cunning of reason gives rise to the modern world in which war is minimized and where, ultimately, even sovereignty itself becomes nothing other than a mere form. To Hegel, the conciliation and mediation typified in the modern world blunt the edge of international conflict as well, and the world is about to enter an era of cooperation and universalism:

States in the modern world seek independence of one another, and this is their honour. This obstinate tendency toward an absolute position to autonomy they have in common with the Greek city-states . . . But despite all the differences between the individual states . . . there also obtains a unity among them, *and therefore we should view even political independence as a merely formal principle.* Today there is not the same absolute chasm between the states of Europe which prevailed between Greece and Persia. When one state is annexed to the territory of the other, it loses, to be sure, its formal independence; but its religion, its laws, the concrete in its life remain intact. The trend of the states is, therefore, towards uniformity. There prevails among them one aim, one tendency, which is the cause of wars, friendships, and the needs of dynasties. But there also prevails among them another uniformity, which parallels the idea of hegemony in Greece, except that now it is the hegemony of spirit.[36]

Thus, though Hegel had begun with the immanence of war – in the end he emerges with a vision of One World, united by culture and reason, progressing towards a system wherein sovereignty, though acknowledged, will wither away, and wars, though immanent, will gradually disappear.

[35] *Ibid.* § 340.
[36] G. W. F. Hegel, *Vorlesungen über die Philosophie der Weltgeschichte*, ed. G. Lasson (Leipzig, 1920), p. 761 (my italics).

Chapter Eleven

THE ENGLISH REFORM BILL – THE SOCIAL PROBLEM AGAIN

Hegel's last published work was a long essay on the English Reform Bill, which originally appeared in the *Preussische Staatszeitung* in 1831. Hegel died a short while later, and the last installment of the essay was suppressed when the Prussian censorship forbade its publication.[1]

Since in this essay Hegel casts doubts on the Reform Bill, it has become customary to view it as one of Hegel's most conservative, if not outright reactionary, pieces of writing. True, its argument runs contrary to what has come to be considered conventional wisdom regarding the course of parliamentary reform in nineteenth century England. The essay, however, is far from being a defence of the *status quo* and the unreformed House of Commons; if read carefully in its entirety, it appears as a most thoughtful piece of social criticism, revealing an attempt to transcend the mere political platitudes of the supporters of parliamentary reform and to identify the fundamental *malaise* of nineteenth-century English society, a *malaise* sometimes too conveniently overlooked by the sponsors and supporters of parliamentary reform.[2]

The crux of Hegel's argument is that a mere reform of the franchise cannot by itself cure the social problems of English society. Hegel's essay is one of the most scathing indictments of English social conditions to come from a continental writer. Yet his critique is aimed not only at existing conditions in early industrial Britain, but also at the liberal attempts to overcome them through a purely electoral reform of parliament. Behind these attempts Hegel sees the self-interest of the new middle class which identifies reform with its own coming into power. Hegel believed that English conditions could not be changed unless Britain underwent a social, as

[1] See Marie Hegel's letter to Niethammer, 2 December 1831, in *Hegel in Berichten seiner Zeitgenossen*, ed. G. Nicolin (Hamburg, 1970), p. 498.
[2] See Rosenkranz, *Hegels Leben*, p. 418.

well as political, transformation; little wonder then that the Prussian authorities were far from happy to see that such an argument was being voiced by the most respectable of their political philosophers in the official *Preussische Staatszeitung.*

Hegel's attitude to the various provisions of the Reform Bill is extremely complex, and was further complicated by the spectre of recurrent revolutionary turmoil which seemed to have been set in motion again by the 1830 July Revolution in France. In his later years Hegel appeared to be confident that the ghosts of revolution – the moment of negativity – had been finally laid to rest by the emergence of the modern, post-Revolutionary political order. The 1830 Revolution seemed to have shattered all this and Hegel dolefully remarks in a letter to a friend that all which seemed certain appears to have become 'problematical' again.[3] Henceforth, he became constantly afraid that Europe might again be on the threshold of a new revolutionary era.[4] As far as English developments are concerned, Hegel remarks at the outset of his essay on the Reform Bill that the recent events in France should serve as a warning to those 'whose advantage lay in . . . the obstinacy of privilege' to change their mind and support reform, otherwise the storm may not spare them next time.[5]

For despite all the misgivings Hegel has about the adequacy of the Reform Bill presented to Parliament, he warmly welcomes the attempt at reform itself. On no account whatsoever can Hegel's position be construed as if it were in support of the unreformed House of Commons:

The prime object of the Reform Bill now lying before the English Parliament is to bring justice and fairness into the allotment of the parts played by the different classes and divisions of the people in the election of members of Parliament, and to do this by substituting a greater symmetry for the most bizarre and haphazard anomalies and inequalities which prevail at present.[6]

In his Württemberg essay a decade and a half earlier, Hegel had already remarked that the English constitution lived by its abuses.[7] Now, however, Hegel says that 'it must be recognized as a good sign of the reawakening of a moral temper in the English people that one of the feelings which the need of a reform brings with it is an antipathy to the [political] depravity [to which I have referred]'.[8]

[3] Hegel to Göschel, 13 December 1830 (*Briefe von und an Hegel*, III, 323).
[4] Hegel to Schultz, 29 January 1831 (*ibid.* III, 333).
[5] *Political Writings*, p. 295.   [6] *Ibid.*
[7] *Ibid.* p. 258.   [8] *Ibid.* p. 297.

Yet there is a far more fundamental reason why Hegel welcomes the Reform Bill. Despite the fact that he is far from happy about some of the concrete changes the Bill is about to introduce, the very fact of reform is to Hegel a welcome sign that England is abandoning its traditional reliance on a customary, 'positive' law. From *The German Constitution* to the essay on Württemberg, we have seen Hegel's opposition to 'positive' law on the ground that its sole legitimacy was its traditionalism. Everywhere else – first in France, later in Germany – Hegel perceived that these traditions had yielded their place to modern, conscious and rational legislation. England, with its Common Law tradition, remained the last bastion of this archaic, pre-modern and irrational system; and though there was much in the English political system which Hegel admired, the arbitrariness and historicity of its basic legal principles were always unacceptable to him. Now, for the first time in English history, a conscious attempt was being made to apply rational criteria to existing political institutions. England was catching up with the *Zeitgeist* of Europe:

On the other hand another legal principle especially characteristic of England is indeed attacked by this Bill. This is the character of 'positivity' which preponderates in the institutions of English law, public and private alike. It is true that every right and its corresponding law is in *form* something positive, ordained and instituted by the supreme power in the state ... But at no time more than the present has the general intelligence been led to distinguish between whether rights are purely positive in their material *content* or whether they are also *inherently* right and rational. In no constitution is judgement so strongly induced to attend to this distinction as in the English, now that the continental nations have allowed themselves to be imposed on for so long by declarations about English freedom and England's pride in her system of law ... This inherently disconnected aggregate of positive provisions has not yet undergone the development and recasting which has been carried out in the civilized states of the Continent.[9]

Hegel thus grasped that the Reform Bill had a significance far above and beyond the immediate changes it aimed at introducing:

The English principle of 'positivity' on which, as I have said, the whole of English law rests, does through the Bill actually suffer a shock which in England is entirely new and unheard of, and one instinctively suspects that more far-reaching changes will issue from this subversion of the formal basis of the existing order.[10]

The ultimate effect of this overcoming of 'positive' law is that no privilege will be secure any longer; nothing will now be able to

[9] *Ibid.* p. 299.   [10] *Ibid.* p. 301.

be legitimized through simply referring to its longevity and continuity. The social consequence of this are clearly seen and welcomed by Hegel:

There is no escaping the fact that the class that has hitherto dominated Parliament . . . will suffer modification as a result of introducing new men and different principles. The Reform Bill in itself encroaches on this system, i.e. on the principle of purely positive rights which secure the possession of privileges, no matter what relation, if any, they may have to the rights of actual freedom.[11]

Hegel is quite outspoken about what he considers the abuses of the unreformed House of Commons. The oligarchic nature of British political life draws special sarcasm from Hegel: 'Nowhere more than in England is the prejudice so fixed and naïve that if birth and wealth give man office, they also give him brains.'[12] To the conservative apologia for the system of rotten boroughs, that it allows bright young men to secure a seat with comparable ease, Hegel retorts that 'examples of this kind may be ascribed to the realm of chance, where one probability may easily be set against another, and a possible advantage against a possible disadvantage'.[13] Both the rotten boroughs and the fact that a significant number of parliamentary seats was purchasable and 'a recognized marketable commodity', are to Hegel examples of how principles of civil society have become dominant in the state; they are all symptoms 'of a people's political corruption'.[14]

This explains what Hegel saw as the beneficial results of the Reform Bill: the aristocratic element in politics will suffer, since parliamentary patronage will be seriously weakened and 'many other individuals will appear in place of those belonging to the present circle'.[15] Hegel welcomes this on wider grounds, since the entry of a new social element into parliamentary life will open the door to the reform of many other aspects of social and political life in Britain. Though Hegel explicitly mentions the dangers involved in the introduction of such novel ideas, he feels that within the pragmatic English context reforms of this kind may pave the way for a gradual and peaceful transformation of social life in

---

[11] *Ibid.* pp. 328–9.
[12] *Ibid.* p. 311.
[13] *Ibid.* p. 323.
[14] *Ibid.* pp. 296–7. What makes Hegel especially angry in the case of the rotten boroughs is that 'a political right has been transformed into a pecuniary asset' (p. 299).
[15] *Ibid.* p. 324; also p. 295.

England rather than lead to a violent revolution as they indeed did in France:

As a result of reform, the route to Parliament may be open to ideas which are opposed to the interest of this [traditional] class and which therefore have not yet entered its heads. Ideas, I mean, which make up the foundations of a real freedom and which affect the matters above-mentioned – ecclesiastical property and organization, duties of the clergy – as well as the manorial and other bizarre rights and property restrictions derived from feudalism, and further sections of the chaos of English life. In France these ideas have been intermixed with many further abstractions and bound up with the violent upheavals familiar to all of us. But unalloyed, they have for long past in Germany become fixed principles of inner conviction and public opinion, and have brought about the actual peaceful, gradual and legal transformation of the [old feudal] rights.[16]

Yet despite this support for the Reform Bill, the general tone of Hegel's essay is critical of the Bill in more than one sense. What disturbed Hegel about those who advocated the Reform Bill was what to him seemed their basic myopia and limited understanding of the social reality around them. In a country beset by social problems of enormous magnitude, it seemed to Hegel to be utter blindness to suppose that a mere reform of the franchise and a re-distribution of parliamentary seats could solve the immense tensions faced by English society. To Hegel, a comprehensive attempt to confront British social realities would call for a far more radical set of solutions. He therefore proceeds to elaborate on these social problems, and the result is, as already mentioned above, an astonishingly perceptive critique of early nineteenth-century English society.

The various points of Hegel's critique of the Reform Bill can be conveniently grouped under two headings: first, his comments about franchise generally; second, his critique of various social, economic and political aspects of English life which need to be rectified and on which the reform of the franchise will have very little effect.

That which above all disturbed Hegel in the liberals' advocacy of a broader – if not universal – franchise was in tune with his general critique of universal, undifferentiated suffrage, as already expressed in the essay on Württemberg and in the *Philosophy of Right*.[17] Universal suffrage, far from calling forth the old republican *virtus* of political involvement, is 'not so attractive as to provoke

---

[16] *Ibid.* pp. 324–5. What Hegel opposed in France was not change itself but the abstract way in which it was introduced, which necessarily led to violence and terror.
[17] See above, pp. 164–7.

strong claims'; when it is provided, 'what seems to prevail in the electorate is great indifference'.[18] Hegel goes into some details concerning the causes of this apathy and cites it as a proof of his thesis that electoral participation alone, unless it is accompanied by a real sense of belonging to a commonwealth and unless it actually has an impact on social life, remains an empty gesture, leading to alienation and indifference.[19] Against this Hegel proposes the system of a differentiated franchise in which legitimate interest groups would be represented and not an abstract electorate. He remarks that, as a matter of fact, such representation had actually been instituted in England unofficially, as when, for instance, it was thought advisable that seats should be found for members of the Board of the East India Co.; but this had been done illegally, through corrupt practices, 'by the route of ordinary trade'. Hegel proposes to recognize the rationale of such practices and to make such a theory of legitimate interest representation the base of the parliamentary structure:

The real basic constituents of the life of the state, granted that they be really distinct, and granted that substanial consideration must be given by government and administration to their distinctive worth, [have to be] consciously and expressly brought to the fore, recognized, and, when they were to be discussed or when decisions were to be taken about them, allowed to speak for themselves without this being left to chance. Napoleon, in a constitution which he gave to the kingdom of Italy, divided the right of representation in the sense of this outlook between *Possidenti, Dotti, Merchanti*.[20]

Hegel further criticizes the conventional wisdom of electoral liberalism by pointing out that mere franchise does not give the electorate any real power over decisions, since constituents cannot even instruct their MP's how to vote.[21] He also remarks that by making the franchise dependent upon property qualifications, the advocates of the Reform Bill manoeuvered themselves into a contradiction: on the one hand, they rightly refused to recognize traditional electoral rights as property rights, and hence no compensation was paid to the electors in rotten boroughs who lost their pecuniary interest by the abolition of their respective seats; on the other hand, introducing a property qualification as the sole universal criterion for the right to vote in the reformed franchise implied that the reformers somehow viewed the right to vote as an extension of property rights.[22]

[18] *Political Writings*, p. 317. Cf. pp. 319–20, where some examples are given of extremely low electoral turnouts in French elections.
[19] *Ibid.* p. 318.   [20] *Ibid.* p. 314.   [21] *Ibid.* p. 319.   [22] *Ibid.* p. 315.

The English Reform Bill

The second level of Hegel's doubts about the adequacy of the Reform Bill directly refers to social conditions in England. 'In England,' Hegel writes, 'the contrast between prodigious wealth and utterly embarrassing penury is enormous.'[23] In the years immediately preceding the writing of the essay on the Reform Bill, Hegel laboriously collected information about social conditions in England. From his notations and the newspaper clippings which he preserved one can see how he arrived at a number of conclusions about the condition of the poor classes in England and how these conclusions were central to his assessment of the English social and political scene. He sees in the Corn Laws a brutal exploitation of the poor; the (unreformed) Poor Laws are an instrument for limiting the population of the lower classes; police procedures make it virtually impossible for the indigent to get adequate legal protection and refrain from self-incriminatory statements at police interrogations; the penalties meted out in accordance with the Common Law for petty thefts are barbarous, scandalous and inhumane, especially as applied to children; the very uncertainty implied in an unwritten criminal code is particularly harsh when applied to the poor who cannot hire lawyers in their defence; there is one law for the rich and one law for the poor; and, finally, the religious intolerance and persecution of Catholics in Ireland fly in the face of every theory of an ordered political life.[24] As for the economic aspects of these conditions, Hegel remarks that 'in England the price of corn and the lease of land have gone up threefold in the last fifty years, while the daily earnings of an agricultural labourer have remained the same'.[25]

Hegel's discussion of English social conditions in the essay on the Reform Bill bears witness to this earlier investigation. Hegel calls the jungle of the unreformed Common Law 'an Augean stable', which he hopes England will clean up before it is too late.[26] What England needs is 'a scientific remodelling of the law [according] to general principles'. Such a comparable remodelling, he remarks, 'has made it possible for the newer continental states to produce statute books and political institutions framed preponderantly on general principles, a process in which, so far as concerns the

---

[23] *Ibid.* p. 325.
[24] For Hegel's excerpts, see *Berliner Schriften*, pp. 718–24.
[25] *Ibid.* p. 723.
[26] *Political Writings*, p. 310. On this occasion he praises the attempts by Sir Robert Peel and Lord Brougham to abolish some of the worst excesses of the old Common Law.

contents of justice, common sense and sound reasoning have been allowed their proper share'.[27] Though England is still far behind such universalistic principles which on the Continent were enunciated by the French Revolution and the Code Napoleon, these 'rights and laws as reconstituted in the civilized states of the Continent . . . grounded on universal reason, cannot always remain so foreign, even to the English understanding, as they have been hitherto'.[28]

Hegel ascribes the causes for England's backwardness to the political power exercized in that country by the priviliged social classes. Legal arrangements reflect the realities of social power in England:

The reason why England is so remarkably far behind the other civilized states of Europe in institutions derived from true rights is simply that there the governing power lies in the hands of those possessed of so many privileges which contradict a rational constitutional law and true legislation.[29]

Hegel then proceeds to a detailed analysis of the class-nature of these conditions. Manorial rights are one of Hegel's first objects of attack: 'For long past these [manorial] rights have not merely brought the agricultural class into subjection; they press as heavily on the bulk of that class as villeinage did, indeed they bring it down to an indigence worse than a villein's.'[30] A further aspect of these rights is the Game Laws, whose social effect on the agricultural population he describes in detail, adding that 'to touch [the Game Laws] is to cut to the heart numerous English Members of Parliament and their connexions, but the nuisance and mischief have become too great for the urging of a change in those laws not to have become inevitable'.[31]

The scandal of ecclesiastical tithes is also dealt with by Hegel; he is particularly dismayed by the incidence of the tithes in Ireland, where they are imposed on a Catholic population for the benefit of the (Anglican) Church of Ireland which is totally alien and inimical to this population. But even in England proper, 'the application of tithes for the maintenance of religious doctrine and the upbuilding and support of the Church has mostly been transformed into a sort of private property revenue'.[32] This usurpation, which, Hegel is

[27] *Ibid.* p. 300.   [28] *Ibid.* p. 325.
[29] *Ibid.* p. 300.   [30] *Ibid.* p. 307.
[31] *Ibid.* p. 309. On p. 310 he remarks bitterly that 'up till now English freedom has put no restriction in these rights which princes in Germany have long ago renounced in the interest of their subjects'.
[32] *Ibid.* p. 304.

glad to point out, had been abolished in Prussia almost a century earlier, is utterly untenable:

> As to tithes, the oppressive character of this tax has been obvious for long past ... Moreover, this tax has been cavilled at on the score of unfairness, because the more the produce of the ground is increased by industry, time, and expenditure, the higher the tax rises, with the result that the improvement of agriculture, in which large capital resources have been sunk in England, is burdened with a tax instead of being encouraged.[33]

To the conventional reasoning of the defender of the *status quo* that the abolition of these arrangements would usher in anarchy and revolution, Hegel retorts by pointing out that it is their persistence that fosters rebellion, while their abolition is in fact one of the fundamental preconditions of a modern state:

> We all know that in other states rights of this kind [viz. ecclesiastical tithes, manorial rights and the Game Laws] have vanished without any such consequences [of anarchy]; not only so, but their abolition is regarded as an important basis of increased welfare and essential freedom.[34]

Conditions in Ireland are analyzed by Hegel with particular care. While he admits that in England proper the Poor Laws do alleviate some of the harsher aspects of poverty, the fact that they do not apply to Ireland makes the conditions in that kingdom even more wretched. Hegel is particularly succinct in pointing out how the religious issue in Ireland is a cloak for blatant social exploitation. Hegel's own quite militant anti-Catholicism recedes completely into the background when he says, in discussing Ireland, that:

> Even the Turks have generally left alone the churches of their Christian, Armenian, and Jewish subjects ... But the English have taken all the churches away from the conquered Catholic population. The Irish ... are compelled, out of the few pence they may have, to pay their own priest and construct a place for their services. On the other hand, they have to pay a tenth of all their produce to Anglican clergy ... [and] the upkeep of the churches that are now Anglican.[35]

There follows a long detailed discussion of social conditions in the Irish village: the system of enclosures, and the peasants' utter helplessness against it, is vividly described. Irish peasants, Hegel remarks, are in a condition so miserable 'that it is not easy to find a parallel example in small and poor districts of continental countries, even in those of them that are backward in civilization'.[36]

---

[33] *Ibid.*
[35] *Ibid.* p. 306.
[34] *Ibid.* pp. 303–4.
[36] *Ibid.* p. 307.

Conditions on the land in Ireland have grown out of the fact that the old feudal order broke down in Ireland in a particularly insidious way: without the peasants gaining possession of the land, the lords of the manor had succeeded in cutting themselves loose from any obligation to look after the welfare of the peasants. This is a system in which the lord enjoys all the privileges of feudalism without any of its obligations, while the peasant bears all the burdens of a feudal system without any of its benefits; in a way, this is much worse than the situation of the French peasantry before 1789. Hegel sees Irish conditions as a unique case of lopsided modernization, which has thus left the peasant in a state worse than feudal bondage. The rigid nature of British law has made conditions even worse:

The moment of transition from feudal tenure to property has slipped by [in Ireland] without giving the farmer class the chance to own land; a chance of achieving this might have been afforded by altering rights of inheritance, introducing an equal patrimony between the children, allowing distraint and the sale of property for the payment of debts . . . But English legislation about property . . . has got too far away from the freedom enjoyed in these matters by continental countries.[37]

Obviously such structural defects in the fabric of British society could not be remedied by a mere change in the rules governing the election of members to parliament. The advocates of the Reform Bill did not, after all, have the political courage, or the social will, to propose a thorough reform of English conditions. To do so would cause injury to too many vested interests:

In order to hit upon radical measures for diminishing the oppressive character of the English political administration, it would have been necessary to trespass too deeply on the inner constitution of particular rights . . . [like] diminishing the prodigious national debt substantially . . .

The exorbitant cost of the chaotic administration of justice (which makes the road to court open to the rich alone), the poor-rate which a ministry could not introduce in Ireland, where need and justice alike demanded it, the utilization of ecclesiastical revenues . . . and many other great branches of society, presuppose, for the making of any change, other changes in the power of the state than those stipulated in the Reform Bill.[38]

The Reform Bill thus appears to Hegel to be a half-measure. Hegel believes that in some instances the Bill will even aggravate existing social conditions. The burden of taxation, falling so heavily on the lower classes, will not become lighter, not only because objective causes will not be affected by the Bill but also because of

[37] *Ibid.* pp. 308–9.   [38] *Ibid.* p. 303.

'the habits of military and naval men and their demand not to fall behind other classes in good living and luxury'.[39] Ecclesiastical tithes and patronage will not disappear and the Church will continue to serve as a refuge for the young sons of the nobility.[40] True, a few seats will be added to Ireland, and they may be occupied by Catholic members; but this will not solve the plight of the Irish peasantry. Hegel goes so far as to maintain that, paradoxically, the Reform Bill may even reinforce the hold of the established social classes on parliamentary representation.[41] The abolition of the rotten boroughs and the tighter control over election procedures will mean that the poor will thus lose some of the few windfalls the old corrupt system sent their way in the form of bribery.[42] Some magnates will certainly present a number of their dependent farmers as possessing the £10 freehold and thus enable them to vote; but the vote of such dependent voters will certainly be controlled by their patrons. Hegel even speculates that ultimately, after some adjustments, the landed interests may be able to retain much of their influence.[43]

However, what troubles Hegel about the composition of the reformed House of Commons is that while the Reform Bill will be able to do nothing about the reform of English social conditions, which will remain as excruciating as before, a door would be opened to social demagoguery. Hegel makes it clear in his critique of English conditions that he sees very little in the English social structure which he would like preserved; but a partial, ineffective reform of merely parliamentary representation may cause the advocates of reform 'to come on the scene only as an opposition to the government and the existing order of things; and the principles themselves would have to appear not in their practical truth and application, as in Germany, but in the dangerous form of French abstractions. The antitheses between *hommes d'état* and *hommes à*

39 *Ibid.* p. 302.
40 *Ibid.* pp. 305–6.
41 *Ibid.* p. 307. Hegel remarks that an 1830 Act of Parliament disenfranchized 200,000 Irish voters by raising the freehold qualification in Ireland.
42 *Ibid.* pp. 315–16.
43 *Ibid.* p. 312: 'But there is a general view ... that landowners and the agricultural interest will not only lose nothing of their influence, but will more likely gain a relative increase, because the proposal in relation to the electoral rights that are to be cancelled is to give the big cities or the trading interest only twenty-five members, while the other eighty-one are to go to counties of the landed interest together with the smaller burghs, where into the bargain the influence of the landed proprietor usually prevails.'

principes which appeared in France at the beginning of the Revolution in just as sharp a form has not yet set foot in England; but it may well be introduced as a result of opening a broader way to seats in Parliament.'[44]

Violent revolution is indeed a danger facing England – not because the Reform Bill is too radical, but because it is not radical enough and so wholly inadequate to deal with the social needs for peaceful transformation in England. In general, the abstract ideas of total revolution popular in France may not take hold of public opinion in England. The relative freedom of English institutions, the pluralism and voluntarism in English social life, 'this free and more concrete condition of civil life may add to the probability that abstract principles of freedom will not so soon find in the class above the lower one . . . the welcome which the opponents of the Reform Bill represent as threatening immediately'.[45] French political centralism is, to Hegel, to a large extent responsible for the abstract nature of French theories about political rights. The more 'concrete' English attitude, representing a 'more practical political sense', may avert such a danger of abstract theories becoming dominant. Hence England has a better chance than France ever had of progressing towards modernization and an overhauling of its political system through peaceful, rather than violent, transformation.

As the last of Hegel's writings, the *English Reform Bill* is thus far from being a conservative defence of the old, oligarchical House of Commons. It is rather one of the most informed and radical critiques of English social conditions. Hegel is well aware of the immensity of England's social and economic problems and cognizant of the inadequacy of purely technical and political solutions. His essay reads like an agenda for social reform in England, and it is remarkable how many of the social and economic reforms advocated by him did indeed become law later during the nineteenth century and thus enabled England to proceed along the path of relatively peaceful social modernization which the reform of the franchise alone would never have guaranteed. Late Victorian England was a very different society from that of the early nineteenth century precisely because it moved along the path described by Hegel as necessary for England if it were to achieve the stage of a modern, more rationally ordered society.

As for Hegel himself, it is indeed noteworthy that his first piece of political writing dealt with the iniquities of the social system

---

[44] *Ibid.* p. 325.   [45] *Ibid.* p. 330.

imposed by the Bernese patriciate on the people of Vaud, while so much of his last political essay concerned itself with the injustices inflicted by the English oligarchic system on the Irish peasantry and the lower classes in Britain generally. In both cases his political argument called for a restructuring and remodelling of an antiquated social system which used political power for social oppression. At the same time, however, Hegel's understanding of the nature of the modern state was somewhat modified. As pointed out by Pelczynski, Hegel's initial theory of politics envisaged a state that deals almost purely with defence; but, later on, he moved to a more comprehensive view, according to which the state, in order to preserve the solidarity of the citizenry, has to deal consciously with social problems, primarily with the care of the poor. Society had changed, and 'a dynamic bourgeois society, engaged in the production, distribution and exchange of wealth'[46] presented challenges far more complex than those of an earlier period. Yet Hegel, who was one of the first to realize the social implications of modern society, also provides in his thought an example of how philosophy by understanding that which is, is also contributing to its transformation.

[46] Introductory Essay to *Political Writings*, p. 67.

Chapter Twelve

HISTORY – THE PROGRESS TOWARDS THE CONSCIOUSNESS OF FREEDOM

In his *Wissenschaft der Logik* Hegel defines actuality as 'the unity of essence and existence'.[1] It is the gradual progress towards the realization of this unity which constitutes the meaning of history for Hegel. Out of what appears as incomprehensible chaos, the philosopher has to distill the hidden meaning written into it by reason. While previous philosophies, and Kant's in particular, tended to divorce the realms of essence and existence and even postulated their ultimate incommensurability, Hegel sees history as the context where the *Nous* is in the process of being realized. In history, spirit externalizes itself and becomes objective and man's consciousness reaches awareness of itself:

The genuine truth is the prodigious transfer of the inner into the outer, the building of reason into the real world, and this has been the task of the world during the whole course of its history. It is by working at this task that civilized man has actually given reason an embodiment in law and government and achieved consciousness of the fact.[2]

That such a view of history could lead to a deterministic theory of development is obvious to Hegel himself and he repeatedly cautions against this eventuality, pointing to the place of consciousness in the process of history. Since spirit is to him the content of history, history is not a spectacle in which the mighty have the last say. The only necessity in historical development is that of freedom's progress towards self-realization in human consciousness, and the unfolding of reason in history is itself a philosophical necessity:

Further, world history is not the verdict of mere might, i.e. the abstract and non-rational inevitability of a blind destiny. On the contrary, since mind is implicitly and actually reason, and reason is explicit to itself in mind as knowledge, world history is the necessary development, out of the concept of mind's

[1] G. W. F. Hegel, *Science of Logic*, trans. W. H. Johnston and L. G. Struthers (London and New York, 1929), II, 160.
[2] *Philosophy of Right*, § 270. Cf. Karl Löwith, *Meaning in History* (Chicago, 1949), pp. 52–9.

freedom alone, of the moments of reason and so of the self-consciousness and freedom of mind.[3]

It is this theme which constitutes the core of Hegel's lectures on the *Philosophy of History*. Like many others of Hegel's lecture courses, the text which we possess is not Hegel's own, but is made up of his students' lecture notes, posthumously edited and published by his disciples. This creates some problems about the reliability of the text, particularly since Hegel lectured on the philosophy of history several times and there are clear variations from one set of lectures to another. But lately these problems have been at least partially solved by a comparison of the students' lecture notes with some of Hegel's own sketches and notes for his lectures. For the English reader the problem is compounded by the lack of a modern textually reliable translation.[4]

The stages of history, which for Hegel represent stages of consciousness, are objectified in a succession of cultures, *Volksgeister*. Hegel discerns four main cultures: the Oriental, the Greek, the Roman and the Germanic-Christian. In each stage of history it is one nation, one culture, which is dominant;[5] but its dominance is not political – and here Hegel's view of a *Volksgeist* diverges from that read into the term by later nineteenth-century political theories. Hegel does maintain that a *Volk* has to found a state, since the very existence of a body politic is an expression of its actuality and its ability to function in the objective world. But this does not imply the emergence of a unitary state, let alone a nation-state, nor is the dominance of any given *Volksgeist* reducible to its political power. The Greek *Volksgeist* is a case in point: the specific expression of the

---

[3] *Philosophy of Right*, § 342. See also Ivan Soll, 'Hegels Rechtfertigung der Geschichte', *Hegel-Jahrbücher* (1968–9), pp. 81–8.

[4] For the textual problems involved, see Hoffmeister's remarks on pp. 272–8 of his edition of *Die Vernunft in der Geschichte* (Hamburg, 1955). Sibree's English translation, originally published in 1858, is unfortunately based on an incomplete German text and is also guilty of a number of gross mistranslations, e.g. rendering *die germanische Welt* as 'The German World', not distinguishing between *Sittlichkeit* and *Moralität*, etc. A newer translation of some portions of the general introduction to the *Philosophy of History* has been published by Robert S. Hartman as *Reason in History* (New York, 1953). Lacking a more authoritative English text I have had to rely upon Sibree's edition, correcting some of the more glaring mistranslations, and have referred on other occasions to Hartman or, when necessary, have rendered my own translation.

[5] *Philosophy of Right*, § 347. It should be emphasized that Hegel's usage of the term *Volk* is still rather undifferentiated: sometimes it means 'nation' in the modern sense, sometimes a group of linguistically related peoples, as when Hegel refers to the Slavic *Volk*.

Greek spirit was the polis, but classical Greece never achieved
political unity; and when Greece became united under the Macedonian dynasty and succeeded in conquering the Orient, the dominance of Greece was already declining. It is the very ability to
create *a* state that is a necessary condition for a *Volksgeist*;
'national' unity is totally irrelevant, as Hegel's preference for
classical, disunited Greece over the Greco–Macedonian Empire
clearly shows. What distinguishes a dominant *Volksgeist* is thus its
overall culture, and not its political or military might: 'We find
poetry, fine arts, science and also philosophy in all world historical
peoples',[6] Hegel remarks, and the post-1815 age, to him the apex of
history, is characterized by a plurality of states in Germany itself as
well as in the wider Western European world in which not one state,
but the spirit, is dominant.

THE STAGES OF HISTORY

Hegel's division of history into periods in his *Philosophy of History*
follows some of his earliest historical fragments very closely.[7] The
following account, which necessarily does an injustice to the richness and complexity of Hegel's views on historical development, will
try to bring out the salient points of the *political* dimension of this
philosophy: the breadth of historical knowledge implied in Hegel's
account of historical development is truly astonishing, and it deserves a close historical critique which, however, cannot be offered
here.

For Hegel, history starts in the East; not in the conventional
Eastern Mediterranean, but in China and India. Hegel is one of the
first European thinkers to incorporate the Asian world into his
scheme of history and emancipate the non-European world from its
historiosophical marginality.[8] According to Hegel, the principle of
the Oriental world is static, epitomized in the absolute power of
the monarch who ascribes to himself divine attributes:

The first phase – that with which we have to begin – is the East. Unreflected
consciousness – substantial, objective, spiritual existence – forms the basis ...
Substantial forms constitute the gorgeous edifices of Oriental Empires in

[6] *Reason in History*, p. 85.
[7] See above, p. 8. For some later historical fragments, see *Berliner Schriften*,
pp. 718–31.
[8] There are also a few passages about Africa, which bear witness to Hegel's
astonishingly wide range of reading (*Philosophy of History*, ed. Sibree, pp.
91–9), but these are of a very rudimentary nature.

which we find all rational ordinances and arrangements, but in such a way, that individuals remain as mere accidents ... The glory of Oriental conception is the One Individual as that substantial being to which all belongs, so that no other individual has a separate existence, or mirrors himself in his subjective freedom ... On the one hand we see duration, stability – Empires belonging to mere space, as it were [as distinguished from time] – unhistorical history ... On the other side, the form of time stands contrasted with this spatial stability. The states in question, without undergoing any change in themselves, or in the principle of their existence, are constantly changing their position towards each other. They are in ceaseless conflict, which brings on rapid destruction ... This history too is, for the most part, really unhistorical, for it is only the repetition of the same majestic ruin. The new element, which in the shape of bravery, prowess, magnanimity, occupies the place of the previous despotic pomp, goes through the same circle of decline and subsidence.[9]

Since consciousness, insofar as it appears in this culture, is expressed only in the one individual person who heads the political structure and not in the totality of the commonwealth, such a culture cannot change itself from within. Hence it is doomed to being static and stagnant. In the Oriental world the individual is totally immersed in substantiality; the sacred has not yet been separated from the profane, and the Oriental absolute despot appears by necessity as the incarnation, in some way or other, of the deity.[10]

The Oriental principle is subdivided according to Hegel into a number of secondary principles. The first is the Chinese, which completely lacks any differentiation between objective existence and subjective consciousness. The static is forever repeating itself: China has really no history, despite all the foreign conquests, and it is 'at once the oldest and the newest' realm;[11] it exists today in the same manner it has existed for over four thousand years. The principle of Chinese ethics is in the family, and this moment appears again in the state, which is thus based on the patriarchical prototype. This makes the Chinese empire into the model of an absolute monarchy; individual morality is totally undifferentiated from political *Sittlichkeit*, and the rulers do not respect any particular interests or opinions. Religion is also attuned to family morality and

---

[9] *Ibid.* pp. 105–6. Marx held a similar view, probably derived from Hegel, on the unchanging and static nature of what he calls 'the Asiatic mode of production'. See Karl Marx, *On Colonialism and Modernization*, ed. S. Avineri (Garden City, 1968), pp. 88–9, 125, 418.

[10] Hegel is extremely critical of the various romantic idealizations of Oriental society, so fashionable in the early nineteenth century. For a devastating critique of Wilhelm von Humboldt's and Johann Josef von Görres' views, especially on India, see *Berliner Schriften*, pp. 85–154, 428.

[11] *Philosophy of History*, p. 116.

The stages of history

hence is a mere instrument for achieving political obedience. The family, civil society and the state are thus one.

Hegel explains that it was this aspect of the Chinese empire which endeared it as a system of government to the people around Louis XIV and later to some of the luminaries of the Enlightenment. The Chinese Emperor epitomized the enlightened absolutist ruler: he is Fénelon's *Télémaque*, the model of Solomonic absolutist wisdom. But, Hegel adds, this form of government was utterly unsuited to Europe, where subjective consciousness had come into its own in the wake of Christianity. It could function only in China, where all were equal in their subservience and were equally dependent on the imperial bureaucracy. European absolutism was thus doomed to failure from the outset.[12]

India, on the other hand, represents a deep socio-cultural differentiation, but the principle of differentiation as it appears in the caste system is arbitrary and naturalistic, completely devoid of a spiritual dimension. The caste system, based as it is on the accident of birth, has already been harshly criticized by Hegel in the *Philosophy of Right*, where it is linked to the Platonic order of society: it leaves no room for consciousness, man is reduced merely to his function and the distinction between what is human and what is animal-like disappears. Hence the state itself is left with only arbitrary functions, utterly unrestricted by any ethical considerations.[13]

The third sub-division of the Oriental realm is the Persian: in Zoroastrian religion the Persians had, according to Hegel, discovered reason as well as its opposite, but never were they able to go beyond this opposition. The King stands for what is good, and though the multi-national Persian empire, in its basic tolerance and pluralism, seems already a transition to the Occident, freedom is still embedded in the abstract action of the monarch, not in any consciousness acting in the populace.[14] Similarly, the Mosaic law is a blind, unreflective obedience imposed on a people as yet unconscious of the inner, reflective truth.

The second cultural sphere or 'world', following the Oriental, is the Greek. What distinguishes the Greek *Volksgeist* is the multitude of forms, represented in the plurality of city-states. The Greek world is the realm of beautiful freedom, which discerns the ethical and the beautiful in the multiplicity of forms and nuances. Subjective freedom does already appear, but it is still embedded (*eingebettet*) in the substantial unity of the polis. The polis is a given, not a willed

[12] *Ibid.* p. 124.   [13] *Ibid.* pp. 145, 161.   [14] *Ibid.* pp. 173–6.

entity.[15] Ethical behaviour is imbued in the individual naturally, and it is not an outcome of a conscious moral choice.[16]

What Greek culture lacks is individual subjectivity, hence the difference between classical and modern democracy: classical democracy is based on the assumption that the popular decision gives expression to the citizen's identification with the republic, annunciating the fundamental tenet of the polis that there is no tension between the will of the individuals and the common will. Modern democracy, on the other hand, based as it is on subjective freedom as initially introduced by Christianity, is a completely different phenomenon.[17]

Hence living democratically for the Greek meant living traditionally, not being faced with the agonizing choices of modern life, where the tension between the private and the public is at the core of civil life. The ancient Greeks knew nothing of this; they still lived in a totally unmediated political structure:

> Of the Greeks in the first and genuine form of their freedom we may assert, that they had no conscience; the habit of living for their country without further [analysis or] reflection, was the principle dominant among them. The consideration of the state in the abstract – which to our understanding is the essential point – was alien to them. Their grand object was their country in its living and real aspect; this actual Athens, this Sparta, these temples, these altars, this form of social life, this union of fellow-citizens, these manners and customs. To the Greek his country was a necessity of life, without which existence was impossible.[18]

This beautiful, unmediated harmony was disrupted, first, in a negative way, by the Sophists and later by Socrates; Plato's attempt to combat this spirit, this free indefinite personality, was itself 'precisely the pivot on which the impending world revolution turned at that time'[19] – ultimately leading to Christianity. The lack of subjective freedom in the classical world was, according to Hegel, the cause of the quest for an objective dimension that would decide arbitrarily what the will really is: since the individual could not say 'I will', he had to have recourse to magic symbolism – the Delphic oracle, the *auspicium* and so on. Because man did not yet dare to attribute to himself the power of ultimate decision, he needed a

---

15 *Ibid.* pp. 106–7.
16 Rectorial Address, 2 September 1813 (*Nürnberger Schriften*, p. 363).
17 *Philosophy of History*, p. 251.
18 *Ibid.* p. 253.
19 *Philosophy of Right*, p. 10. G. W. F. Hegel, *Lectures ·on the History of Philosophy*, trans. E. S. Haldane (London, 1892), I, 384–447.

higher, insurmountable authority to make this decision for him.[20] Consequently Hegel even sees the sack of the temple at Delphi by the Phocii as a symbolic indicator of the decline of classical Greece.

While Hegel's critical account of Greece is accompanied by his obvious admiration for the culture of the polis – an admiration already evident in the description of the polis in his earliest writings – he shows very little sympathy for what is represented by the third state of history, the Roman world. Rome stands for sheer arbitrary, external power:

The Roman principle thereby exhibits itself as the cold abstraction of sovereignty and power, as the pure egotism of the will in opposition to others, involving no ethical element of determination, but appearing in a concrete form only in the shape of individual interests.[21]

To the Roman, the state is the ultimate end, not the totality of social life, as it was to the Greek. The individual is a mere instrument in the hands of the state and the polis is turned into a universal empire, which thus ceases to be the realm of beautiful, though unmediated freedom, and becomes the sphere of hard work and servitude. This universal entity engulfs the individuals and they have to disappear in it – persons, peoples, all particular and distinct units. This is the utter abstraction of power, and with the growth of empire the struggle for power within Rome itself became worse, since nothing could satiate the infinite drive for more and more power. The transformation of the republic into the empire is nothing else than an expression of this unlimited craving of power for power's sake.[22] Caracalla's edict which made all subjects of the empire equal before the law was merely the ultimate stage in this stripping of the subject of all independent power *vis-à-vis* political power as represented by the emperor: *imperium* became indistinguishable from *dominium*.[23]

Ultimately, Christianity emerged as an answer to this utter lack of mediation between the subject and political power. Hegel's account of Christianity in the *Philosophy of History* follows the path already to be found in his earlier writings, though the implications are different. Christianity introduced the element of subjective consciousness, and though this had to pass through a number of stages, culminating in the Lutheran Reformation and ultimately in

[20] *Philosophy of History*, p. 254.   [21] *Ibid.* pp. 308–9.   [22] *Ibid.* p. 311.
[23] *Ibid.* pp. 313–14. Cf. also Hegel's historical fragments from the Frankfurt period, where the Roman empire is similarly described as the ultimate in enslavement (*Dokumente*, p. 265).

the French Revolution, history since the emergence of Christianity is a continuous unfolding of the principle of subjective freedom in the world.[24] If the Oriental world knew only *one* man to be free – the despot – and the polis knew already that *some* men are free, Christianity announced the principle that *all* men can be free. That the principle of subjective freedom in Christianity leads to the political and social freedoms of the French Revolution is noted by Hegel in a revealing discussion on property:

> It is about a millenium and a half since the freedom of personality began through the spread of Christianity to blossom and gain recognition as a universal principle from a part, though still a small part, of the human race. But it was only yesterday, we might say, that the principle of the freedom of property became recognized in some places. This example from history may serve to rebuke the impatience of opinion and show the length of time that mind required for progress in its self-consciousness.[25]

But the historical context within which Christianity became dominant was unique, since it was carried by an historical agent – the Germanic peoples – who were originally alien to it. Hegel calls the fourth stage of history 'the Germanic world' (*die germanische Welt*), and this term is coeval with Western Christendom – with the states which were established by the descendants of the Germanic peoples on the ruins of the Western Roman Empire: the 'Germanic world' thus encompasses not only Germany and the Nordic nations, but France, Italy, Spain and England as well. The Romance peoples, as well as the more narrowly defined Teutonic peoples, are expressly included by Hegel in his 'Germanic world', and any attempt to view the last and fourth stage in Hegel's philosophy of history as connected with the nationalistic or ethnic-linguistic views of later German romanticists and nationalists has no foundation in Hegel's usage of the term 'Germanic world'. Sibree's translation of *die germanische Welt* as 'the German World' has misled many English readers, creating the understandable but incorrect notion that Hegel was referring to German supremacy.[26]

[24] On the role of the Reformation, see esp. Hegel's address on the occasion of the tricentenary anniversary of the Augsburg Confession (*Berliner Schriften*, pp. 32–55).

[25] *Philosophy of Right*, § 62. On the philosophical significance of the French Revolution, see *Philosophy of History*, pp. 449–54, and *Political Writings*, p. 234. On the lopsided impact of the French Enlightenment on Germany, see Hegel's critique of Hamann's writings in *Berliner Schriften*, pp. 224–5.

[26] For the explicit inclusion of the Romance people in the 'Germanic world', see *Philosophy of History*, p. 349. For a painstaking distinction between *deutsch* and *germanisch*, see the historical fragment printed in *Berliner Schriften*, p. 734.

The stages of history

There is a further element here which is of considerable interest: despite the fact that Hegel attributes the final stage to the Germanic peoples, he views with disdain the original culture of the ancient Germanic tribes. The Germanic *Ur-Volk*, so much idolized and mythologized by the romantic tradition in Germany, is to Hegel a complete irrelevance. On several occasions he even viciously ridicules some of the romanticizers of the mythical Teutonic *Ur-Volk*.[27] The role of the Germanic peoples in history is due solely to the fact that they received Christianity from the Romans, and though they destroyed the Roman empire, they absorbed its culture which included at that time the Christian religion:

It is extremely important to stress how different is the course of Germanic history from that of the Greeks and Romans. The latter embodied their own original principles, the impulse to Germanic development was imparted to the Germanics by alien culture. Their culture (*Bildung*), their laws and religions are alien.[28]

Hegel also casts aside the pet theory of freedom emanating from the forests of Germany:

We will not follow the Germanics back into their forests, nor investigate the origin of their migration. Those forests of theirs have always passed for the abodes of free peoples, and Tacitus sketched his celebrated picture of Germany with a certain love and longing – contrasting it with the corruption and artificiality of that world to which he himself belonged. But we must not on this account regard such a state of barbarism as an exalted one, or fall into some such error as Rousseau's, who represents the condition of the American savages as one in which man is in possession of true freedom. Certainly there is an immense amount of misfortune and sorrow of which the savage knows nothing; but this is a merely negative advantage, while freedom is essentially positive. It is only the blessings conferred by affirmative freedom that are regarded as such in the highest grade of consciousness.[29]

As we have seen in our earlier discussions, it is this conscious freedom which Hegel sees as actualized in his contemporary world. We shall yet have to see how final this stage really is.

[27] For such an attack on Arndt's romanticization of the old Teutonic *Ur-Volk*, see *Berliner Schriften*, p. 677.
[28] G. W. F. Hegel, *Vorlesungen über die Philosophie der Weltgeschichte*, ed. G. Lasson (Leipzig, 1923), p. 758. Sibree's translation omits this passage. He cites, however, similar passages such as: 'The process of culture they underwent consisted in taking up foreign elements and reductively amalgamating them with their own national life. Thus their history presents an introversion – the attraction of alien forms of life and the beginning of these to bear upon their own . . . The Germanic World took up the Roman culture and religion in their completed form . . . In art and philosophy a similar alien influence predominated.' (*Philosophy of History*, pp. 341–3).
[29] *Ibid.* p. 347.

THE CUNNING OF REASON AND THE
WORLD HISTORICAL INDIVIDUAL

One of the distinctive traits of Hegel's philosophy of history is the dialectical tension postulated between intent and outcome. History is the unfolding drama of man's coming into himself, and in this drama Hegel allots a central role to the works of 'great men'; but these appear as mere agents of a higher purpose which, unbeknownst to themselves, moves them towards goals of which they are rarely fully cognizant.

The great men of history – 'the world historical individuals' to follow Hegel's terminology – thus occupy an ambivalent place in his scheme of history. They are judged by Hegel not by their motives but by the objective result of their work. Already in his early fragment on Württemberg, Hegel warned against a motivational, psychological approach to history:

The so-called secret motives and intentions of single individuals, as well as anecdotes and subjective impressions, have been regarded as the most important thing in the psychological view of history which was still in vogue not so long ago. But this view has now been discredited and history strives once more, in accordance with its dignity, to set forth the nature and the march of the thing in its substantial being, and to afford an understanding of men of action from what they do.[30]

The role of the individual in history is strongly linked in Hegel's thought to changes in political structures. Since the operational legitimacy of the political order is completely divorced in his thought from the historical circumstances in which it came into being, Hegel faces no problem in presenting historical states as originating not in contract but in the act of a 'great man', although he explicitly states that the power of the 'great man' has very little to do with physical coercion:

All states have thus been established by the sublime power of great men: not through physical strength, since the many are stronger than [any] single person. But the great man has something in his traits which makes all others call him their master; they obey him against their own will ... All gather around his banner: he is their God. Such was the way in which Theseus founded the state of Athens; similarly, in the French Revolution, a terrible power held the state, everything. This power is not despotism, but tyranny, pure horrible (*entsetzliche*) power; but it is necessary and just insofar as it establishes and preserves the states as [such] an actual individual.[31]

[30] *Political Writings*, p. 247.
[31] *Realphilosophie II*, 246. Both here and in 'The German Constitution' (*Political Writings*, pp. 219–23), Hegel refers to Machiavelli as the originator of this theory of a constitutive dictatorship. For another reference to Theseus, see *Political Writings*, pp. 219, 241.

The cunning of reason and the world historical individual

Hegel's ambivalent attitude toward such a constitutive dictatorship is thus most clearly expressed. Its role is dialectical: it has to educate the populace towards obedience, to instil in it the habit of obeying the general rather than the particular will. But once it accomplishes its task, it becomes redundant and withers away, it is *aufgehoben*:

By thus educating towards obedience ... tyranny becomes superfluous and the rule of law is being introduced. The power which tyranny exercises is the power of law in itself; through obedience it ceases to be an alien power, becomes the conscious general will. Tyranny is overthrown by the peoples because it is abhorrent, degrading, etc. The real cause for this is that it has become superfluous.[32]

Consent, according to Hegel, has been introduced historically by means not based on consent. Hegel thus eschews the *petitio principi* implied in so many liberal theories when they are confronted by the prickly question of, for example, how majority rule was decided upon and legitimized in the first place. Hegel, on the other hand, is fully conscious of the uncomfortable fact that every foundation of a new state, and every revolutionary change in history, are events which can find their legitimacy only within themselves and not in any previous criteria. The foundation of a new state, or the introduction of a new social order, by definition, cannot be based on initial consensus, and within traditional theories of legitimacy such an event will always have a mark of bastardy written on its face. For all his elaborate system of legitimizing revolt under clearly circumscribed circumstances, Locke always remained uneasy about it, and to Hegel the recourse to 'self-evident truths' is an exercise in chicanery on the part of a victorious revolution: the rebels of yesterday parade in usurped legitimate garb.

But in another sense, the 'great man' of history does speak for his age, expresses its will, though this will may not always be explicit. Had he not given expression to latent forces in the social order of his generation, he would have never succeeded in accomplishing anything: 'The great man of his age is the one who can put into words the will of his age, tell his age what its will is, and accomplish it. What he does is the heart and essence of his age, he actualizes his

---

[32] *Realphilosophie II*, 246–7. Similarly, Hegel explains Robespierre's fall because 'power has abandoned him since necessity abandoned him and he was overthrown' (*ibid.* 248). It is fascinating to speculate that Marx's thought about the dictatorship of the proletariat and the ultimate *Aufhebung* of the state has a similar dialectical structure. Cf. also the dialectics of Master and Slave (*Phenomenology*, pp. 233–40).

age.'[33] Writing about Richelieu in *The German Constitution*, Hegel similarly points out that his enemies 'gave way not to Richelieu as a man but to his genius, which linked his person with the necessary principle of the unity of the state . . . Herein lies the political genius, in the identification of an individual with a principle.'[34]

Hegel is thus able to put a distance between a historical person's motives and the consequences of his deeds; reason works in history through the instrumentality of subjective elements. This is the cunning of reason, *List der Vernunft*. On the one hand, the world historical individual has a central place in historical development as an agent of change, innovation and upheaval; on the other, he is a mere instrument in the hands of superior forces and his own views or ideas are of little importance. Nor is it these subjective notions that are being realized in history; rather it is something which transcends the individual himself.[35] As a matter of fact, the motivation of a Caesar or a Napoleon may have been petty ambition rather than an overall view of historical destiny; yet the hidden hand of reason managed to fit even these ambitions into a wider perspective. Passions, ambition, jealousy, greed and the like are thus viewed as the handmaids of reason working in history. Consequently, there is a basic difference between the way in which Hegel views the historical hero and, for example, the veneration of a Carlyle. These individuals, according to Hegel,

are the living instruments of what is in substance the deed of the world mind and they are therefore directly at one with that deed though it is concealed from them and is not their aim and object. For the deeds of the world mind, therefore, they receive no honour or thanks either from their contemporaries or from public opinion in later ages. All that is vouchsafed to them by such opinion is undying fame in respect of the subjective form of their acts.[36]

The personal fate of the world historical individual is also of secondary importance; in terms of their own goals, these historical figures often end up in failure. But it is what they have accomplished that counts:

Once their objective is attained, they fall off like empty hulls from the kernel. They die early like Alexander, they are murdered like Caesar, transported to

[33] *Philosophy of Right*, addition to § 318.
[34] *Political Writings*, p. 216.
[35] Sidney Hook, *The Hero in History* (London, 1955), pp. 59–66, does not always take account of this dialectical relationship.
[36] *Philosophy of Right*, § 348. For an interesting view on Pericles in this context, see Hegel's letter to Döderlein, 29 April 1817 (*Briefe von und an Hegel*, II, 157).

The cunning of reason and the world historical individual

Saint Helena like Napoleon ... They are fortunate in being the agents of a purpose which constituted a step in the progress of the universal spirit. But as individuals ... they are not what is commonly called happy, nor did they want to be.[37]

Yet this dramatic scenario contains an epistemological difficulty which points to a number of questions that must have remained unsettled in Hegel's own mind. When Hegel calls the world historical individual an 'agent' or an 'instrument' this implies not only that the individuals involved might have been motivated by considerations far inferior to the ultimate ends of history, but also that they might not have been aware at all of the historical importance of their work. What is intriguing is that Hegel seems unsure of himself about the exact extent to which the world historical individuals were aware of the historical significance of what they were doing. We have already quoted above Hegel's view that 'the great man of his age is the one who can put into words the will of his age' as well as his saying that the deeds of the world mind are 'concealed from them and [are] not their aim and object'. In the passages of the *Philosophy of History* dealing with the historical figures one can further discern at least three variations on this theme:

(a) The historical men, world historical individuals, are those who grasp ... a higher universal, make it their own purpose and realize this purpose in accordance with the higher law of the spirit ... The world historical persons, the heroes of their age, must therefore be recognized as its seers.[38]

(b) Caesar was motivated not only by his own private interest, but acted instinctively to bring to pass that which the times required.[39]

(c) Such individuals have no consciousness of the Idea as such. They are practical and political men.[40]

We thus find Hegel describing the world historical individual as, alternatively, (i) wholly conscious of the idea of history and its development, (ii) only instinctively conscious of it and (iii) totally unaware of it. With all the possible allowance for the varieties of expression and nuance, no adequate explanation can be given for what must in the last resort be viewed as a series of contradictory statements. And though it is obvious that the argument of Hegel – that the progress of history is mediated through subjective motives wholly unrelated to the *telos* of history – is apparent in all the variations quoted above, the crucial problem of how far the world

[37] *Reason in History*, p. 41.   [38] *Ibid*. pp. 39–40.
[39] *Ibid*. p. 39.   [40] *Ibid*. p. 40.

233

historical individuals are aware of the historical dimension of their deeds remains unsolved.

A further problem is involved here. The periods of history signify for Hegel successive stages in the development of self-consciousness. What is surprising in Hegel's account of the world historical individual's subjective awareness of the significance of his own actions is that, whatever the ambiguities just pointed out, there is no development over time of this awareness. One might expect that later historical individuals, representing a higher and more differentiated stage of history, would also be more aware of their own role in the historical process. Yet there is nothing in Hegel to suggest that there is such a development of the historical consciousness of the historical actor. Though the deeds of a Napoleon represent a higher stage than those of a Caesar, Napoleon's historical understanding of his own role seems to be on the same level as that of Caesar. Thus, at the core of Hegel's philosophy of history there remains a strangely static, a-historical element.

This also raises another problem in connection with the relation between history and consciousness. If the historical actor is unaware of the reason implied in the historical process, who then is aware of it? To Hegel the answer is obvious: the philosopher, whose *Nach-denken*, by painting 'its grey on grey' implies that 'a shape of life has grown old'. The philosopher, as we have however seen, should not give 'instruction as to what the world ought to be', nor should he participate in any way in the shaping of the world to come or try to put on the mantle of the historical actor. For philosophy, 'always comes on the scene too late', it 'appears only when actuality is already there, cut and dried after its process of formation has been completed'.[41]

An intriguing paradox is thus presented by Hegel: those who make history do not understand it, and those who understand it do not (and should not) make it. At the end of Hegel's long road, consciousness and action, subject and object, doer and knower, are still separate and the tension between them has not been *aufgehoben*.

GLIMPSES OF THE FUTURE?

Hegel's insistence that philosophy, as *Nach-denken*, deals with that which has already objectified itself in the actual world and not with

[41] *Philosophy of Right*, pp. 12–13.

preaching, prophesying and predicting, is strongly brought out in his *Philosophy of History*. It is in the modern, post-1815 world of Western Europe that Hegel sees the apex of historical development. It is here that 'the empire of thought is established actually and concretely ... Freedom has found the means of realizing its Ideal – its true actuality.'[42] Hegel admits that there is still 'work to be done'; but this, he claims, belongs to the 'empirical side'.[43] The absolutization of the present period in history is thus very strongly emphasized.

Yet we have already seen that in his discussion of modern society Hegel is aware that its mechanism creates problems to which it does not seem to have an adequate answer; the system is, ultimately, much less a closed one than it appears to be at first sight. Similarly, it is extremely interesting to note that on the margin of Hegel's seemingly closed horizon of history there appear a few instances in which he oversteps, however cautiously and reluctantly, the boundaries set down by his own system. These instances have to do with the future roles of Russia and America in world history.

Hegel mentions the Slavs several times in his account of European history. On the one hand, he maintains, they perpetuate within the Christian-Germanic world 'the connection with Asia'.[44] On the other, he adds, 'this whole element has not yet appeared in the development of the spirit, and we do not have to be detained [in our discussion] by them'.[45] Perhaps too much weight should not be attributed to the 'not yet'; but on another occasion, in his most extensive comment on the Slavs, Hegel has the following to say:

We find, moreover, in the East of Europe, the great Slavonic nation, whose settlements extended west of the Elbe to the Danube ... These people did, indeed, found kingdoms and sustain spirited conflicts with the various nations that came across their path. Sometimes, as an advanced guard – an intermediate nationality – they took part in the struggle between Christian Europe and un-Christian Asia. The Poles even liberated beleaguered Vienna from the Turks; and the Slavs have to some extent been drawn within the sphere of occidental reason. Yet this entire body of peoples remains excluded from our consideration, because hitherto it has not appeared as an independent element in the series of phases that reason has assumed in the world. Whether it will do so hereafter, is a question that does not concern us here; for in history we have to do with the past.[46]

---

[42] *Philosophy of History*, p. 110.
[43] *Vernunft in der Geschichte*, p. 257.
[44] *Philosophy of History*, p. 102.
[45] *Vorlesungen über die Philosophie der Weltgeschichte*, p. 758.
[46] *Philosophy of History*, p. 350.

History – the progress towards the consciousness of freedom

Again, one should perhaps not attach too much importance to these asides; yet we also possess a much stronger statement by Hegel, included in a private letter to a Russian Baltic nobleman of Estonian extraction, who attended Hegel's lectures in Heidelberg. Urging his erstwhile student to enter the Russian Imperial service, Hegel says:

You are lucky, sir, to have a fatherland that occupies a conspicuous place in the realm of world history and which has undoubtedly an even higher vocation. It looks as if the other modern states have already passed the pinnacle of their course and their position has become static. Russia, on the other hand, which is perhaps already the strongest power of all, carries in its womb an immense possibility of developing its intensive nature.[47]

A similar set of remarks is made by Hegel about America: a new culture is emerging there, formed out of an amalgam of European, American-Indian and African elements.[48] 'America,' Hegel remarks in a footnote to his 1826–7 lectures on the philosophy of history, 'is clearly the land of the future, which is still in the process of becoming.'[49] The most explicit statement about America's future role is, however, coupled with a caveat against predicting the future – a remark very similar to the one appended by Hegel to his aside about the Slavs:

America is therefore the land of the future, where, in the ages that lie before us, the burden of world's history shall reveal itself – perhaps in a contest between North and South America. It is a land of desire for all those who are weary of the historical lumber-room of old Europe. Napoleon is reported to have said: 'Cette vieille Europe m'ennuie.' It is for America to abandon the ground on which hitherto the history of the world has developed itself. What *has* taken place in the New World up to the present time is only an echo on the Old World – the expression of a foreign life; and as a land of the future, it has no interest for us here, for, as regards history, our concern must be with that which has been and that which is. In regard to philosophy, on the other hand, we have to do with that which (strictly speaking) is neither past nor future, but with that

---

[47] Hegel to Boris von Uexküll, 28 November 1821 (*Briefe von und an Hegel*, II, 297–8). That an offshoot of Hegelian philosophy, Marxism, became the motive force in making Russia into such a world power, only adds to the dialectical irony of this statement as read from our contemporary perspective.

[48] *Philosophy of History*, p. 82. Hegel adds that the Negroes are 'susceptible to European culture' and mentions the examples of blacks who became competent clergymen, doctors, etc. as an indicator of the future possibilities open to the black population in the United States. Needless to say, this is contrary to the prevailing opinion in Europe – and America – at that time. But Hegel's insistence that the blacks can absorb European culture is accompanied by a very low view of African culture itself; no idealization here either.

[49] See appendix to *Vernunft in der Geschichte*, p. 265.

which *is*, which has an eternal existence – with reason; and this is quite sufficient to occupy us.[50]

This is, of course, a remarkable statement for Hegel, and his closing remark shows that he is aware how much he may be straying beyond the pale. But these remarks about Russia and America, preceding by several years Tocqueville's famous dicta,[51] clearly indicate that while Hegel considered history as having attained its apex as the march towards man's self-consciousness in his own age, he was well aware that the future was still open in terms of the emergence of new cultures. Of course, this would then somehow have to relativize the absolute status given by Hegel to his own philosophy as well as to his own age. There is no way of escaping this conclusion which is obviously difficult to square with Hegel's own philosophy. What remains open, however, is whether the future development of Russia and America would signify new 'principles' of world history or just an extension of the principles already achieved; the texts themselves are obscure.

One should therefore recognize that, contrary to some of the accepted views about Hegel, there always remained a question mark beside what appears as his total absolutization of his contemporary age. The dialectical irony implicit in Hegel's systematic treatment of history is thus also brought out. We have seen how many caveats against prediction and projection Hegel has expressed in the course of his philosophy of history; again and again, he has maintained that every philosopher, as an individual person, is a child of his time and that 'it is as absurd to fancy that a philosophy can transcend its contemporary world as it is to fancy that an individual can overleap his own age, jump over Rhodes'.[52] Yet it is intriguing to contemplate that it was precisely that philosopher who always looked for the realization of reason in actuality, who systematically shied away from any attempt at predicting how things

---

[50] *Philosophy of History*, pp. 86–7. Hegel also draws a very instructive picture of the way he conceives of North American society. Since all attention is given to work, 'the desire of repose, the establishment of civil rights, security and freedom' became the basis of the Americans' existence as a united body. The community that thus arose in America was 'the aggregation of individuals as atomic constituents'; hence the state became 'merely something external for the protection of property' (p. 84). Hegel goes on to explain that in North America 'the general object of the existence of [the] state is not yet fixed and determined ... For a real state and a real government arise only after a distinction of classes has arisen, when wealth and poverty become extreme ... But America is hitherto exempt from this pressure' (pp. 85–6).

[51] Alexis de Tocqueville, *Democracy in America*, ed. P. Bradley (New York, 1954), I, 452.   [52] *Philosophy of Right*, p. 11.

would or should be, that it was he who would be able to get a glimpse of what lay beyond his own particular Rhodes.

It could be argued quite convincingly that not too much importance should be read into these fragmentary statements about the future. They are, after all, not much more than mere footnotes to a very impressive and comprehensive corpus of philosophical thinking, and the system should be judged by what is in it, and not by a few notes on its margin. This is easily granted; yet these footnotes indicate that on this issue – just as on the dialectical relationship between the rational and the actual and, on another level, when discussing the social fabric of modern civil society – Hegel's system remains a far more open-ended one than the structure of the system would lead us to believe. The dynamic nature of the dialectics is not, despite appearances, foreclosed. Thus when Moses Hess, following August von Czieskowski, asked in 1841, 'If it is within the possibilities of reason to comprehend the essence of God, freedom and immortality, why should the essence of the future be excluded from it?',[53] then he was asking a question already implicit in the Hegelian system itself.

[53] Moses Hess, 'Die europäische Triarchie', in *Philosophische und sozialistische Schriften*, ed. A. Cornu and W. Mönke (Berlin, 1961), p. 83.

EPILOGUE

Nothing could better express the prejudices and ignorance connected with Hegelian political philosophy in English-speaking countries than the following statement by Bertrand Russell:

It follows from his metaphysics that true liberty consists in obedience to an arbitrary authority, that free speech is an evil, that absolute monarchy is good, that the Prussian state was the best existing at the time when he wrote, that war is good, and that an international organization for the peaceful settlement of disputes would be a misfortune... What he admired were... order, system, regulation and intensity of governmental control.[1]

Labouring under such enormous prejudices, it is not easy to restore a more balanced view of Hegel's political thought. What we have tried to bring out in our discussion is not only how false such a view as expressed by Russell is, but also that Hegel has to be seen as the first major modern political philosopher who attempted to confront the realities of the modern age. While many among eighteenth-century philosophers undoubtedly helped to shape the emergent modern world, their basically a-historical approach made them incapable of facing the challenges of the new society; and Rousseau, who deeply sensed this inadequacy of the *philosophes* and perceived the novelty of his age, retreated in disgust from what the new world had to offer to man. Some of the more extreme antics of the Jacobins bear witness to this turning away from the realities of modern, contemporary life: their reversion to the virtuous republican simplicities of the ancient polis was not a mere rhetorical device – it expressed a deep aversion to the complexities of modern society. While many of the German romantics echoed much of the same theme, though the immediate political implications were anti-revolutionary rather than pro-Jacobin, British utilitarianism could be seen as a courageous, though simple-minded, attempt to throw overboard the whole heritage of Natural Law as well as of historical experience, and see modern man *qua homo economicus* as the

[1] Bertrand Russell, *Unpopular Essays* (London, 1950), p. 22.

239

Epilogue

measure of all things. French Jacobinism ended up by proclaiming terrorism as political virtue; British utilitarianism made the horrors of modern life into a new law of nature.

It is in this context that Hegel's attempt to construct a new political theory becomes significant. Its main theme is perhaps best expressed by Hegel's ambiguous attitude to civil society: on one hand, it is the major achievement of the modern world; on the other, woe to that society of men that allows the forces of civil society to rule unimpeded. This *Golem*, expressing as it does man's creativity and subjective freedom, should not be allowed to run free.

Hence Hegel's insistence on institutional means for the curbing of civil society; hence even his tortured view of war as the power of negation to which even the most obstinate forces of the 'realm of needs' have to bow. In pieces of writing as different from each other as *The German Constitution* and the *Realphilosophie* there emerges the model of a modern state, free as much as possible from the shackles of the old absolutism, based on representation, served by a rationally oriented bureaucracy, allowing ample space for voluntary associations and trying to strike a balance – perhaps an unattainable one – between *homo economicus* and *zoon politikon*. It is in this sense that what Hegel tried to achieve, despite what might appear very old-fashioned because of his sometimes obscure language, is so strikingly contemporary.

What is also contemporary is the feeling which we have seen creeping into Hegel's thought from time to time that the solution offered by him may not be good enough and that the fabric of modern society, trying to reconcile man's craving for unlimited self-expression with his need for a common restraining factor, may be bursting at the seams.

Engels was probably right when he once remarked that no-one has harmed Hegel more than his own disciples.[2] But this might be said of any major thinker. Hegel's main fault, however, may lie somewhere else, and it is a failure as judged by Hegel's own standard of philosophy being 'its own time apprehended in thoughts'. Much as Hegel succeeded to an astonishing degree in reading correctly and in deciphering some of the more vexing problems of the modern period, he also shared some of the illusions common to his own age. Not least among these was his certainty that nationalism had no future: we have seen how vigorously Hegel opposed the

[2] Engels to Friedrich Graeber, 21 December 1839, in: Marx/Engels, *Werke* (Berlin, 1967), Engänzungsband/2. Teil, p. 440.

manifestations of nascent German nationalism, thinking the ethnic ties were just an extension from the past. On this point, however, he misread the signs of the times. Hegel's failure to see nationalism as one of the major forces of the nineteenth and twentieth centuries is perhaps the major flaw in the claim of Hegelian philosophy to express adequately its own *Zeitgeist*. It is the irony of the fate of Hegel's philosophy that in the twentieth century Hegel has been mistakenly and ignorantly branded as the harbinger of modern, and specifically German, nationalism. But with the rise of ethnic, romantic nationalism so much of what Hegel described as characterizing the modern state became irrelevant, and it can be easily understood how his theory of the state became misconstrued; similarly, Hegel's vision that ultimately wars could be limited and minimized in the modern world became a mere wishful thought. The combination of nationalist ideology and total war, which buried under it the relative achievements of the Victorian Age, made Hegel's philosophy also one of its main victims.

Nothing in what has been said until now should be construed to imply that the answers Hegel gave to the other questions raised by him should always be regarded as satisfactory or adequate. But the ability to ask the right kind of questions about the nature of post-1789 society and to incorporate them into a general philosophical system, as well as the realization that consequently classical political theory stands in need of rectification and renaissance – all this makes Hegel into more than a mere chapter in the history of ideas. His questions – if not always his answers – point to the direction of understanding that which is, today as much as in his own time.

BIBLIOGRAPHY

WORKS BY HEGEL

In the original German

Werke, vols. I–XVIII. Berlin, 1832–45.
Sämtliche Werke, vols. I–XX, ed. H. Glockner. Stuttgart, 1927–30.
Werke, vols. I–XX, eds. E. Moldenhauer and K. M. Michel. Frankfurt/Main, 1970–1.
Theologische Jugendschriften, ed. H. Nohl. Tübingen, 1907.
Schriften zur Politik und Rechtsphilosophie, ed. G. Lasson. Leipzig, 1913.
Politische Schriften, Nachwort von Jürgen Habermas. Frankfurt/Main, 1966.
Jenaer Realphilosophie I: Die Vorlesungen von 1803/4, ed. J. Hoffmeister. Leipzig, 1932.
Jenaer Realphilosophie II: Die Vorlesungen von 1805/6, ed. J. Hoffmeister. Republished under the title *Jenaer Realphilosophie. Hamburg*, 1967.
Jenaer Kritische Schriften (Gesammelte Werke, Bd. IV), eds. H. Buchner and O. Pöggeler. Hamburg, 1968.
Phänomenologie des Geistes, ed. J. Hoffmeister. Hamburg, 1952.
Nürnberger Schriften, ed. J. Hoffmeister. Leipzig, 1938.
Wissenschaft der Logik, ed. G. Lasson, 2 vols. new edition. Hamburg, 1966–7.
Grundlinien der Philosophie des Rechts, ed. J. Hoffmeister. Hamburg, 1955.
Vernunft in der Geschichte, ed. J. Hoffmeister. Hamburg, 1955.
Vorlesungen über die Philosophie der Weltgeschichte, ed. G. Lasson, new edition, 4 vols. Hamburg, 1968.
Enzyklopädie der philosophischen Wissenschaften (1830), ed. F. Nicolin and O. Pöggeler. Hamburg, 1959.
Berliner Schriften 1818–1831, ed. J. Hoffmeister. Hamburg, 1956.
Briefe von und an Hegel, ed. J. Hoffmeister, 4 vols. Hamburg, 1952–60.
Dokumente zu Hegels Entwicklung, ed. J. Hoffmeister. Stuttgart, 1936.
Hegel-Archiv, ed. G. Lasson, 3 vols. 1912–17.

English translations

Early Theological Writings, trans. T. M. Knox, introduction by Richard Kroner. Chicago, 1948.
Political Writings, trans. T. M. Knox, with an introductory essay by Z. A. Pelczynski. Oxford, 1964.

Bibliography

The Phenomenology of Mind, trans. J. B. Baillie, with a new introduction by G. Lichtheim. New York, 1967.

Science of Logic, trans. W. H. Johnston and L. G. Struthers, 2 vols. London and New York, 1929.

Philosophy of Right, trans. T. M. Knox. Oxford, 1942.

Reason in History, trans. R. S. Hartman. New York, 1953.

The Philosophy of History, trans. J. B. Sibree, with a new introduction by C. J. Friedrich. New York, 1956.

Lectures on the History of Philosophy, trans. E. S. Haldane and F. H. Simson, 3 vols. London, 1892.

Philosophy of Nature, trans. A. V. Müller, foreword by J. N. Findlay. Oxford, 1970.

Philosophy of Mind, trans. W. Wallace and A. V. Müller. Oxford, 1971.

The Philosophy of Hegel, ed. by C. J. Friedrich. New York, 1953.

Hegel: Selections, ed. J. Loewenberg. New York, 1929.

OTHER WORKS

Absolutulus von Hegelingen [O. H. Gruppe], *Die Winde, oder ganz absolute Konstruktion der Weltgeschichte durch Oberons Horn*. Leipzig [1831].

Adams, G. P., 'The Mystical Element in Hegel's Early Theological Writings', *University of California Publications in Philosophy*, 1910, vol. II, No. 4.

Anon., *Der verderbliche Einfluss der Hegelschen Philosophie*. Leipzig, 1852.

Asveld, Paul, *La pensée religieuse du jeune Hegel: Liberté et aliénation*. Louvain/Paris, 1953.

Bachman, Carl Friedrich, *Anti-Hegel*. Jena, 1835.

Bahnsen, Julius F. A., *Zur Philosophie der Geschichte*. Berlin, 1872.

Barth, Paul, *Die Geschichtphilosophie Hegels und der Hegelianer, bis auf Marx und Hartmann*. Leipzig, 1890.

Bense, Max, *Hegel und Kierkegaard*. Köln and Krefeld, 1948.

Beyer, Wilhelm Raimund, *Zwischen Phänomenologie und Logik*. Frankfurt/Main, 1955.

'Hegels Mitarbeit am *Würtembergischen Volksfreund*', *Deutsche Zeitschrift für Philosophie* XIV (1966), 709–25.

Bloch, Ernst, *Subjekt-Objekt: Erläuterungen zu Hegel*. Berlin, 1951.

Bockelmann, Paul, *Hegels Notstandslehre*. Berlin and Leipzig, 1935.

Buchner, Hartmut, 'Ein unbekannter politischer Text Hegels?' *Hegel-Studien* IV (1967), 205–14.

von Buggenheim, Erich Arnold, *Die Stellung zur Wirklichkeit bei Hegel und Marx*. Rodofzell a. Bodensee, 1933.

ten Bruggencate, H. G., 'Hegel's Views on War', *The Philosophical Quarterly*, October 1950, 58–60.

Bülow, Friedrich, *Die Entwicklung der Hegelschen Sozialphilosophie*. Leipzig, 1920.

Busse, M., *Hegels Phänomenologie des Geistes und der Staat*. Berlin, 1931.

Caird, Edward, *Hegel*. Edinburgh and London, 1883.

Carritt, E. F., 'Hegel and Prussianism', *Philosophy*, April 1940 (190–6), July 1940 (315–17).

Bibliography

Chamley, Paul, *Economie politique et philosophie chez Stewart et Hegel*. Paris, 1963.

Creuzinger, P., *Hegels Einfluss auf Clausewitz*. Berlin, 1911.

Croce, Benedetto, *What is Living and What is Dead of the Philosophy of Hegel*, trans. Douglas Ainslie. London, 1915.

Čyževskyj, Dmitrij, *Hegel bei den Slawen*. Reichenberg, 1934.

Dilthey, Wilhelm, *Die Jugendgeschichte Hegels*. Berlin, 1905.

Dittmann, Friedrich, *Der Begriff des Volksgeistes bei Hegel*. Leipzig, 1909.

Dulckheit, G., *Rechtsbegriff und Rechtsgestalt: Untersuchungen zu Hegels Philosophie des Rechts und ihrer Gegenwartsbedeutung*. Berlin, 1936.

Engel, Otto, *Der Einfluss Hegels auf die Bildung der Gedankenwelt Hippolyte Taines*. Stuttgart, 1920.

Fackenheim, Emil L., *The Religious Dimension in Hegel's Thought*. Bloomington and London, 1967.

'On the Actuality of the Rational and the Rationality of the Actual', *Review of Metaphysics* XIII (June 1970), 690–8.

Fahrenhorst, Eberhard, *Geist und Freiheit im System Hegels*. Leipzig and Berlin, 1934.

Falkenheim, Hugo, 'Eine unbekannte politische Druckschrift Hegels', *Preussische Jahrbücher* CXXXVIII (1909).

Findlay, J. N., *Hegel: A Re-Examination*. New York, 1958.

Fischer, Kuno, *Hegels Leben, Werke und Lehre*, 2 vols. Heidelberg, 1901.

Fleischmann, Eugène, *La philosophie politique de Hegel*. Paris, 1964.

Foster, Michael B., *The Political Philosophies of Plato and Hegel*. Oxford, 1935.

Friedrich, Carl J., 'The Power of Negation: Hegel's Dialectic and Totalitarian Ideology', *Hegel Symposium*, ed. D. C. Travis (Austin, 1962), pp. 13–35.

Gabler, Georg Andreas, *Die Hegelsche Philosophie*. Berlin, 1843.

Germino, Dante, 'Hegel as a Political Theorist', *Journal of Politics* XXXI (1969), 885–912.

'Hegel's Theory of the State: Humanist or Totalitarian?', *Statsvetenskaplig Tidskrift* XIX (1970), 293–313.

Giese, G., *Hegels Staatsidee und der Begriff der Staatserzichung*. Halle, 1926.

Goldstein, Leon J., 'The Meaning of "State" in Hegel's Philosophy of History', *The Philosophical Quarterly* XII (1962), 60–72.

Göschel, Karl Friedrich, *Hegel und seine Zeit*. Berlin, 1932.

Gropp, R. O., 'Die marxistische dialektische Methode und ihr Gegensatz zur idealistischen Dialektik Hegels', *Deutsche Zeitschrift für Philosophie* II (1954), 344–83.

Haering, Theodor, *Hegel: Sein Wollen und sein Werk*, 2 vols. Leipzig and Berlin, 1929.

Haldar, Hiralal, *Hegelianism and Human Personality*. Calcutta, 1910.

Harms, Ernst, *Hegel und das zwanzigste Jahrhundert*. Heidelberg, 1933.

Harris, William T., *Hegel's Logic*. Chicago, 1890.

Haym, Rudolf, *Hegel und seine Zeit*, Berlin, 1857 (reprint, Hildesheim, 1962).

Heidegger, Martin, *Hegel's Concept of Experience*. New York, 1970.

Heimsoeth, Heinz, *Hegel: Ein Wort der Erinnerung*. Erfurt, 1920.

Heller, Hermann, *Hegel und der nationale Machtstaatsgedanke in Deutschland*. Leipzig and Berlin, 1921.

Bibliography

Hoffmeister, Johannes, *Die Problematik des Völkerbundes bei Hegel und Kant*. Tübingen, 1934.

Hyppolite, Jean, *Genèse et structure de la Phénoménologie de l'Esprit de Hegel*, 2 vols. Paris, 1946.

Studies on Marx and Hegel, trans. J. O'Neill. London, 1969.

Jakovenko, Boris, *Untersuchungen zur Geschichte des Hegelianismus in Russland*. Prag, 1938.

Kahle, Karl Moritz, *Darstellungen und Kritik der Hegelschen Rechtsphilosophie*. Berlin, 1845.

Kaufmann, Walter, *Hegel*, Garden City, 1965.

(ed.) *Hegel's Political Philosophy*. New York, 1970.

'The Hegel Myth and Its Method', *Philosophical Review* LX (1951), 459–86.

'Hegel's Early Anti-theological Phase', *Philosophical Review* LXIII (1954), 3–18.

Kedney, J. S., *Hegel's Aesthetics – A Critical Examination*. Chicago, 1885.

Kelly, George A., *Idealism, Politics and History: Sources of Hegelian Thought*. Cambridge, 1969.

Kelly, M., *Hegel's Charlatanism Exposed*. London, 1911.

Kimmerle, Heinz, 'Dokumente zu Hegels Jenaer Dozententätigkeit 1801–07', *Hegel-Studien* IV (1967), 22–99.

Kline, George L., 'Some Recent Interpretations of Hegel's Philosophy', *The Monist* XLVIII (1964), 34–75.

Knoop, Bernhard, *Victor Cousin, Hegel und die französische Romantik*. Oberviechtach, 1932.

Knox, T. M., 'Hegel and Prussianism', *Philosophy*, January 1940 (51–63), July 1940 (313–14).

Kojève, Alexandre, *Introduction to the Reading of Hegel*, ed. Allan Bloom. New York, 1969.

Köstlin, Karl, *Hegel in philosophischer, politischer und nationaler Beziehung*. Tübingen, 1870.

Leo, Heinrich, *Die Hegelingen*. Halle, 1839.

Lim, Sok-Zin, *Der Begriff der Arbeit bei Hegel*. Bonn, 1966.

Litt, Theodor, *Hegel: Versuch einer kritischen Erneuerrung*. Heidelberg, 1953.

Lobkowicz, Nicholas, *Theory and Practice*. Notre Dame and London, 1967.

Löwith, Karl, *From Hegel to Nietzsche*, trans. David F. Green. New York, 1964.

Meaning in History. Chicago, 1949.

Lukács, Georg, *Der junge Hegel*. Zürich and Wien, 1948.

Mackenzie, Millicent, *Hegel's Educational Theory and Practice*. London, 1909.

Mager, Karl W. E., *Brief an eine Dame über die Hegelsche Philosophie*. Berlin, 1837.

Maihofer, Werner, 'Hegels Prinzip des modernen Staates', *Festschrift für Gerhart Husserl* (Frankfurt, 1968), pp. 234–73.

Marcuse, Herbert, *Reason and Revolution*, new edition. Boston, 1960.

Marković, Mihailo, 'Economism or the Humanization of Economics', *Praxis* V (1969), 451–75.

Mehta, V. R., *Hegel and the Modern State*. New Delhi, 1968.

Mewes, Erika, *Hegel und das deutsche Richterideal: Versuch einer Fortführung rechtsphilosophischer Gedanken Hegels*. Urach, 1937.

Morris, George S., *Hegel's Philosophy of State and of History*. Chicago, 1887

Bibliography

Müller, Emil Gustav, *Hegel: Denkgeschichte eines Lebendigen*. Berlin and München, 1959.

Müller, Emil Gustav, 'The Legend of "Thesis-Antithesis-Synthesis"', *Journal of the History of Ideas* XIX (June, 1958).

Mure, G. R. G., *An Introduction to Hegel*. Oxford, 1940.

Myers, Henry Alonzo, *The Spinoza–Hegel Paradox*. Ithaca, 1944.

Ogienski, Immanuel, *Hegel, Schubart und die Idee der Presönlichkeit in ihrem Verhältnis zur preussischen Monarchie*. Trzemessno, 1840.

Peperzak, Adrien, *Le jeune Hegel et la vision morale du monde*. La Haye, 1960.

Plenge, Johann, *Hegel und Marx*. Tübingen, 1911.

Popper, Karl R., *The Open Society and Its Enemies*. Princeton, 1950.

Pringle-Pattison, A. Seth, *The Philosophical Radicals and Other Essays*. Edinburgh and London, 1907.

Rehm, F., *Goethe und Hegel: Eine historische Parallele*. Oels, 1849.

Reyburn, Hugh A., *The Ethical Theory of Hegel: A Study of the Philosophy of Right*. Oxford, 1921.

Riedel, Manfred, *Theorie und Praxis im Denken Hegels*. Stuttgart, 1965.

Ritchie, David G., *Darwin and Hegel and Other Philosophical Studies*. London, 1893.

Ritter, Joachim, *Hegel und die französische Revolution*. Köln and Opladen, 1957.

Rohovsky, J. J., *Unvereinbarkeit der Hegelschen Wissenschaft mit dem Christentum und der christlichen Theologie*. Breslau, 1842.

Rosenkranz, Karl, *Georg Wilhelm Friedrich Hegels Leben*. Berlin, 1844 (reprint, Darmstadt, 1963). Excerpts translated into English were published in the *Journal of Speculative Philosophy* VI (1872), 258–79, 340–50.

Apologie Hegels gegen Dr R. Haym. Berlin, 1858.

Hegel als deutscher Nationalphilosoph. Leipzig, 1870.

Rosenzweig, Franz, *Hegel und der Staat*. Berlin and München, 1920.

'Das älteste Systemprogramm des deutschen Idealismus', *Sitzungsbericht der Heidelberger Akademie der Wissenschaften*, Phil.-hist.-Klasse, Jahrgang 1917, 5. Abhandlung.

Rubinstein, M., 'Die logischen Grundlagen des Hegelschen Systems und das Ende der Geschichte', *Kant-Studien* III (1906), 40–108.

Sandkühler, Hans Jörg, 'Hegel – Theoretiker der bürgerlichen Gesellschaft', *Politik und Zeitgeschichte*, Beilage zur Wochenzeitung *Das Parlament*, 22 August 1970, 11–23.

Schmidt, Werner, *Hegel und die Idee der Volksordnung*. Leipzig, 1944.

Schubart, K. E., *Über die Unvereinbarkeit der Hegelschen Staatslehre mit dem obersten Lebens- und Entwicklungsprinzip des preussischen Staats*. Breslau, 1839.

Sedlak, Francis, *A Holiday with a Hegelian*. London, 1911.

Shastri, Prabhu Dutt, *The Conception of Freedom in Hegel, Bergson and Indian Philosophy*. Calcutta, 1914.

Sigwart, H. C. W., *Die Propädeutik der Geschichte der Philosophie*. Tübingen, 1840.

Simon, Ernst, *Ranke und Hegel*. München, 1928.

von Sommer, Ferdinand, *Hegels Philosophie widerlegt aus dem Standpunkte des Systems selbst, dem anderer Philosophen und der gesunden Vernunft*. Berlin, 1842.

Bibliography

Soll, Ivan, *An Introduction to Hegel's Metaphysics*. Chicago and London, 1969.

'Hegels Rechtfertigung der Geschichte', *Hegel-Jahrbuch* (1968/69), pp. 81–8.

Stace, W. T., *Hegel*, new edition. New York, 1955.

Staudenmaier, Franz Anton, *Darstellung und Kritik des Hegelschen System aus dem Standpunkte der christlichen Philosophie*. Mainz, 1844.

Stirling, James Hutchinson, *The Secret of Hegel*. 2 vols. London, 1865.

Trahndorf, K. F. E., *Wie kann der Supernaturalismus sein Recht gegen Hegels Philosophie behaupten*. Berlin, 1840.

Trescher, H., 'Montesquieu und Hegel', *Schmollers Jahrbuch* XLII (1918).

von Trott zu Solz, Adam, *Hegels Staatsphilosophie und das internationale Recht*. Göttingen, 1932.

Weil, Eric, *Hegel et l'État*. Paris, 1950.

Wendel, J. A., *Beurteilung der Hegelschen Philosophie*. Coburg and Leipzig, 1839.

Wenke, Hans, *Hegels Theorie des objektiven Geistes*. Halle/Saale, 1927.

Verhandlungen des Ersten Hegelkongresses (Haag), ed. B. Wigersma, Tübingen and Haarlem, 1931.

Verhandlungen des Zweiten Hegelkongresses (Berlin), ed. B. Wigersma, Tübingen and Haarlem, 1932.

Verhandlungen des Tritten Hegelkongresses (Rom), ed. B. Wigersma, Tübingen and Haarlem, 1934.

Hegel-Studien, vols. I–IV.

Studies in Hegel (Tulane Studies in Philosophy IX), New Orleans, 1960.

Studien zur Hegels Rechtsphilosophie in der UdSSR. Moskau, 1966 (in mimeograph).

INDEX

249

Index

England, civil service in, 159; influence in Empire, 56; law of, 75 n46, 210, 214–16; poor in, 149 n50; 1832 Reform Bill, 208–20; representation in, 7, 163–4, 212–13; social conditions in, 214–20; system of taxation in, 6–7

Enlightenment, German, 1–2, 22, 62, 66, 125; view of Jews, 17, 19; view of religion, 15

equality, in early Church, 27; in modern society, 145

ethics, social (*Sittlichkeit*), 2, 31–2, 84–6, 87, 121, 132, 133; distinguished from individual, 32, 103, 137; of estates, 105 n63; in Oriental culture, 224

family, 133–4, 139–41, 224

fate, Hegel's concept of, 28

Ferguson, A., 141 n28

feudalism, 50–2, 180; breakdown in Ireland, 217

Feuerbach, L. A., 14, 113

Fichte, J. G., compared with Hegel, 5, 54 n50, 83; in Hegel's education, 1; views of, 34, 35, 47, 62, 82

folk religion, 16–17, 29

founding, of states, 21, 230–4

France, centralization in, 48–9, 168, 219; freedom of speech in, 173 n55; Hegel's view of, 35, 63, 164, 212; representation in, 51–3, 213 n18; 1830 Revolution in, 209; *see also* French Revolution

Frankfurt, Hegel at, 8–12, 15, 34

freedom, destruction of, 9; in nature, 145; and positivity, 14–33; of the press, 67, 173; progress towards, 42, 132, 221–38; and representation, 6–7; within state, 11–12, 124–5, 167, 179–84, 225

French Revolution, causes of, 16, 51; effects of, 52–3, 62, 66, 198; Hegel's view of, 7–8, 47–9, 74, 83, 125, 184; impact on Hegel, 3

Friedrich Wilhelm IV of Prussia, 116, 189

Fries, J., 119–21, 130

Germanic world, 228–9

Germany, modernization of, 3, 34–61, 66–80, 90, 198, 212

Goethe, J. W. von, 62

Greeks, 2; culture of, 153, 222–3, 225–7; religion of, 14; state of, 9, 19–24, 28, 32–3, 111–12, 128–9, 179–80, 195–6

groups, *see* organizations

Habsburgs, 57–8

Haller, L. von, 44, 182–3, 187, 188 n48, 190

Hardenberg, Prince von, 116, 189

Heidelberg, 115, 116

Henning, L., 130

Herder, J. G. von, x, 14, 16, 17, 21, 39

Hess, M., 113, 238

history, as manifestation of ultimate reality, 65; meaning of, 221–38; related to political philosophy, x, 55–6

Hobbes, T., 41, 83, 99, 134

'Holy Alliance', 201

Hungary, 56

idealist philosophy, programme of, 4, 10–12

India, 30; culture of, 225

individual, in Empire, 25–6, 38, 227; in Greek state, 112; in modern state, 50–1, 69, 76–8, 101–4, 105, 143, 147, 165, 167, 179; relation with social life, 87; relations between, 137; religious rights of, 30–3; world historical, *see* leader

industrialization, effects of, 91–8, 146

Ireland, 214, 215–18

Italy, 8–9, 10, 30, 53

Jacobinism, 7–8, 9, 239–40

Jena, 116; Hegel at, 34, 38 n13, 62

Jesus, 18, 19, 24–5, 27, 32

Judaism, 14, 17–19, 21–4, 28, 29; anti-Semitism, 119–20, 170–1

Kamptz, von, 131

Kant, I., compared with Hegel, 64–5, 82, 118–20, 125, 137–8, 139, 200, 201, 221; in Hegel's early education, 1, 3; influence on Hegel, 13–15, 182; theories of, 194, 197 n6

Kierkegaard, S., foreshadowing of, 14

Klopstock, F. G., 21–2

Kotzebue, A. F. F., 119

Index

labour, 89–101, 141, 143–54; in class structure, 105
language, in definition of state, 45–6
law, 132, 178, 183, 186; in Berne, 6; English, 210, 214–16; in Germany, 39–40, 42, 58–9; 67, 74–5; international, 200–7; Mosaic, 17–19; Roman, 9; rule of, 102, 121, 190–3
leader, in Hegel's theory, x, 20, 54, 71, 110-11, 174–5, 230–4
league of nations, Hegel's view of, 201–4
Locke, J., 134, 231
Lombardy, 56.
love, in Hegel's theories, 28, 30, 32, 140

Machiavelli, N., 53–4, 230 n31
marriage, 139–40
Marx, K., comparison with, 104, 107, 128, 199; foreshadowings of, 11, 14, 50, 94, 95 n35, 103 n61, 111 n76, 125, 140 n22, 144 n37, 224 n9, 231 n32; view of Hegel, 90 n25, 97 n44, 160 n15
mediation, by classes, 155; by education, 133; by labour, 89–94, 143; in large state, 23, 52, 77–8, 105, 108, 148, 161; by law, 192; money as, 95
Mendelssohn, M., influence of, 2, 15, 30–1
Messiah, Hegel's explanation of, 18–19
Metternich, Prince, 201
middle class, 105–6, 158, 168; in England, 208
Mill, John Stuart, 163
monarchy, constitutional, 185–9; function of, 43; modern, 66, 110–12, 168 n39; Oriental, 223–4
money, Hegel's theory of, 95, 107
Montesquieu, Baron de, influence of, x, 4, 16, 185, 186, 187
morality (*Moralität*), 14–20 *passim*, 24, 31, 132, 133; distinguished from social ethic, 32, 103, 137; law concerning, 191–2; in Oriental culture, 224
Müller, A., 182, 188 n48

Naples, 56
Napoleon, 63, 66-7, 71-2, 168, 175, 185, 189, 213; Code of, 67, 215

nationalism, in Hegel, 34-6, 45, 69, 79, 115, 228, 240–1
natural law, 82–6, 194
Nazism, 15, 119, 122
needs, human, 143–7, 149
Niethammer, 63, 67–8, 70, 71, 121 n17
Nuremberg, Hegel at, 63, 67

objectivity, in morality, 138; in religion, 15–16
organizations, political, 78, 160, 162, 164–8
Oriental society, 8, 52, 152, 169, 171, 223–5

paganism, 14, 17–24, 29
peasantry, 105, 106, 156; in Ireland, 216–18
Peel, Sir Robert, 214 n26
Persia, culture of, 225
philosophy, Hegel's view of, 64, 68, 99, 101, 113, 118–30, 132, 221, 234–5
Pitt, William, 7
Plato, 84, 128, 226; comparison with, 86 n11, 96 n42, 112 n78, 136, 158, 171–2
pluralism, 46–7, 167–75, 180–1
Poland, 56, 235
polis, *see* Greeks, state of
positivity, in politics, 74, 123, 210; in religion, 14–33
poverty, 24, 96–8, 136–7, 146–51, 166; in England and Ireland, 214–18; state policies regarding, 99–101, 151–4
price control, 100
property, in Britain, 217; in Christianity, 27–8; defence of, 196; of family, 140–1; in Germany, 38, 41–2; in Greece and Judea, 23–4; in modern state, 9–10, 40, 84–5, 102; in Roman Empire, 25; as social attribute, 88–89, 106, 135–7, 157, 171, 228; as voting qualification, 213
Prussia, after 1815, 115–22; civil service in, 159; government of, 48–9, 164, 173n; modernization of, 35, 56–8, 79; in Napoleonic wars, 62–3, 189 public opinion, 67, 110, 172-5
public realm, compared with individual, 10, 38, 41–4, 50–1, 75, 84, 101–2, 167, 226

251

Index